# SEX AND FANTASY

# SEX AND FANTASY

*Patterns of Male and*
*Female Development*

ROBERT MAY

W·W·NORTON & COMPANY

NEW YORK    LONDON

Grateful acknowledgement is given to the following publishers for permission to reprint already published material:

The Loeb Classical Library (Harvard University Press: William Heinemann, (London, 1916), *Hesiod, the Homeric Hymns and Homerica,* translated by H. G. Evelyn-White and Ovid, *Metamorphoses,* translated by F. J. Miller.

Indiana University Press (Bloomington, Indiana, 1955), Ovid's *Metamorphoses,* translated by Rolfe Humphries.

Pergamon Press, *Journal of Child Psychology and Psychiatry,* 1973, vol. 14, "Sex differences in newborns with special reference to difference in the organization of oral behavior," by Anneliese Korner.

John Wiley and Sons (New York, 1966), *The Adolescent Experience,* by Elizabeth Douvan and Joseph Adelson.

Harper & Row, Publishers, Inc. (New York, 1955), Henry Murray, "American Icarus," *Clinical Studies of Personality,* edited by Arthur Burton and Robert Harris.

# Acknowledgments

It would be an impossible, and even embarrassing, task to thank all those whose influence lies behind this work. I can only trust that they will recognize their imprint. But I would be negligent if I did not thank those who have had a more immediate role in this project. Others' interest in continuing the research into fantasy patterns has often rekindled my own, and here I am particularly indebted to the skill and enthusiasm of Phebe Cramer. In addition to interesting empirical results, her work and that of Jean Saunders and Carolyn Saarni has provided many of the story examples I use in chapter II. The refining and application of the fantasy scoring system owed much to the incisive and orderly mind of Diane Furtney. The preparation of the manuscript owed as much to the patience and persistence of Hyde Meissner.

Edward Kaplan and Kim Townsend generously gave me careful and helpful readings of earlier drafts of the manuscript. The Austen Riggs Center provided the opportunity for the clinical studies and for one phase of the empirical research. Amherst College, and its president, John William Ward, underwrote the year's leave that provided the crucial time and space in which to write this book. And the Adult Department of the Tavistock Clinic, with the unflappably helpful staff of the Tavistock Joint Library, gave me invaluable material support and intellectual stimulation during that time.

R.M.

# Contents

# Introduction

This book is an exploration of the experiences of maleness and femaleness. It comes out of more than a decade's interest, both empirical and therapeutic, in the area of sex differences. How does our gender effect our growth and development, our view of the world, our character traits, our inner life? This book is a response, though hardly an answer, to such questions.

The existence of male and female is a basic aspect of human reality and as such it has always been explained according to the dominant theory of the times. Thus for centuries we would have believed that man and woman existed the way God created them and that the differences between them rested on the foundation of Natural Law. In the nineteenth century this notion began to give way to one based on the supposed Law of Natural Selection: men and women have been shaped, over countless generations, by the pressures of evolution and thus what is now is what ought to be for the continuance of the species. This form of Social Darwinism is so easily just an apology for the status quo that it has been vehemently rejected by all the movements for social change that have been so characteristic of our century.

This justified reaction against Social Darwinism has joined in America with our environmentalist ideology. We tend to believe that we come into the world as the proverbial blank slate, to be written upon by experiences and by the training to which society subjects us. As with any reaction, this one runs the risk of going too far. We risk losing sight of what I mean to be the central perspective of this book: what we know as male or female is the result of an interplay of our bodies and our social reality. The history of the study of gender is rife with misguided assumptions about the inevitability, even sanctity, of certain sex differences. But we do ourselves no intellectual favor by rushing, now, to assert that everything about male and female is a matter of external convenience.

This exploration of gender will rely at times on the study of fantasy. Some might wonder why we should pay attention to mere products of the imagination, to "fantasy." Although the word has a degraded public meaning in our culture, akin to "unreal" or nonsensical, I use it to refer to the rich and varied theater that plays in our heads all the time. Scenes of hope and of fear, incidents of anger or of lust, retroactive rewritings of history, and tender anticipations of the future—all these are part of the constant buzzing and scuttling that goes on in the darkened backstage areas of our mind. This activity, to which we rarely attend except in our sleep or particular moments of stress, is an inherent human faculty (even very young infants show the rapid eye movements characteristic of dreaming). It is here that we interpret the events of our life and distill them into a collection of vivid tableaux, which help to guide our next actions. Thus fantasy is both a vital indicator of what people really care about and is also the emotional reservoir that powers our actions.

There are a number of predictable difficulties that people will have in reading this book. They are some of the same difficulties that plague any discussion about men and women. Given our tendency to envy the other sex, women are likely to feel that the male part is more desirable and that the book slights women; men are likely to feel the opposite. There will also be a problem in staying with the notion of an interplay between our bodies and our social context. Because I suggest that the body *does* matter, some will read me as saying that sex differences are entirely a matter of genes and hormones.

There is also a troublesome urge to turn statements about overall differences into absolutes. To say that men and women, as groups, differ in a particular way is *not* the same as saying that all men are this way and all women that. Such statements are not meant to apply to *everyone,* nor are they disproved by one contrary example. On the whole there may be an important difference, yet there is still considerable individual variation, there is still overlap between the sexes on almost every dimension. It is too burdensome to qualify one's language constantly, so I want to state the caveat now: the focus of this book is on some ways in which men and women differ, but I am not implying an absolute, categorical distinction.

Is it legitimate and allowable for a man to write about women? There is a current separatist position that would say no, would say that any man's understanding of women is bound to be so defective as to be useless if not actively destructive. Obviously I do not agree. One of the disturbing trends in our cultural and intellectual life is a kind of Balkanization that is ultimately based on the narcissistic assumption that only like can understand like. We have not only the right, but the positive obligation to follow our imagination across these boundaries and try to understand the nature of others' experience.

One theme of this book is that there *are* significant psychological differences between the sexes, and that these differences are worth thinking about; a mild point, it would seem. In fact there is a tendency, at least in America these days, to think that anyone who raises the question of sex differences is at best mean-spirited and at worst a reactionary bigot. We are eager to talk as if there were a level of humanness that is independent of gender. I think this is a mistaken way to put it. I would rather say that each of us comes to a level of humanness *through* our maleness or femaleness. From the moment of conception we are either female or male; from early in life we are psychologically *both* male and female, and we are so by way of a complex inner structure, not an amorphous mixture in which black and white make grey.

Diana Trilling laments ". . . a woman's liberation movement which has failed to locate and to hold the place where sexual equality supports rather than violates biology."[1] Apparently it has been necessary in the course of that movement to mount an assault on the body and on sex differences in general. It may be time for the pendulum to begin its slow swing back again. With rare exception* sex differences have come to be seen as a *problem,* an affront to human dignity and social progress. Our sore need is for a language and a space in which to talk about the distinguishing characteristics of men and women without its being demeaning to either. I hope that what follows can contribute to this process.

*Jean Baker Miller's deeply humane *Toward a New Psychology of Women* (Boston: Beacon Press, 1976) is a good example.

# SEX AND
# FANTASY

# Chapter I

❧⟨ᴍ⟩❧

# Two Myths of
# Male and Female

Myths are fantasies shared by a whole culture. Out of the ambiguities of the surrounding world, the change of the seasons, or the movements of the sun, a people constructs a tale that embodies its important concerns and its sense of what matters in human life. Such stories are shaped over centuries and only survive if they continue to have an important common appeal. We begin this inquiry into male and female with two myths from ancient Greece.

### PHAETHON

The archetypal male myth is the story of Phaethon.[1] Phaethon is a young man whose mother has told him that his father was Phoebus, the sun god. But Phaethon has come to doubt this and he sets off to find out. He climbs up to the palace of the sun and begs Phoebus, "Give me a proof, so people will believe me, know me for what I am, and let my mind be free from doubting." His father embraces and welcomes him. As proof of paternity he offers to grant any favor Phaethon might ask. Phaethon asks to drive the chariot of the sun.

Too late to take the oath back, but the father
Repented having sworn it; over and over
He shook his shining head. "Your words," he said,
"Have made mine rash: could I take back the promise,
This is the only thing I would deny you.
So, let me try persuasion. What you want,
My son, is dangerous; you ask for power
Beyond your strength and years: your lot is mortal,
But what you ask beyond the lot of mortals.

The father warns and pleads, offering his anguish as the proof Phaethon demands:

Beware, my son! I do not want to give you
The gift of death; there is time to change your prayer.
Of course you want the most convincing proof
I am your father. That I give you, surely,
By fearing as I do. I am proved a father
By a father's fear. Look at me! You see my face;
Would you could see my heart and all the cares
Held there for you, my son.

But Phaethon insists and his father, full of regret, honors his pledge
and gives over the gleaming chariot with its fierce, winged horses:
"The boy was in the car, and stood there proudly, / Holding the
reins, all happiness, and thanking / His father for the gift he gave
unwilling."

But as soon as they have begun their course through the heavens
it is apparent that Phaethon cannot control the horses.

But the weight was light,
Not such as they were used to, and the yoke
Without its usual pressure; so, as schooners,
Unballasted, career and roll and yaw
Out of the proper course, so the bright chariot
Tosses and bounds, as if there were no driver.
It did not take the horses long to know it,
To run away, beyond control; the driver,
In panic, does not know in which direction
To turn the reins, does not know where the road is,
With those wild plunging animals.

Already terrified by the height and by his own abject helplessness, Phaethon is paralyzed by the sight of the monsters (the constellations) that inhabit the heavens.


Out of his senses, with cold fear upon him,
Phaethon dropped the reins.
                         And when the horses
Feel them across their backs, and none to check them,
Bolting, they charge the air of unknown regions,
Wherever impulse hurls them, lawless, crashing
Against high stars; they keep the chariot bounding
Through pathless ways, now high, now low, toward Heaven
Or plunging sheer toward earth. The Moon, in wonder,
Watches her brother's horses running lower
Than her own steeds. The scorched clouds smoke. The
   mountains
Of earth catch fire, the prairies crack, the rivers
Dry up, the meadows are white-hot, the trees,
The leaves, burn to a crisp, the crops are tinder.


Earth is on fire, the fields smoldering and the oceans drying up. To save the world from destruction Zeus strikes Phaethon and the chariot with a lightening bolt.


                         And Phaethon,
His ruddy hair on fire, falls streaming down
The long trail of the air. A star, sometimes,
Falls from clear heaven, so, or seems to fall.
And far from home, a river-god receives him,
Bathes his poor burning face, and the Western Naiads
Give burial to the broken body, smoking
With the fire of that forked bolt, and on the stone
They carve an epitaph:
                         *Here Phaethon lies,*
*Who drove his father's chariot: if he did not*
*Hold it, at least he fell in splendid daring.*

The myth of Phaethon had many purposes. On one level it embodied a theory of the structure of the universe and an explanation for the apparent movement of the sun, in addition to various lessons in geography and geology. But our concern will be with another level: the lessons about human emotion, and the rules for right living, which this vivid and moving story puts forward.

It is a cautionary tale in that it warns, as do many of the tales of classical Greece, against the dangers of human pride. It speaks of the disastrous results of the overreaching arrogance that the Greeks called *hubris.* The fact that pride is the major motive force in this drama is even more apparent when we learn what started Phaethon on his extravagant errand. He had been boasting of his supposed lineage when a male companion, the product of another godly dalliance but in this instance on the part of Jove, ridiculed Phaethon's inflated idea of himself: "You are a fool to believe all your mother tells you, and are swelled up with false notions about your father." Phaethon's injured pride is clear when he then demands some proof from his mother: "I, the high-spirited, the bold of tongue, had no word to say. Ashamed am I that such an insult could have been uttered and yet could not be answered."[2] The issue of who his father is matters less now than does his damaged pride and his sense of having been defeated and rendered speechless by another man. He must prove that he is indeed of "high birth" in order to assuage the sting of this competitive defeat. The situation is not far removed from the arguments of little boys about whose father is stronger. But Phaethon is not a young child. His masculine pride is more stubborn, more driven, more destructive in its consequences.

So the story proper begins with Phaethon seeking out his father. The themes of pride and power are stated in the first image of the poem, the royal palace of the sun. The emphasis on splendor and on height (the high palace, the lofty columns) is typical of the whole story. Its imagery focuses around pride and ascension throughout. Ascension carries power with it; the high is identified with the strong. And the primary area is power over nature and material things: "Manner there had conquered matter. . . ."

In this first encounter with his father Phaethon embodies the opposite pole. He is lowly (he must climb up) and overawed. He trembles and speaks of his doubt. This doubt is the servant of his shame—the fear that rules him is the fear of being exposed as a pretender and of being ignored or dismissed. Is he my father, am I rightfully his son? Phoebus answers the question immediately and without hesitation. But then comes another sign that Phaethon's shame and doubt is only the dark side of his intense pride and competitiveness. If he is not a lowly nothing, if he indeed *is* Phoebus's son, then he must be *everything*, he must drive the chariot of the sun. Phoebus's words are not enough and his son shows no sign of being touched or even relieved by his father's embrace. All the reassurance does is to loose his need to *do* something, his need to carry out an act that will prove his power. It is a peculiar and concrete proof of paternity that he demands: if I am my father's son then I must be entitled, and able, to do what he does. This is not just a wish to be acknowledged as son but also a competitive drive for equality with one's father.

Phoebus points out the pretension: "you ask for power beyond your strength and years." But Phaethon is as little moved by this as he is by his father's touching concern ("I am proved a father by a father's fear"). We may suppose that he hears his father's warnings as an attempt to deprive him of the honor and excitement of taking his father's place (the Miller translation refers to Phaethon at this moment as "ambitious" and "burning with desire"). And alongside his prideful desire to exert "control . . . over the winged horses," there is now a battle of wills between father and son. Phaethon is determined to force his father to keep his promise; he will prove his influence by compelling his father to give the thing he least wants to give. Phoebus's own pride, in the form of his sense of honor, requires him to keep his word even though he knows it to be murder. Having reduced his father to impotent pleas and warnings, Phaethon assumes the splendor of the golden chariot: his doubt is gone and he basks in the reflected light of the marvelous machine. "The boy was in the car, and stood there proudly / Holding the reins, all happiness and thanking / His father for the gift he gave unwillingly."

But this moment of narcissistic inflation is abruptly shattered. It is one thing to want to be able to control the power that father controls, quite another actually to manage it. Phaethon is literally too lightweight to master the chariot. And now his prideful fantasy of control and ascension turns into a nightmare of fear and helplessness.

The very qualities he hungered for, height and power, now strike him with blind, trembling terror. The language of the poem emphasizes the loss of control: "lawless," "unmastered," "chaos." The horses are mindless energy, force that has escaped all restraint or guidance, and thus has turned destructive. This is central to the moral of the tale in that the horses are Phaethon's own pride become demented and run wild. As they protray impulsive and irresistible power, he collapses into the opposite: abject fear and timidity. The wish for mastery and even triumph has outrun the ability to control, direct, and modulate these basically aggressive urges. And great indeed is the destruction that results.

"Earth, our mother" is dying by fire. As an image she stands in opposition to Phoebus and his errant son. She is associated with "sinking down," with being low rather than high, and with living in darkness rather than blinding light. And far from imposing on others, her life is one of endurance: "Is this what I am given / For being fruitful, dutiful? for bearing / The wounds of harrow and plowshare, year on year?" She calls on "the almighty father," the source of ultimate sanction and control. He is the highest of all and from "the very peak and pinnacle" he fights fire with superior fire, striking Phaethon down. It is interesting to note that the punishment falls on Phaethon, not on the wild-running horses. *His* is the blame for not controlling them. They represent a part of him that has slipped its fetters and become dangerous.

Phaethon's fiery plunge is fully as dramatic and vivid as was his rise. But what of the epitaph? "Here Phaethon lies, / Who drove his father's chariot: if he did not / Hold it, at least he fell in splendid daring." This seems a sudden change of tone and stance. Up until this point Phaethon has hardly been an admirable character: boastful, easily insulted, demanding, impulsive, blindly proud, and fool-hardy. But now we are supposed to admire his "daring." This is a staggering request in view of the catalog of havoc we have just finished reading. A rash and feckless boy comes near to destroying the world in order to satisfy his own pride, and we should admire that? Since there is little to idolize in Phaethon's character, so we can only turn to pity over his death and awe about the sheer magnitude of what he tried to do, how far above himself he tried to rise. Our sympathy with him as he is struck down overrides our judgment of what he was doing a moment before. Once he has died we can acknowledge that there is part of him in us, that Phaethon embodies a pride that we ourselves cherish even as we sense its potential destructiveness.

So this "cautionary tale" turns out to be deeply ambivalent. It warns of the dangers of unmodulated pride, but ends on a note of admiration for the splendid but doomed attempt. While hubris is a punishable sin, dangerous to the community as well as the individual, yet pushing to get as high as one can is still an ideal. One is admired for one's most self-destructive trait and must always be walking an obscure line between extraordinary aspiration and inevitable punishment.*

## The Story of Demeter

We turn now to a quite different epic, that of Demeter and Persephone. It is an archetypal myth of women.

The text here is the Homeric Hymn to Demeter. Being much closer to the original oral tradition than Ovid's polished and literary restatements, the story as it appears is complex and rambling and full of genealogical asides. For these reasons the quotations from the text will be more fragmentary.[3]

Demeter is a goddess, "lady of the golden sword and glorious fruits." As the story opens her daughter, Persephone is "apart from [her]" gathering flowers with a group of other young girls in a lovely and fragrant meadow. The richest and most radiant of the flowers, the narcissus, has been put there as "a snare for the bloom-like girl."

---

*Here we must note that Phaethon exemplifies characteristic and troublesome qualities of the classical Greek personality. His story was riveting for the ancient Greeks because he was truly one of them. Alvin Gouldner's lucid book *The Hellenic World* (New York: Harper & Row, 1965) points out the many ways in which classical Greece was a society organized around the notion of contest and prideful competition. Phillip Slater, in *The Glory of Hera* (Boston: Beacon Press, 1968) takes the analysis of the Hellene character even further. His more enthusiastically psychoanalytic approach leads to a book that is chaotically rich in insight. Although he does not deal directly with the story of Phaethon, he cites several similar tales, and the personality pattern that Slater outlines is very relevant to our discussion.

The more recent Christian tradition offers similar stories of pride and downfall in the Faust legend and in Milton's treatment of Satan in *Paradise Lost.*

As she reaches out "to take the lovely toy," the earth opens up and Hades, lord of the underworld, springs out in his chariot to seize her. "He caught her up reluctant on his golden car and bare her away lamenting."

Demeter hears Persephone's cries as she is carried off: "Bitter pain seized her heart, and she rent the covering upon her divine hair with her dear hands: her dark cloak she cast down from both her shoulders and sped, like a wild bird, over the firm land and yielding sea, seeking her child." In her grief she gives up food or any physical comforts and wanders the earth looking for "my daughter whom I bare, sweet scion of my body. . . ." When she discovers what has happened, and that it was with Zeus's connivance, "grief yet more terrible and savage came into the heart of Demeter." She shuns the gatherings of the gods and instead goes disguised ("disfiguring her form a long while") among "the towns and rich fields of men. . . . And she was like an ancient woman who is cut off from childbearing and the gifts of garland-loving Aphrodite. . . ."

And here we come to a story within a story. Demeter meets four young women and tells them a tale of having been abducted by pirates and recently having escaped from them in this foreign land. The women are kind and solicitous and invite her to their mother's, Metaneira's, house. All are touched by Demeter's mourning. "A long time she sat upon the stool without speaking because of her sorrow, and greeting no one by word or by sign, but rested, never smiling, and tasting neither food nor drink, because she pined with longing for her deep-bosomed daughter. . . ." Twice the women offer her the same words in consolation: "Mother, what the gods send us, we mortals bear perforce, although we suffer." Metaneira asks this sorrowing old woman to be nurse to her newborn son. Demeter immediately comes to life and promises to raise a rare child indeed. Under her care he grows amazingly. Demeter has embarked on a regimen to make the child "deathless and unageing," until Metaneira discovers that part of the technique involves burying the infant in the fire at night. On seeing this Metaneira cries out in "grief and bitter sorrow" and her assertion of a mother's concern enrages Demeter, the divine foster mother. She reveals herself as a goddess and demands that a temple be built and rites established in her honor.

But even this does not appease her rekindled rage and grief:

Then she caused a most dreadful and cruel year for mankind over the all-nourishing earth: the ground would not make the seed sprout, for rich-crowned Demeter kept it hid. In the fields the oxen drew many a curved plow in vain, and much white barley was cast upon the land without avail. So she would have destroyed the whole race of man with cruel famine . . . for she vowed that she would never set foot on fragrant Olympus nor let fruit spring out of the ground, until she beheld with her own eyes her own fair-faced daughter.

Zeus is finally moved, not out of compassion but rather because a barren earth means the end of gifts and sacrifices for him. On Zeus's order Hades tells "his shy mate" that she may return. "When he said this, wise Persephone was filled with joy and hastily sprang up for gladness. But he secretly gave her sweet pomegranate seed to eat, taking care for himself that she might not remain continually with grave, dark-robed Demeter."

There is an ecstatic reunion, marred only by Demeter's accurate suspicion:

And when Demeter saw them, she rushed forth as does a Maenad down some thick-wooded mountain, while Persephone on the other side, when she saw her mother's sweet eyes, left the chariot and horses, and leaped down to run to her, and falling upon her neck, embraced her. But while Demeter was still holding her dear child in her arms, her heart suddenly misgave her for some snare, so that she feared greatly and ceased fondling her daughter and asked of her at once: "My child, tell me, surely you have not tasted any food while you were below? Speak out and hide nothing, but let us both know. For if you have not, you shall come back from loathly Hades and live with me and your father, the dark-clouded Son of Cronos and be honoured by all the deathless gods; but if you have tasted food, you must go back again beneath the secret places of the earth, there to dwell a third part of the seasons every year: yet for the two parts you shall be with me and the other deathless gods. But when the earth shall bloom with the fragrant flowers of spring in every kind, then from the realm of darkness and gloom thou shalt come up once more to be a wonder for gods and mortal men.

Persephone confesses that she *has* eaten, "against my will." But this is a small flaw and it is quickly drowned in a flow of emotional and agricultural abundance: "So did they then, with hearts at one, greatly cheer each the other's soul and spirit with many an embrace: their hearts had relief from their griefs while each took and gave back joyousness. . . . And rich-crowned Demeter did . . . straightway make fruit to spring up from the rich lands, so that the whole wide earth was laden with leaves and flowers."

On the most general level we recognize the story of Demeter and Persephone as a fertility myth. The richest and most consistent thread of image and simile concerns birth, growth, and fecundity: young girls are like flowerful meadows or "as hinds or heifers in spring time, when sated with pasture"; daughters are compared to the shoots used in grafting and propagating plants, and children are considered a blessing from the gods; in contrast to the earth, the air is called "fruitless"; Demeter's revenge is in kind, barrenness for barrenness. Little distinction is made between people and plants. Thus Persephone at one moment is picking flowers and at the next *is* a flower in the eye of her mother or of the storyteller. Demeter's retaliation makes clear the analogy: so long as Persephone remains hidden underground, so will all grain and fruit. And it is the seed Hades insinuates into Persephone that ties her to him.

Emotions are seen to have a direct, we would say magical, effect on the world. In this way the myth constructs an explanation of events that are both crucial and puzzling for an agricultural people: the alternation of the seasons and capricious variations in fertility. These powerful phenomena are reduced to a drama of very human emotion, though the emotions are attributed to gods. The world dies in the fall and comes to life again in the spring because Persephone is journeying back and forth, and both Demeter's grief at separation and her joy at reunion are sympathetically expressed in the natural world. Likewise famine, or long periods of human barrenness, can be understood as the goddess's loss or anger writ large. With the cause thus located in one humanlike figure, people can at least hope to affect the harvest, whether of barley or of babies, by proper respect and worship.

The Homeric Hymn to Demeter existed both as an explanation of and as a text for a set of religious rituals that survived in Greece for centuries. Referred to as the Eleusinian Mysteries, they were dedicated to Demeter and her daughter.[4] Jane Harrison suggests that in fact one of the distinctive qualities of the Eleusinian Mysteries was that it was a cult primarily of and for women.[5] Whether that is historically true or not, any description of the myth needs to begin with the fact that it is a story of women. All the important characters, save Hades and Zeus, are female. Although these two men are certainly important to the story, neither are fully or sympathetically developed characters and they each rather play the role of a malevolent but awkward deus ex machina. The real life of the drama rests with Demeter, Persephone, Metaneira, and her daughters. The important settings are the meadow where young girls gather flowers, the "Maiden Well" where Demeter meets the daughters of Metaneira, and then the interior space of Metaneira's house, where the only male we see is an infant. No doubt this may be an accurate reflection of the sexual segregation that was typical of Greek society. But it also gives the mythmakers room to elaborate their notions of the concerns and qualities of women.

It is a story full of the complex play of human emotion. Physical action is quite peripheral in comparison to the emotional bond between mother and daughter. It is this bond that is the prime motive and source of energy. All that happens stems from Demeter's terrible longing for her daughter. Attachment and separation are the basic and persistent issues in this tale. It begins with Persephone "apart" from her mother, with the implication that that was the first mistake. She is snatched and becomes totally separate, lost, from her mother. Her mother then separates herself from *her* place with the gods, and while disguised as a sad and barren old woman, invents a tale of *her* abduction from a distant home. And finally, Metaneira rekindles Demeter's depressive anger by voicing her own fear of losing her child and thereby shattering Demeter's surrogate motherhood. And at the positive end of this polarity, we are shown repeatedly the life-giving and sustaining nature of human relationships. Contrasted with Demeter's ravaged and bereft wandering are the kindnesses of Metaneira and her daughters, the miraculous recovery of Demeter when given an infant to care for, and the deliberately elaborated ecstasy of the reunion between mother and daughter.

The central theme of human attachment and loss also shows itself indirectly throughout the narrative. We are presented with two counterpoised states: having, which is being full, happy, and in bloom; and losing, which is barren, sad, and withered. There is a literal level on which having is associated with physical closeness, with being almost a part of someone, while losing is associated with being far away. It is on this level that we can understand the myth's persistant images of reaching and touching: Persephone "reached out with both hands to take the lovely toy," Hades "caught her up," Demeter tenderly holds Metaneira's baby and later will "cast him from her," Metaneira's daughters fail to comfort the infant because "handmaids much less skilful were holding him now," and the reunion of Demeter and Persephone is replete with embraces.

Eating and nursing are also literal representations of emotional ties and are used in this myth to further fill out the theme. The generosity and tenderness of Metaneira and her daughters is symbolized by the special drink they prepare for the sorrowing Demeter. Demeter's power is first revealed by her supernatural abilities as an infant nurse ("And the child grew like some immortal being, not fed with food nor nourished at the breast"). Finally, Hades ties Persephone to him by giving her something to eat. In this last we see a merging of the notions of feeding and impregnation, of being a baby and having a baby. The whole myth derives part of its power from the way in which it blurs such distinctions and thus gives us a sense of the complex interlocking of *all* attachments and relationships of caring.

In response to the question "what happens in this story?" we might be tempted to focus on Persephone's abduction and release, and perhaps on Demeter's laying waste the earth. Those are events that can be clearly and simply described. But to seize on them would distort the myth. The important *event* here is Demeter's grieving. This is what receives the most attention in the story itself and what was taken as the core of the accompanying religious rites. It is likely to be hard for us to think of an emotional state, or even an emotional process, as an event. We are tempted to emphasize the *acts* associated with the feeling—Demeter tore her garments and wandered the earth—rather than the feeling itself. But this is one of the remarkable aspects of this particular myth, its assertion that feelings matter as much or more than actions. The myth devotes itself to following the course of a complex emotion, grief. We are shown its vicissitudes, its ebbing and flowing, its alternation between self-laceration and angry attack on others, its precarious hunger for another child to make good the loss, its need for kindness and feeding from others, and its slow and demanding rhythm. Much respect is paid.

Of the many morals implicit in this tale, one is that such emotions indeed deserve respect and attention. Another might be that we should not underestimate the strength of the tie between mother and daughter. And another still: "Yet we mortals bear perforce what the gods send us, though we be grieved." In case we should miss this lesson it is said twice, and said to Demeter while she is in the depths of her sorrows. This lesson has to do with necessity and endurance. Things must be borne. Demeter must grieve, Persephone is helpless against the force and guile of Hades, Metaneira must accept the chances lost by having disrupted Demeter's plan for her son. But yet the lesson is not a pessimistic one. Two things are spoken of as being "borne": grief and babies. But each holds promise as well as pain. The counsel of endurance is not merely aimed at a stoic bearing-up-under. Instead the bearing is to be creative; something will come out of it. A vital function of this endurance is to protect and keep alive inside us a fertile hope.

The myth of Demeter shows us caring confirmed and endurance rewarded. Demeter's suffering is followed by intense joy—a joy stronger than she would have felt had the sorrow and separation not preceeded it. Persephone's fearful descent into the underworld is followed by a joyful ascension. And the earth's period of barrenness is followed by an eruption of fruit and flowers. Attachment and loss are necessarily intertwined. Genuine caring requires a willingness to suffer the loss of what we care for. Not only is the potential loss not a threat to the attachment, it is the surest sign of the attachment and is the experience (in reality or merely in repeated anticipation) that defines and heightens the caring. The myth and its associated rituals spoke to the integrity of this pattern: pain followed by joy, separation followed by reunion, death followed by renewal, winter followed by spring. And we are told that our proper participation in this rich fabric requires the capacity for creative endurance in the service of caring. As opposed to Phaethon's rise, full of pride and self-importance, and his consequent disastrous fall, Demeter and Persephone show us a pattern of sorrow, loss, and suffering followed by an ecstatic return to fullness and growth.

# Chapter II

⌒✦⌒

# Fantasy Patterns

Consider the following two stories, told in response to a picture of two trapeze artists, man and woman, in mid-air:

They are a very famous man and wife trapeze act. They have been unable to perform on the high wire because of certain marital conflicts. They have tried many times to regain their previous skills, but each time they are in the air, ready to catch one another, either the husband or the wife realizes something about himself or his wife and finds themselves unable to reach out for the other. They have tried desperately to come to some sort of answer, and tonight they feel they've reached it. But they both wonder if they will be able to reach each other, and by clasping hands, become man and wife again. They reach each other, and eventually learn to communicate and to enjoy one another.

Sam gripped Martha's wrists, tensed, and flipped her into the air. She turned in the air much as a leaf turning during that second in which it hangs suspended upon the wind. The audience was silent except for scattered gasps and an occasional licking of lips. Again Sam caught her by the wrists, thrilling to the sensation of strength which violently surged from his arms into hers. Sweat formed in glistening beads upon the bulging sinews of his thickly corded arms. "Sam, I love you," sighed Martha. "And I you," said Sam, releasing her wrists with the steel-trap reflexes for which he was famous, watching her fall towards the up-turned faces.

At first glance these contemporary imaginings may seem to have little in common with the myths of the previous chapter. But brief and humble as these two stories are, there are important structural links. The first story, told by a woman, has the same sequence or trajectory as the Demeter myth: it moves from pain to pleasure, from difficulty, effort, and doubt to success and reunion. The second story, told by a man, follows the trajectory of Phaethon: soaring strength ending in destruction.

Here is another pair of stories. Again the first was told by a woman and the second by a man.

Husband and wife who've been given an opportunity in a first-class circus after many discouraging months in carnivals. She's discovered she's pregnant after having had several miscarriages. She's been warned not to indulge in strenuous physical activity. However, knowing that this would be an opportunity for her husband, she goes ahead without his knowledge. She feels joyous, being partner to his success and suppresses thoughts of a possible miscarriage. They're a standing success. They perform with discipline and artistry. She does not lose the child.

This is a husband and wife team flying through the air before a packed house. He has just caught her and they both feel a thrill of excitement. He met her as a young girl and fell in love with her and trained her to fly with him. He was very anxious for her at first but now he feels a sense of pride and relief. But too soon—in the next pass he reaches for her hands and misses. She falls to her death. He spends the rest of his life feeling guilty. He loses his confidence and his ability to fly.

The woman's story takes us through a time of suffering and doubt and then on to final success and happiness. The man's story begins in both physical and emotional excitement, even pride, but soon collapses into failure and despair.

In this chapter I wish to establish the fact that this sort of sex difference in fantasy patterns is typical of men and women in our culture. But to do so will require some narrowing of focus and definition of terms. In order to make the material manageable, and comparable from person to person, we will be looking at fantasy patterns as manifested in the stories people make up about this ambiguous picture of a man and woman on the trapeze.* It is then possible to develop a relatively objective way to evaluate the pattern of movement in such stories.†

First we need an anchor point in the story, a moment that separates the "before" from the "after." Most such brief stories do indeed have a dramatic turning point, a hinge around which the story turns, a crucial act or emotional state, which is the transition between the opening scene that the author has set and the final outcome. In the

*This technique, of studying imaginative stories told in response to ambiguous pictures, is known generally in psychology as the Thematic Apperception Test, or TAT. The method has proven successful with a number of different pictures, but it will simplify the discussion to limit ourselves to the trapeze picture. For background on the use, in psychology, of this technique, see: Christiana Morgan and Henry Murray, "A Method for Investigating Fantasies" (1935) in Robert Birney and Richard Teevan, eds., *Measuring Human Motivation* (Princeton: D. Van Nostrand, 1962); John Atkinson, ed., *Motives in Fantasy, Action and Society* (Princeton: D. Van Nostrand, 1958); Bernard Murstein, *Theory and Research in Projective Techniques* (New York: John Wiley & Sons, 1963).

†The notion that there might be such a sex difference in fantasy was first suggested to me by David McClelland. The evolution of his ideas can be seen in his paper on "The Harlequin Complex," in Robert White, ed., *The Study of Lives* (New York: Atherton Press, 1963) and in chapters 3 and 5 of *Power: The Inner Experience* (New York: Irvington Publishers, 1975).

scoring system\* this hinge is called the "pivotal incident" and various
rules are set up to help identify it. Once this has been done we then
proceed to locate all the "units" (words or coherent phrases) that
have a definite emotional tone. These are noted as either positive or
negative, or in the more general language of the scoring system, as
Deprivation or Enhancement. Deprivation includes physical need or
tension, failure, injury, painful effort, falling, unpleasant feelings, and
so forth. Enhancement includes physical satisfaction, ability and
success, growth or ascension, good feelings, being helped by others,
insight, and the like. These units are scored according to their position before or after the pivotal incident: a plus one for a Deprivation
unit before or an Enhancement unit after, and a minus one for the
opposite. Thus the scoring system gives a positive score to stories that
move from Deprivation to Enhancement and a negative score for
those that move from Enhancement to Deprivation.

For instance:

> This is in a circus and *the girl has just been thrown out of the arms of
> another trapeze artist* (D +1) who's not in the picture. And *the man
> in the picture has just caught her* (E −1) and [he'll swing her back to
> the platform on the other side] and *let her down safely* (E +1).
>
> (Total score = +1)

> These are acrobats who *use their skills* (E −1) to entertain other
> people. Like *the audience that's down below* (E −1) watching them.
> [And after the show they'll go out] and *get drunk together and laugh*
> (E +1) at *all the people below them* (E +1).
>
> (Total score = 0)

We should note two things inherent in this method of scoring. First
the overall tone of the story, its general optimism or pessimism if you
will, should not be an issue since the same sort of references on either
side of the pivotal incident will cancel themselves out numerically.
It is a system designed to be sensitive to *shifts* in tone. Secondly, the
scores themselves do not distinguish between absolute and relative
shifts. That is to say, a story that has only gloom, but moves from a
lot of gloom to only a little, will receive a positive score. This is an
intentional aspect of the scoring system since people certainly vary
a good deal in terms of their typical mood and we do not want to

\*A full copy of the scoring system is in appendix A.

exclude those for whom success means going from disaster to mere misfortune, or whose idea of failure is slipping from splendid to only good.

There is a remarkable range of content and tone in the stories one gets when one asks people to say what they think is happening in the trapeze picture. All of the following, for instance, came from a relatively homogeneous group of college students:

Gerry's just started flipping out after shooting some acid. He's imagining that he and his chick Doris are just flying around, free from any kind of obstacles. They're really together here, which is probably the first time they've been so in about six months, even if it is only in his mind. During his trip, Gerry and Doris are both naturally high and they're both getting into each other's minds. It's like a real communion for them. When he starts to come down, though, he finds that it was really just a trip, and while he enjoyed it, he knows things can never be the same again. Doris has begun to realize that she doesn't want to be tied down to one guy, and she's started messing with a couple of guys that she really digs. Gerry's really hung up on her and he knows he won't be able to handle the situation.

This is a painting. The people are acrobats. The artist's parents were circus acrobats and the artist spent his youth among these circus people. The artist is seeking unity of movement and form as if the male and female are merely extensions of one another. The artist will lament the loss of his parents and preserve his remembrance of them on canvas.

This man and woman had climbed a mountain. They reached a certain point where no gravitational force existed and went flying off into space. Now they are concentrating all of their energy into trying to hold on to one another. They are not fighting their flight into space, but just kind of being carried by some strange unknown forces. Again their only concern is that they remain together. The lights in the bottom of the picture are just some kind of satellites sent up by some country on earth. They get carried into a place where there is no past, present, or future, and remain transfixed there together.

How would you like to be a trapeze artist and constantly catch your wife in the act? Well, Joe was sick of the circus life, the make-believe, the shiny costumes, the fake smiles, the drama of the drums as they came to the final triple somersault. He had to get out. He had to escape from Liz. She was so possessive. She didn't let him do anything. He had to

get rid of her to be free. Tomorrow, yes, tomorrow, when they came
to Gary, Indiana, they would work without a net. The daring Darius's
would cause great excitement in the crowd with their courage. Then
he'd drop her. He would miss and she would fall on the ground, a
crumpled body in gold lamé.

But concealed in this variety is a structural consistency: stories told
by men tend to move from enhancement to deprivation (negative
scores by the scoring system) and stories told by women tend to move
from deprivation to enhancement (positive scores). Ten separate
studies have shown this to be true.

These male and female fantasy patterns begin to emerge in early or
middle childhood. Several studies by Phebe Cramer have established
that boys and girls begin showing significantly different fantasy patterns somewhere between the ages of six and nine. (Appendix B lists
the published research work on these fantasy patterns. The studies
referred to in this chapter are summarized in more detail there.) It is
not possible to fix a precise beginning in part because one runs into
methodological troubles with preschool children: they are not inclined
to tell the sort of well-organized story, with a beginning, middle, and
end, that the scoring system calls for. At the same time the simplicity
of the stories often reveals the pattern even more starkly.

> Once there were two trapeze. The people kept thinking they were
> going to miss each other in the air. They felt very fritin. Now it was
> time! They did their trick in the air and the man caught the lady. And
> they lived happily ever after [girl].

> Once there was a man and a lady and their names were Mike N. and
> Gina G. and they were friends. They are practicing and Mike N. thinks
> he is going to fall before a man took their picture they were climbing
> a tight rope and he fell and killed himself [boy].

As the occasionally novel spelling and grammar indicate, the above
stories were written by the children themselves. With even younger
children it makes more sense to have them tell the story out loud
while the interviewer writes it down. And the oral method seems to
liberate even more flights of fancy, as shown in the following series
of stories from Cramer's extensive researches. A young boy responded:

I think they're over water. Oh, I know what they're on, they're on a string, And he's over and she's like this. But, when she gets done doing that she going to go away. When she goes away she is going to fall somewhere . . . in a deep, deep hole. And then she'll be bitten by alligators, "Ough" and that's all.

Other boys are similarly alive to the destructive possibilities in the picture (in parentheses are questions asked by the interviewer):

He's trying to kill this one. And this one here is trying to kick this one in the mouth. And he feels like he is trying to pull off his leg. That's what I think he feels like. Where's his head. I can't see it. I can't even see what he's feeling like. (What happens?) This thing here is going to break off. (How does it end?) With them two dead.

It's sort of a trapeze, ballet sort of thing, and they do twirls around in the circus. But I think this is just practicing, rehearsing and stuff like that. And I think the man is about to drop the lady and I think the lady is going to land on her back. And maybe she's going to be flattened. The man will get put in jail and I think he will be gassed in a gas chamber.

Sometimes the sin is merely one of stealing the show, and the punishment routine:

The lady and the man joined the circus to do a job. Then they're in the air doing the high trapeze. Then the lady slips and she goes into the trampoline the next row on down, that she wasn't suppose to be in. Then she does the trampoline really high and does the highest record. And then the man caught her and the lady went on to the other side where the elephants were, and she landed on the elephants. Later the man caught the girl again and then they landed. And the two got fired for being in all three acts. (How do they feel?) They feel horrible, misery.

Sometimes the boys' fantasies even echoes the mythic destruction by fire that we saw with Phaethon:

The man and woman are swinging. The man is trying to get to the ceiling but the woman is pulling him down. Some animal may get them both and eat them up. And then the room will catch on fire and burn down. The fireman will try to pour water in. (How does it end?) Maybe they're going to get burned by the fire, and get shot by big hammers like my daddy has.

Once upon a time there was a man and a woman who really wanted to be some acrobats. They joined an acrobatic school and they studied up how to be a really good acrobat. And then they joined the Thomas circus and they went around playing. Then they went to this city called Seattle. They were practicing in it, doing their stunts. And then when the lady was doing her fancy flip in the air and catch the man's hands she missed. She went all the way down, hit the net, went through the net, in the ground, through the center of the earth, come back up, and back down through the center of the earth and then barely gets to reach her hands to the net she fell though. And she keeps going back and forth through the center of the earth till she hits the fire ball and gets burned up.

The stories told by little girls are more complex, less addicted to catastrophe, and more likely to chronicle the passage from bad to good:

They're in the circus and they're practicing for a big circus, the president is going to come. And when the president comes they're doing it really good and then the girl falls off and jumps into a net, and the president thought that was part of the act. She became very good in jumping and he [the president] thought it was real good. (How do they feel?) They feel really surprised that they fooled the president.

Looks like they were in the circus and now they have to say they're going to . . . the guy said they have to climb a trapeze thing. Right now, she just flew off the trapeze, and he, this other one, got her and they're going to do some somersaults and they're going to do some really good flips and she's land on her feet on a big cushion. And he going to swing and then he is going to stop and then he going to hold on to another man's arms. Then it's going to stop all together right there. (What are they feeling?) She's feeling, "uh-oh, I hope we make it," and he's feeling, "Uh, I hope I have my muscles on good today".

That lady used to live in the country and she was very poor. But one day the circus passed by her window and they stopped by and asked her for some food and drink. And she said she didn't have any so they said they would go on further. But she wanted to be in the circus so she just walked along behind them. Finally they came to the circus. The lady who usually does this said she was sick and she couldn't do it. The girl came running up and said she would do it and she would try it. So she acted it up, and right here she is thinking how she would love to keep with this job. The other lady and the end of this performance, the lady came and she told them that she couldn't stay with them because they had found her a better job as a secretary. So she became the lady who swung on the trapeze for the rest of her job. And she got money and she didn't live in the country anymore. (How does she feel?) She likes it a whole lot.

Throughout the school years the male and female patterns become more developed and clearly established. This differentiation accelerates as puberty approaches, occurring earlier in girls as does puberty itself (See Cramer, 1975). Phebe Cramer's developmental studies of Deprivation/Enhancement patterns included thirty-one children who were tested twice, a year apart, while entering adolescence. Twenty-eight of these boys and girls showed a shift in Deprivation/ Enhancement scores, with twenty of these shifting in the direction we would predict for their sex. Here are some examples of this shift:

### Age eleven and one-half

This is a man and a lady that worked in the circus for a long time. They practice a lot and they get a lot of money. There was this one day, they put on the circus and there was millions of people there. It was their turn and they did this cannon act, where they get shot out of the cannon. They get shot out of the cannon and everybody claps. There were these other people who asked if they could play at their park; put the circus on at their park. They go to the park and they get up on the stage and they start to practice for the circus. They practice getting shot out of the cannon. There are two cannons that they get shot out of like that. The girl got shot out of the cannon first and then the boy. The girl fell down first on the net and then the boy fell down right on top of her. She got her neck broken so she couldn't play in the circus. She went to the hospital and they didn't know if she was going to survive or not. The guy was really worried. They had to figure out some sort of way to cure the neck so they can make it feel better. They sew her neck together and she's all right.

### Age twelve and one-half

Well, this is a brother and a sister and they work for a circus, Barnum and Bailey Circus, and they like acrobatting for the circus and they like it a lot. And they had a cannon act too where they got shot out of a cannon and so they liked acrobatting and getting shot out of a cannon a lot. One time in an act, they were getting shot out of a cannon, and they hit each other and fell on the net and the lady broke her neck and the guy broke his arm so they couldn't acrobat for a long time, two years. The girl had to stay in a wheelchair and the guy had to stay in bed. So they stayed there for two years in the hospital. After that when they got through, they asked if they could work in the circus again and the doctor said no they wouldn't be able to because of the muscle spasms, in the guy's arm and the neck conditions in the lady's neck so they couldn't be in any more circus acts and that's all. (How did they feel?) They felt bad because that was their living.

This young man stays with the same theme but the pattern becomes more extreme: there is more clearly stated positive feeling in the beginning of the story, and then a more definitely damaging outcome. Together these changes make for a story with a much more severe fall (as reflected in the score shift from $-3$ for the first story to $-13$ for the second).

### Age ten

I know what it is, these two both climbed up on stands, with lots of people watching. And there is no net below them. And that is the assistant and that is the star. They both climb up on to their trapeze stands. They jump on their trapeze, the girl flips and grabs on to the man. Then before that, on to one stand. Then the man flips over the other trapeze and this goes on and on until about one hour is up and then they dive into a net they have brought out there now. (What do they feel?) They felt a little nervous because it was their first time in front of an audience, they've practiced many times. The net, uh, the first time the net gave them sort of a fright but the men first told them to jump into the net. And they had a lot of trouble and they kept falling. But after a while they got more confident, made it alot easier.

### Age eleven

That's a coincidence. That's a circus in the night, and they are both thinking, "Well hold on tight and good luck." They're doing the trapeze stunt in the Ringling Brothers Circus. (What happens?) That guy's legs are going to catch a muscle and they're going to fall. I don't like thinking of that. (How does it end?) There's going to be a net below them so nothing will happen. And it will look like part of the act. (How do they feel?) When they hit the net they felt, "Well, this is it." (How does it end?) Nothing happens except they got a cut in their pay.

The story at age ten shows a complex pattern of overt skill but underlying anxiety, followed by trouble and then ultimate recovery. As judged by the scoring system the overall movement is positive (a score of +6). But by age eleven this boy's story has become almost entirely an unwilling meditation on the degree of the final disaster: the author says he doesn't like thinking about the fall, but he can in fact think of little else and the only question open in his mind is the extent of the damage.

### Age ten and one-half

There was this man and wife and they had a trapeze act. So late at night when they weren't suppose to go into the tent and practice, they wanted to practice. And they were practicing, and practicing, and practicing, and they were doing flips and somersaults, and holding on to the trapeze with one hand, and hanging by the heels. And then the man caught her and she slipped out of his hands and fell on to the net and bounced right back up and the man caught up her and she got on to the other trapeze and she slipped again she fell on the net again, and she bounced and she caught hold of the man and she went on over to the tightrope and she walked across and then she went on the trapeze again and she swung over to the platform. The next day was the circus. She fell and she missed the net but nothing happened to her, she didn't have one bruise or anything. But her husband thought the trapeze was too dangerous and they started on clown.

### Age eleven and one-half

It's the nighttime and they're practicing on the trapeze but no audience is there, but they're practicing and the man when he's hanging by one of his knees, one of his legs comes undone from the rope and there's no net underneath, and they're still practicing and his leg's still slipping out but he doesn't know it and then his leg comes out all of a sudden. And the girl she doesn't want him to die because he's important to the circus, so she waits until the next trapeze comes and she gets on the trapeze and she swings over and helps him get his leg back under the trapeze. But she can't do it so she slides down the rope and she lowers the trapeze thing so he can get out of there. So they were all happy and they were a little afraid to practice again but they waited until somebody else was with them just in case they needed some help so they didn't go up there again until they had somebody else with them. Their act went pretty good cause they had a whole bunch of people there.

This young girl's fantasy shows a shift in the other direction. The first story is a series of falls followed by recoveries. It ends on a note of withdrawal or resignation. The later story has some of the same up and down pattern, but the story as a whole has crystallized into a sequence of anxiety overcome and danger survived. And this story differs from the male examples in another way also: it testifies to the importance of other people as sources of help and comfort.

By late adolescence the sex difference in Deprivation/Enhancement fantasy patterns is well-established enough to be statistically significant in five of the seven studies done with young adults.*But the evidence so far is also limited in several important ways. Most of the work has been done with middle-class men and women of college age or younger. There are, however, two studies, one by Sharon Wilsnack (1972) and one by Carolyn Saarni (1976), that found positive Deprivation/Enhancement scores for older, working-class women. Saarni got fantasy stories from a group of twenty-three skilled workers (average age forty-three, and high-school education). When scored, the trapeze stories turned out to be highly positive. Many were extreme and melodramatic examples of deprivation followed by enhancement. For instance:

> Clarice ran up the ladder as quickly as she could. Her heart pounded with the excitement. As she reached the platform, she glanced down at the spotlights throwing their glare up at her. She remembered John's words: "Don't look down. Keep your eyes on me." She looked anxiously across the tent, and saw he was watching her.

*There is the suggestion in the data that Deprivation/Enhancement patterns peak in intensity in early adolescence, though we have little information for the period between age thirteen and twenty. In some as yet unpublished work, Cramer found that the spread between the sexes decreases in the junior high school years and may even reverse itself in the first year of college, with males being somewhat more positive in Deprivation/Enhancement score than females. This is indeed intriguing, since the Deprivation/Enhancement sex difference is again well-established by the middle years of college. If Cramer's results hold up we will need to think in terms of an initial extreme differentiation of fantasy patterns in early adolescence, followed by a period of moderation or even reversal in middle adolescence and then a new but less extreme separation of the sexes in later college and adult life.

When he saw he had her attention, he gave her the signal, and she started counting. All of her practice had not quite prepared her for this first time performing before an audience. John smiled at her confidently, then swung off into space. As she counted, she pushed herself off on her trapeze. Her heart pounded in her throat; her stomach felt empty and fluttery. For a moment she panicked, thinking she had missed him. Then she saw him smiling at her, and she launched herself into space. She felt his hands grab hers and instantly she knew everything was alright. She would make it.

Whether such classic stories are more typical of older or working class women, it is too soon to say. But we can say that the Deprivation/Enhancement fantasy pattern is not limited to young, middle class women. For men there is less evidence about the possible effects of age and social class. As we will see in chapter VI, there is some closely related work by David Gutmann that strongly suggests a shift in fantasy pattern in the mid and later years of a man's life.

Saarni's study also included a group of "politically and organizationally active feminists." These women, curiously enough, are the only example, in the many studies which have been done, of a group of women with solidly negative Deprivation/Enhancement scores. They do not seem to get these scores in the same way the typical man does: with a story moving from pride to disaster. Instead what we see in the stories of these feminists is pride and self-confidence without the catastrophic end:

The trapeze artist is in top form tonight and despite the lurching in her stomach which is still there each time she feels gravity taking hold in the middle of a descent, she is pleased with the precision of the swings, aware that all eyes are on her and her performance is flawless. She has an additional glow of satisfaction that her anchor man is envious of her prima donna status, the spotlight role that has been choreographed for her while he must swing back and forth on the sidelines giving her the firm grips and steady flips she needs to follow her pattern.

The trapeze artists are a famous team—the woman is the more agile and daring of the two—she performs the most thrilling feats—she relies on her partner's excellent sense of timing—They have agreed not to be intimately involved with each other because they have agreed that it would be difficult to do their death-defying act if they carried over daily life situations literally into the act.

These stories offer a dramatic contrast with the saga of feminine anxiety, the tale of "Clarice," from which we just came. Not the least of the differences is the firm way in which these latter fantasies place the man in a minor and supporting role. It is a general confirmation of our approach to find that a group of women whom we would expect to wish to separate themselves from traditional sex roles, and to work against male domination, to find such women producing these stories.

The design of Saarni's study does not allow us to go much farther, nor to know what part of her results may be due to the fact that her "feminists" are also the most highly educated group that has yet been tested. These are the directions in which we need to go now: to try to understand the meaning of these fantasy patterns by looking at stories from widely varying groups, and to begin to study smaller groups more closely. Now that we can say that this fantasy difference between men and women does exist, the really interesting questions appear. What might it mean? *Why* does it exist, and what might it be connected to?

Of the various groups of men who have been given this fantasy test, the only one to cross over the boundary to the usually female territory of positive Deprivation/Enhancement scores is a group of acknowledged homosexuals (May, 1975). These men's stories also point to another important aspect of such fantasies. There was a wide range of patterns in these stories, as can be seen in these two examples:

> Two people swing on the trapeze in the circus act and there're three people in the act and she's the flier who's supposed to go—swing to the other person who catches her and there's this jealous relationship going on between the three of them and the other one really likes the guy and the guy likes the girl and so the guy—the catcher—when she goes —intentionally drops her. And she gets very hurt and breaks her neck and dies. And the other man successfully makes it with the second guy.

> Acrobats in a circus. He's the catcher and she's uh I don't know what the term is. She does all the somersaults and turns in the air and catches onto his arms. There was another acrobat in the act but she fell and

hurt herself rather badly. And this girl's had to take her place. She was the second one in line. He's terribly scared that she wants to give it up. And he keeps asking her wait wait wait til I get somebody else. She feels a large risk, more, being as nervous as she is. The more chance she has of having an accident. But she doesn't have an accident but he hurts his back one night as he grabs her awkwardly and he has to stop doing it. He can't do it for many many months so she gets out of it that way. She's very happy about it.

The first story shows a more typically male pattern, getting a negative score, while the second story moves the opposite way and receives a positive score. At the same time we notice that the male figure is at the center of the first story while the second revolves around the woman. It was with this group of stories that it first became clear that it may matter whether the story is told with a male or female hero. When the stories were classified as to the sex of the central figure, it turned out that stories with male heroes tend toward negative scores while stories with female heroes tend toward positive scores. The male homosexual group scores more positively overall not just because their neuter (the male and female figures equally central) stories are positive while those of a nonhomosexual comparison group are negative, but also because the homosexual group shows a greater preference for female heroes.

There have been two studies that have attempted to increase our understanding of Deprivation/Enhancement patterns by seeing whether they are affected by experiences that we would expect to be relevant. Sara Winter was interested in the psychological effects on the mother of nursing an infant. Her research showed that mothers who made up a fantasy story while nursing their child revealed an intensified form of the female Deprivation/Enhancement pattern. Michael Bramante used an equally inventive experimental procedure to discover that viewing a film calculated to heighten one's awareness of gender and sexuality results in more extreme fantasy scores, in the predicted direction, for both men and women. He also found evidence that the shift to a hypermale pattern was greatest in those men who feel least secure in their masculinity.

Information from personal interviews (May, 1969) allows us to begin sketching in the context and correlates of Deprivation/Enhancement fantasy (throughout this discussion the words "high" and "extreme" refer to fantasy patterns more in the direction typical of one's sex, that is, positive in score for women and negative in score for men): Men high on Deprivation/Enhancement are in awe of their father's aggression or competence and wish to show both father and themselves that they can do as well. Their striving has not been smoothly successful. At some point in their growing up they have felt quite inadequate, and the humiliation has involved some imagined physical or sexual failing. At present they value such qualities as strength, independence, and fortitude. They envision men as inherently tougher than women and thus properly the leaders and initiators in relations with women. They are uncomfortable when not in control. At the same time they speak of envy for what they see as a woman's license to be warm and emotional, and to follow or depend on someone. They feel that one of the prices of being male lies in a constant pressure to prove one's masculinity or competence.

Women high on Deprivation/Enhancement see their mothers as enforcers of an unwanted set of standards. These standards are variously described as "acting like a lady," being loving, associating with "nice" boys, and having good manners. Politeness, gentility, and pleasantness seem to be the crux of it. The daughter resented this pressure, and even more resents what she sees as the bad side of being a woman: a certain passivity, a sense of having to stifle her own initiative and quietly endure while waiting on the whims of men (women low on Deprivation/Enhancement share this image of femaleness but paint it in positive terms and value it). Men are envied or imitated and there is often the recollection of having been forced to give up one's "tomboy" aggressiveness.

For each sex a period of isolation and estrangement from peers in the preadolescent and early adolescent years is associated with extreme Deprivation/Enhancement patterns. This can be seen as indicating either a genuine historical lack of an important chance to moderate and make more human one's self conception, or it can be seen as a reflection of a current sense of loneliness and strain in the high Deprivation/Enhancement types. More securely in the realm of historical reality is the curious fact that having an older brother tends to raise a boy's Deprivation/Enhancement score (Johnson, 1974). Perhaps it does so by way of a heightened atmosphere of male competition in the family.

For both sexes extreme Deprivation/Enhancement patterns go with a feeling of strain about gender. There is a sense of standards that may be actively distasteful or simply difficult of attainment, but which in any case require effort, struggle, and a certain pain. But the struggle is in different areas. For men high Deprivation/Enhancement is associated with a high need for achievement; for women the more extreme pattern is linked with the absence of a concern about achievement and instead with an investment in nurturance, succorance, and endurance (Malmaud, 1975). This division of psychological labor is congruent with the traditional outline of male and female roles.

On a more cognitive level the male pattern is associated with an unrealistically high evaluation of one's own abilities and chances of success. The female pattern is associated with the tendency to downgrade and underrate one's performance (Rabinovitz, 1976). And in women, high Deprivation/Enhancement scores go with greater perceptual "field dependence," the unwillingness to wrench a context apart and seize on one element to the exclusion of the surround (May, 1975).

Now we come to the more complex question of basic character or personality structure. In the one study (May, 1975) in which diagnostic assessments on the basis of intensive clinical study were available, we find that the most feminine group in Deprivation/Enhancement terms is those women classified as "hysterical." This is a diagnostic term with a long history, and a close association with the troubles of women ever since the Greeks invented the term for female disturbances, which they attributed to a wandering womb. As a character description it is used to refer to some combination of the following: a serious sexual conflict or dysfunction, often in the context of repetitive triangular relationships; an engaging interpersonal style involving elements of seductiveness and high emotional drama; a certain childlike innocence, conventionality, and concern with pleasing; a mental style that tends toward the romantic, the fuzzy, and the forgetful; and a persistent experience of being the victim of others' aggression, sexual or not (the fear of rape is often hovering in the background).

The notion that the female Deprivation/Enhancement pattern may have links to this character pattern even in a less troubled group is supported by Cramer and Carter's (1978) study of college students.

"Reversal," the defense that they found most positively tied with high Deprivation/Enhancement women, refers to a series of strategies for dealing with conflict, which focus on changing one's feelings or perceptions even at the cost of falsifying reality. Included are repression ("I can't remember"), Pollyannalike denial ("I don't see it"), and reaction formation ("I don't hate him, I love him"). These have long been considered defenses typical of the hysterical character. And as Cramer and Carter found, they are associated in high Deprivation/Enhancement women with an inhibition of the opposite strategy of solving conflict by an aggressive attack on someone or something outside.

The personality context of Deprivation/Enhancement in men is not as clear. There were no significant diagnostic correlates. There is one hint in the fact that the diagnostic category that showed the largest difference in men was that of paranoid (they have a more "male" score than the average) versus nonparanoid (a less "male" score). Once again Cramer and Carter come to the rescue. Their work with a "normal" group of young men shows that the psychological defense most characteristic of high Deprivation/Enhancement men is projection. Projection is defined as "the justification of the expression of aggression toward an external object through first attributing to it, without unequivocal evidence, negative intent or characteristics." So the character style linked to male Deprivation /Enhancement scores involves responding to stress by first locating an enemy somewhere out in the world and then proceeding to attack, and to be angry at, this enemy. And these men are particularly low in the tendency to turn anger inwards against the self, to react to conflict with guilt and self-blame. They are also low in what was, for Cramer and Carter's group, another typically female defense: "principalization." This group of maneuvers includes intellectualization, rationalization, and other methods of holding the conflict inside and trying to neutralize it. In this sense it is the opposite of the outward-facing, aggressive response, which seems to typify high Deprivation /Enhancement men.

On the evidence so far we can comfortably say that the female Deprivation/Enhancement pattern is related to "hysterical" character traits and particularly to psychological defenses that inhibit anger and treat conflict as an internal matter, something to be metabolized or absorbed. With rather less assurance we think that the male Deprivation/Enhancement pattern is tied to a "paranoid" character style, or at least to defenses that transform conflict into an external matter and try to solve it through aggressive attack. The two types of fantasy pattern would be thus linked to different ways of managing frustration and anger. The female pattern is associated with holding the feeling inside and endeavoring to neutralize it or turn it into something more pleasing. The male pattern is associated with deflecting the feeling away from oneself and using it to prod or batter someone else.

So out of these empirical studies there has emerged at least an outline of a coherent picture: many of the studies point to similar emotional and cognitive correlates of our fantasy patterns. But the picture is a complex one. It looks, for instance, as if a particular pattern has different roots in each sex. Cramer's work on defenses indicates that the pattern of deprivation leading to enhancement in its typical female context is linked with the strategies of "reversal," whereas when a man produces such a fantasy pattern it goes along with quite different strategies ("turning against the self" and "principalization"); likewise the typically male pattern coexists with "projection" in men, but when a woman thinks that way it is in the context of "turning against the other."

Or, to take another question, what is the function of anxiety and ambivalence about one's sexual role? It does appear to be part of the extreme fantasy patterns. Should we think of it as simply part of the extremes, or as an important component of the male and female patterns at any point along the scale? To begin to answer these questions we must move from studies of groups to a more fine-grained look at the complex interior of an individual life.

# Chapter III

❦

# Two Lives

## JONATHAN W. LANGLY III

It's a picture of two trapeze artists, a man and a woman. They're
married and they're very happy in the circus and they like performing
and they do it very well . . . [Here he trails off into silence and the
interviewer asks him what happens next.] I was thinking he might drop
the woman . . . but then I think he likes her a bit too much to drop
her.

Jonathan's story begins with considerable good fortune and happiness
and rather abruptly slides into danger and doubt. The couple are
together, happy and competent. They enjoy their work and are good
at it. But this idyll cannot be maintained. The author falls silent,
perhaps struggling to save the robust and joyous world he has built,
or perhaps stunned by its collapse before his inner eyes. When we
ask, we find that murder has intruded: the man might drop the
woman. This seems to come from nowhere, as if the bottom has
suddenly fallen out of the world we were feeling admiring and comfortable about. The Snake has appeared in the Garden. The author
does his best to save things, but all he can manage is a note of doubt.
This near escape is based on a thin reed of mood; apparently if he
liked her just a bit less, down she would go. We note, though we don't
know what to make of it at this point, that the destructiveness is
located in the male.

Jonathan Langly was the second child, and first son, born into a family of weighty tradition. He was named for his paternal grandfather, a socially prominent and quite wealthy judge. In spite of his considerable success, the grandfather was said to have always felt himself overshadowed by his even more successful brother. As we shall see this is one of those malignant patterns, one of those hereditary taints, passed on through the generations. The grandfather died before Mr. Langly was born. Grandfather's son, Jonathan Wordsworth Langly II, had paid his respects to this patriarch by also becoming a prosperous and influential judge. His professional success has been signaled by his peers having elected him to head virtually every important professional group, and by the many glamorous members of high society who are known to seek his advice. He married a woman of beauty, respectable education, and considerable wealth. Mrs. Langly upholds the social honor of the family fully as well as her husband upholds the professional, performing good works and keeping a sharp eye on others' opinions of the Langlys. The few blemishes on this family stand out against the well-groomed background: secrecy veils the life of one of the father's sisters, a woman who has been in a mental hospital for several decades. Another of the father's sisters died young of a heart attack (the same disease that killed her mother, for whom she was named). This fatal tradition is a fearful unspoken presence in the family. And though the father is portrayed as a man totally lacking in vices, there is an undertone of detachment and chilliness about him. The son speaks of feeling out of touch with both his parents—several years have passed since they last wrote to him.

Jonathan Wordsworth Langly III was born just as Europe began to experience the demented attentions of Adolf Hitler. As befitted Mr. Langly's social class, nursemaids and servants saw to his early needs. Aside from being a finicky eater early on, his development appears to have gone smoothly until age two when his father left to serve in the war. During the five years his father was away Jonathan was prone to illness, easily frightened, and difficult to control (particularly with the younger brother who came on the scene about the same time as his father left). His mother took him into her bedroom during this difficult period.

Jonathan's first memories are of happy muscular activity. Throughout his school years he was very good at sports and physical games.

Active, well-coordinated, and popular are the adjectives that run through this period. But there was also a dark side, which stands in stark contrast. He has a memory of being restrained as a child, being tied down to his bed with a harness. He speaks of being terrified of school, fearing that he would be beaten and laughed at. That the fearfulness about school may have been more than incidentally connected with his father's return is suggested by a memory from these same years of his father beating him, eyes red with anger. His interest and success in sports was counterbalanced by a poor academic performance, such that he had to repeat a grade. And his preadolescent years were marked by numerous injuries, some of them serious, stemming from his boisterous and impulsive activity. Around the time of puberty he went away to boarding school. This was in the context of a growing independence, which frightened his mother considerably: he liked to go to baseball games by himself, freely struck up conversations with strangers, and associated with disreputable boys who were involved in projects such as stealing gun powder.

The first public crisis in his life seems to have been precipitated in part by continuing academic failure at boarding school. In the process of refusing to return to school he alarmed his family by his agitated overactivity and by being, for the first time, argumentative and rebellious. After a time that must have been quite difficult on both sides, his career of psychiatric treatment and hospitalization began (at age 15). His understanding of the hospitalization was that it meant he was an embarrassing failure to his family. He felt considerable shame and guilt. After a number of months of psychotherapy, both in hospital and out, he entered another prep school. Once again he excelled at sports, was popular and respected by his peers, but unable to do much serious academic work. During his junior year he had an anxious period with considerable drinking, and was admitted to the school infirmary. This seems to have been triggered by having had intercourse with a girl, in circumstances in which she might have become pregnant. His fears centered around how her father would react.

He was able to apply himself more to his work during his final year and he did graduate and get into a college, although it was a little-known school about which he felt chagrined. This failure fed his growing envy and resentment of his younger brother. The brother was doing well academically and appeared to be increasingly ahead in the race to be father's favorite and follow in the family professional tradition.

Jonathan did well enough to transfer to a university that he thought represented "the big time," a place of academic pressure and social prestige of which his father would approve. He experienced severe anxiety in the course of trying to work, but forced himself to stay with it and after much pain did in fact graduate. But he was unable to decide what to do next. After several abortive and anxious forays into various fields, he settled on investing in and helping to manage a small business. In less than a year this turned into a humiliating failure for him. With the help of further psychotherapy, and some discreet use of influence by his family, he picked himself up to try again, this time as a teacher. He seemed to do quite well indeed and was thought of as successful, competent, and popular in the all-male world of the boarding school where he worked. As he reflects back on this time, however, he sees it as one of intense, if private, anxiety.

Everything collapsed when he was suddenly promoted to a very responsible position. On the day following this success he felt absolutely unable to continue. He was now twenty-seven years old and the next few years were a tangle of broken relations with therapists, hospitals entered in hope but left in anger and disappointment; overall, the picture of a life fraying itself out. We hear repeatedly the note of dependent resentment toward older men: he needs something from his father and his doctors, and is bitterly furious that they have let him down or neglected him. This pattern is so persistent, and his disillusionment so obviously touched with scorn, that we are entitled to wonder whether there is a contorted form of competitiveness at work. By not being helped he turns his failure into the failure of those trying to help him.

What can we learn from this rather brief description of a complex life-in-process? There are a number of themes that deserve our attention. Let us take, to begin with, the matter of lineage. It does not take extraordinary empathy to feel the oppressive weight of those illustrious forebears. No doubt Jonathan's birthright also included the more positive elements of pride and a sense of entitlement. But the sharper echo is the troubling question: can I live up to this revered and powerful heritage? Can I prove that I belong in this family, that I am a true son of this father? The question is made more keen by the fact that the image has been formed in isolation. Jonathan was named for a dead grandfather, was without his father for a number of important early years, and even after that seems to have been contending more with a distant picture of perfection than with a real person. This is a situation offering endless possibilities for idealization and worship. And the absence or inaccessibility of the father also opens the door to a special and possessive relation with the mother, which may complicate even further the son's working out a sane sense of his own powers and competence.

One of the remarkable things about this family is the clarity with which one can hear the undertone of failure beneath the song of success. Death haunts the scene. It is a family where one's heart can give out in the middle of the race. The mother regularly warned father and son that they were risking a heart attack by exerting themselves too vigorously. And even short of death, the lesson of the family story about the grandfather is that one can achieve great things and still feel inadequate. There is no clear sense of how much would be enough, of when a person can slow down and enjoy the fruits of achievement. Perhaps never; certainly one is urged on by the example of what happens to those who stumble or fall behind. They fade into oblivion and might as well be dead, though the family rites of interment are presided over by psychiatrists rather than morticians. What appears to be a happy and successful life is constantly on the verge of sudden and disastrous collapse; good work cannot be trusted to last.

The notion of physical activity is central in Jonathan's life. This family clearly values activity, doing and accomplishing, but also fears activity as dangerous—it leads one into bad company or heart attacks. Motility, the ability and pleasure in moving one's body, and mobility, the ability to move in the social and interpersonal world, are persistent themes in the story of Jonathan. He defines himself in these terms by his earliest memory of "chasing a ball down the street." And others soon came to see him as a man of action too: "uncontrollable" action with his younger brother while his father was away and later a more modulated and praised activity. In fact the only area that stands out as one of consistent success is his ability to move his body.

From the joy of being "a fantastic runner" in grade school to the eager waiting for the weekend touch-football game in prep school, sports gave him a chance to do something and feel good about it. And early in his life we also see the theme of activity's counterpart, restraint. He remembers being put in a "straitjacket" in bed, a mechanism that "tied me down when I wanted to go out." We can imagine his raging and helpless struggles against this restraint, and his inevitable conclusion that someone important viewed his activity as inconvenient, bad, or downright dangerous. His later penchant for injuring himself is likely to have been both an enactment of this lesson about the dangers of activity and a sign that the successful modulation of his activity was proving a hard task. His activity polarizes into paralyzed restraint on the one hand and chaotic discharge on the other.

His crisis at age fourteen comes after having moved further away from home than he ever had been allowed previously, and one of the things that alarmed his family was his "overactivity." He is finally restrained through hospitalization. After this point his troubles take on more and more the metaphor of inhibited activity. His recurrent anxiety interferes with his getting anywhere in life and his mobility, both professional and physical, becomes more and more impaired. At the time of his second major crisis, at age twenty-seven, he has been struggling for quite some time with a fear of going out of his room.

In some way activity, once his greatest hope and talent, has become deeply dangerous and hemmed in with fear. His worst distress occurs at moments in his life that offer the prospect of a new step forward, a new mastery. Thus adolescence, a stage that always involves the question of leaving home and of providing space for one's growing strength and potency, is the scene of his first catastrophe. While it is likely that his continued poor academic performance after going to boarding school caused him pain, there is also reason to think that the prospect of success was just as anxiety-laden. For there is no evidence that his school work went any more poorly than in previous years and in fact he had spent a peaceful first year away from home and had been making progress in venturing off on his own despite his mother's fearful concern. It is as if the anxiety mounts as he approaches the point of a successful takeoff. The disturbing behavior that aborted this process has the quality of independence run self-destructively wild: he can't sit still, he can't stop talking, he disobeys and generally abuses his parents. His hyperactivity is so anxiously driven that others feel the need to restrain him. The next episode we hear about, two years later, also comes after a period of athletic and social success at school: While on a vacation trip with a friend he has intercourse with a woman and proceeds to get acutely anxious, drink himself insensible, and commit himself to the school infirmary. It appears that sexual progress does not sit very well either. And the most recent collapse is more telling yet: a promotion to a prestigious position brings him down.

How are we to understand this paradoxical pattern of snatching defeat from the jaws of victory? On a simple level we may want to relate it to the combination of high expectations and underlying threat that seems to have existed in his family. The road to be traveled seems endless and one is burdened with the constant awareness of possible humiliation or death. Thus each step is only a further commitment to this terrifying journey, and it wouldn't surprise us that Jonathan would want to invalid himself out of it all. His fears of not being able to make it turn out to be only a prelude to the continuing fear of not being able to keep it up. Having a success only gives you further to fall next time.

But there is another mode of explanation, not contradictory but certainly more complex. We take our lead from Freud, who describes a character type he calls "Those Wrecked by Success."[1] Freud starts with the puzzle of people who collapse into illness upon attaining something, a promotion or a marriage, for which they have long wished. He tells us that our puzzlement about this sequence is partly due to our unwillingness to recognize that an internal frustration can be just as important as an external one. Although a person may seem to have gotten what he or she wants externally, he can still arrange to deprive himself of any pleasure in it. Freud offers both clinical and literary examples of people who collapse upon the successes of their plans. He constructs the argument that, firstly, it is our consciences that punish us at the moment of success, and secondly that the crime for which we must suffer was originally located in our lusts and angers toward our parents. It was an Oedipal crime, and the present success revives our guilt.

Although we by no means have all the information we'd like, let

us see how we might apply this notion to what we do know of
Jonathan's life. We would begin by paying attention to his father's
absence: from ages two through seven Jonathan's was a fatherless
household, and, but for all of the first of those years, Jonathan slept
in his mother's bedroom. It was during this time that his fearfulness
and uncontrollable behavior first became evident. We know precious
little about the actual quality of the relation between mother and son,
or about what other important figures there were in the household
then. Nonetheless we can venture some likely guesses. The young
wife's loneliness must have focused on this eldest son, especially since
he seemed to need her care very much. So they moved closer together, even it seems at the expense of the newly born younger son.
Here indeed is an Oedipal victory, with its sense of power and
exclusive possession of the mother.

But from what we hear it does not seem to have been a happy
victory. The anxiety and disruptiveness continue in spite of sharing
a bedroom with his mother, and in fact he is beset by screaming
nightmares for a year at age four. Here is the prototype of a victory
that Jonathan can't stand. Such is the nature of Oedipal victories;
they are always Pyrrhic. Insofar as there is a primitive sexual fantasy
involved, the son has won himself a prize that he can't possibly do
anything with. The fantasy of sexual domination over, or union with,
the mother may be quite exhilarating but the more it becomes a real
possibility the more one's simple physical inadequacy is bound to
shatter those hopes. Even more important, in the psychoanalytic
view, is the fear of punishment. Such an audacious project is felt as
bound to bring retaliation from this woman's *real* husband. As evidence here we can point to Jonathan's vivid memory of a furious and
vengeful father, so at odds with the overall picture of this man as calm
and mild, and the disabling episode of fear at age seventeen, a fear
that centered on what the father of the woman he had had intercourse with might think or do.

Erik Erikson has usefully expanded psychoanalytic theory by elaborating the context of the various stages and pointing to the ways in
which physical and social development interlock with sexual development to shape particular modes of action. He points out that what
is traditionally referred to as the Oedipal stage is also the time when
the child first gains reliable control over his or her own movement.

The salience of "locomotor mastery" on the level of physical development is paralleled by a playing out of the "intrusive mode" on an
interpersonal level: "the intrusion into other bodies by physical attack; the intrusion into other people's ears and minds by aggressive
talking; the intrusion into space by vigorous locomotion; the intrusion
into the unknown by consuming curiosity."[2] Erikson sees the "psychosocial" issue at this stage as one of "initiative," of coming to a
comfortable sense about one's ability to start things, to make things,
to act aggressively on the world. A miscarriage here is likely to leave
one burdened with a guilty fear of one's own potential for action.
"The danger of this stage is a sense of guilt over the goals contemplated and the acts initiated in one's exuberant enjoyment of new
locomotor and mental power: acts of aggressive manipulation and
coercion which go far beyond the executive capacity of organism and
mind and therefore call for an energetic halt on one's contemplated
initiative."[3] The reverse side of initiative is paralysis and impotence,
which serve as a defensive denial of any aggressive capability.

Having begun trying to understand Jonathan by way of some
Freudian notions about the Oedipal stage, we now find that Erikson's
elaboration and expansion also fits well. We have already seen the
extent to which activity and physical movement are dominant
themes in Jonathan's story. And it is often activity that cannot be
reliably modulated and controlled. The correspondence between
Erikson's description of the various childhood aspects of intrusiveness
and the offensive behavior that first got Jonathan hospitalized is
striking: incessant movement, incessant talk, and an attacking attitude. As further confirmation of the coherence and relevance of this
stage, we notice in Jonathan a devotion to activity that then collapses
into its opposite: the sort of paralyzed and impotent denial of one's
initiative that Erikson sees as the result of unmanageable conflict at
this stage.*

The Oedipal stage, or the stage of Initiative vs. Guilt in Erikson's
terminology, is also the time when the crystallization of sexual identity occurs. Classical psychoanalytic theory sees the link in the boy's

---

*It is interesting to note that this inhibition extends even to the style of his thought
processes. The report of a psychological testing done during one of Mr. Langly's
periods of crisis refers to his mental style as characterized by constriction, passivity,
an unwillingness to "extend himself," and a general "cognitive flabbiness." (!)

fearful identification with his father. The desire to possess mother runs up against fears of retaliation by father. This dilemma is solved by identifying with father, thus at one stroke both trying to become the sort of person who *could* have mother and at the same time to joining father rather than contending with him. The boy's eventual sense of his own maleness depends to a considerable extent on this complex transformation of his infantile assertiveness. Erikson's approach is broader but not significantly different. He sees this stage as determining the shape of one's initiative and the modulated use of the intrusive mode, both of which are intimately related to a male identity as we generally think of it. So this line of theory would expect to find some problem of sexual identity in Jonathan, an area in which his various difficulties are reflected in a troubled sense of his own maleness.

Once again we do not have all the information we would like and we are left making inferences from small hints. On the face of it there *is* reason to doubt that Jonathan has arrived at any patterning of his sexual life that can provide him satisfaction within a productive relationship with a woman. The one episode of sexual intercourse we hear about is disastrous. The woman involved is the only woman outside his immediate family who appears in the story at all, and even she seems to have been upstaged in Jonathan's mind by her father. Jonathan's is a life in which almost all the important characters are men. While it would be rash to talk of homosexuality on the basis of this evidence, it is naturally a question brought to mind by this exclusively male, sports-oriented world. If maleness needs to be asserted by isolation from women we doubt its depth or durability. Of course the saving grace of compulsive athleticism and of drunken male camaraderie is that it provides acceptable outlets for affection and the wish to touch. But for someone who is anxious about his own sexual orientation, this can be a delicate game to play. It is reported that Jonathan's early adolescent sexuality included fellatio with other boys, that he had at least one drunken sexual encounter with another male faculty member, and that after leaving his prep school job he complained of the "homosexual atmosphere" there.

But this is all rather like crossing a stream by jumping from one stone to another and we may soon find ourselves stranded on one of these isolated "facts." Even if we could argue for a strong "homosexual" trend in Jonathan, that would not necessarily settle the question of his sexual identity, since it is possible to have a firm sense of oneself as a man, but be a man who loves other men. More telling perhaps is the fact that Jonathan is neither clearly homosexual nor heterosexual and that it would be more correct to say that his life is characterized by an avoidance of sexuality. One possible reason for such an avoidance is the sense that one doesn't quite know who one is sexually and fears that the intensity of actual sexual experience will overrun already unstable boundaries and thereby bring on the intense anxiety that accompanies the collapse of a sense of self. A glimpse of this is provided by Jonathan's response to an inkblot in the Rorschach test: he sees two women with penises. Given the shapes in this particular inkblot, his perception is not crazy. But it is the sort of anxiety-provoking incongruity that most people, if they allowed themselves to see it in the first place, would feel the need to explain away with a joke or an explicitly magical plot. Jonathan rather blandly presents what he sees, as if the differences between men and women's bodies are not a very stable part of his internal world to begin with.*

Jonathan Langly's life embodies the pattern of collapse in the midst of potential success. And his life helps us to recognize some of the elements behind this pattern: pride and the pressures of lineage, activity and competitiveness gone awry, the haunting fear of failure, and the terrifying prospect of victory.

---

*It is necessary to take a short theoretical side step here. How does a precarious sexual identity square with Jonathan's fear of his father, if we're working from a psychoanalytic approach that sees the boy's identification with father as a result of fear? Taken simply this approach would seem to suggest that the greater the paternal ogre one grows up with, the more solid one's masculine identity. But of course this formulation *is* too simple. The complex psychological process of identification is motivated by love as well as fear. Taking in, and emulating, another person is an affectionate act and it will not happen when the person is totally despised or feared. By the time of the Oedipal crisis the boy has already identified in many ways with his mother and this identification will not be given up or integrated into an alliance with father unless the father seems both approachable and willing to offer something worthwhile. In a sense Jonathan had the worst of both worlds: his father's long absence would be bound to both intensify his bond with his mother and provoke guilt and fear, which would make the later step toward father even harder. What we see is a troublesome split. On the one side father is excluded, unreal, distant, and on the other side he is a terrifying spectre of rage. This is not a situation that lends itself to a boy's establishing a firm and comforting sense of the kind of man he could be.

## JANET LAUDER

This is a story about a sister and brother who had a trapeze act in a
circus. And they hated each other but they stayed together. And they
both always had thoughts of letting go of the other and letting them
fall to the ground, but they never did . . . [The interviewer asked how
the story would come out.] Fine, they stayed together and held on to
each other.

Here the stage is set with hatred and potential murder: each
constantly thinks of letting the other plummet to the ground. But
they don't, and the outcome of the story is a reassurance that this
disaster will be kept in check, that they will stay together and alive.
In that sense we have progressed from anxiety and threat to relief and
relative security. Of course Janet's terse story does not go out of its
way to convince us of the genuineness of the transformation. We are
still left wondering *why* they don't drop each other and where the
hatred has gone. The author insists that we take her word for this and
simply accept that the badness *has* disappeared. The transition in the
story is abrupt and magical. The rather bland optimism of the con-
cluding sentence rests on a complicated psychological maneuver
aimed at banishing evil, most probably some combination of denial
and repression. Perhaps it is the precariousness of this defensive
position that adds an overtone of fearful clinging to that last "held
on to each other"; the couple will stay together *in spite of* the badness
between them, as if they are trapped with it and with each other.
Finally, we should not leave this story without noting that to see the
couple as brother and sister is an idiosyncratic detail, which we would
expect to have roots in Mrs. Lauder's own life history. It is also a
detail that adds to the impact of the story by placing this struggle
against murderousness within the context of a family.

Janet Lauder's family was fulfilling one version of the American
success story. Her father came from a large and impoverished Eastern
European family. His own father died when he was quite young.
Though he speaks only sparingly about those days, one has the sense
that it was out of desperation as much as hope that he and his older
brother emigrated to America. He was then just old enough to be
accepted into the army of his new country and, as he sees it, he won
his right to citizenship by fighting as an American in the trenches of

the First World War. His brother had been rejected by the military and spent the war years establishing a small business, which Janet's father joined when he returned. He stayed with this firm for twenty years in spite of the steady increase of bad feeling between himself and his older brother. This is an area in which there must have been considerable pain, but again it is only hinted at. And on a similar but much more troubling level, the rest of father's family was destroyed in the Nazi concentration camps but this ghastly loss is not spoken of. We can only imagine the spectres lurking around the edges of this family's success, and wonder how much the father's grim reserve and taut facial mask represent his sacrifice of any emotional life in order to keep the past buried.

Janet's mother's journey had not been as long in the sense that the emigration came in the previous generation. But the attempt to find a place continued and a family move west when she was young had to be given up when father's business failed. She herself had hopes of writing poetry and when she was forced to interrupt her education and find work she chose a job that she thought might lead to her poetry being published. It didn't, but it did lead to meeting her husband. She was in her early twenties, ten years younger than he, and probably more romantically inclined about marriage than his comment of "I decided this was the best girl I could find" suggests that he was.

Several years later, after the mother had finished her college education, they had a son. The birth was quite difficult and she was advised not to have any more children. But as her infant grew up she came to feel that she would not be happy with only one child. This need became strong enough so that she risked another pregnancy eight years after the first. Again it was arduous. Among other things she mentions copious bleeding and a postpartum "sickness," which in her mind was due to "sponges" that had been left inside her and that she mistook for another baby when they emerged several days later.

The mother's initial reaction was tinged with disappointment. She had hoped for a pretty girl but the female baby she was presented with was dark and serious, "like a philosopher." But soon, to her delight, her daughter's appearance changed and she became the realization of all her mother's tender hopes: blond, lovely, and happy. Her parents seem to have taken great pleasure in Janet and as they look back now at her childhood they describe her variously as a jewel, a princess, a piece of sugar, a sweet little hostess, and Little Mary Sunshine. There was, we are told, no trouble with her early development, feeding, toilet training, and so forth. The picture that is painted of her as a child is a compellingly altruistic one. Stories are told about her not only never getting ice cream on herself when the Good Humor truck came by but even setting about to clean the other children. And she regularly bestowed a kiss on one of father's friends because she knew he suffered from having no little girls of his own.

These of course are parental recollections subject to the usual vagaries. But we take them even more seriously when we see how similar is Janet's own earliest memory: on the first day of kindergarten a boy was crying and she gave him her coloring paper. Aside from this kind gesture, her memories of childhood are remarkably vague and lifeless. She thinks the family went around "like zombies," that there was much strain in the house because of her father's unhappiness with his job, and that she felt often like an uncomfortable visitor, especially around him. Her father showed his affection by pinching her. It hurt but was better than nothing.

She does not remember the royal treatment reported by her parents: mornings when they would prepare her breakfast, put her favorite record on the phonograph, and her father would then wake her and carry her downstairs. Whatever aliveness and warmth she *can* remember is focused on her maternal grandmother. There were pleasant trips to a warm house where food was plentiful and Janet felt the unfortunately rare sense of "being appreciated for what I was." The grandmother died when Janet was an adolescent. She was saddened by her inability to pay this woman the tribute of grieving.

Two other things stand out in her recollection of middle childhood, both events centered on the home and both troublesome. Janet says she had daily enemas administered by her mother from as early in life as she can remember. Her mother maintains that this happened only during her ninth year. In any case it was a frightening and "awful" experience and each time she would hide in her brother's closet. And each time, of course, her mother would find her. The other memory is of masturbating her brother, Jacob, when she was about eight. What she remembers of that is her feeling that he was angry because she hadn't done it properly, and his telling her to wash her hands afterwards.

Her school years appeared to go smoothly both in terms of her work and her friendships. Menarche was uncomplicated although no one had explained anything to her about sex, babies, or womanhood. What little sexual play occurred in early adolescence was in the context of a boy touching her breast against her will, with Janet's being afraid to object for fear he would get angry. Ironically, this was the same boy she had succored in kindergarten. When it came time for high school she chose to go to an elite boarding school. This was the first of several prestigious schools she attended and this must have meant a good deal to her mother who was fascinated with the upper classes and old New England. Janet consistently felt inferior in these places and not even being chosen junior prom queen was much consolation. She went west for college but returned (as had her mother's family) after a short and uncomfortable stay. Her complaint was that it was too cold in that foreign place.

We should also note, though we don't know much about it, that Janet's adolescence was probably made more difficult by her mother's depression after having a hysterectomy. Her mother began to feel that her life was over and wrote intense notes to her daughter with such phrases as "love will be our bond."

Before reaching twenty Janet met and married a man ten years older. A decent and rather lonely fellow having some success with a private consulting business, he was an occasional associate of her brother. In spite of Jacob's attempts to discourage him, Jim Lauder was entranced with this attractive young woman who seemed to him so "bubbly and alive." But this promise of warmth soured rather badly on the honeymoon. Janet discovered that she had not really thought about marriage as involving sex. The prospect of intercourse was so frightening that she could only lock herself in the bathroom and cry. After several months of this, compromises were worked out to allow at least a tolerable approximation to a happy marriage. Mrs. Lauder pretended to enjoy intercourse when in fact she was able to feel nothing at all. But better anesthesia than fear.

After a dozen years of marriage there are sons aged nine and five. From the outside the picture of a contented family would be quite convincing, save perhaps the continuing hostility and avoidance between Jim and his wife's family. But this strain would only be noticeable at times such as the birth of a child, when Janet's mother moves into her daughter's house and takes charge with a solicitude that tolerates no opposition. The husband's business does well, the wife is helpful in her community, explores her own talents in poetry and painting, and provides a caring and attentive space within which the children flourish. The only problem is that she doesn't feel good. She rarely experiences the pleasure that others might have, and expect her to have, on viewing this scene. She feels phony and, despite tremendous skillful effort as wife and mother, unloving. Her vague but intensely painful depression and her "frigidity" impelled her to start psychotherapy four years ago. But as she became involved in that process with a therapist she steadily "closed up." Silence, even muteness, in sessions was added to her by now chronic constipation and amenorrhea. Finally the only voice that her deepening inner despair and emptiness could find was a violent and shocking one: two suicide attempts within a year. Each of these attempts effectively terminated the therapy she was involved in at the moment.

This brings us up to the present, to the time when Mrs. Lauder, aged thirty, entered residential treatment. Again with a constant awareness of how much we don't know, and of the impossibility of completely comprehending even what we do know, let us pick out some themes of this partial life story. We will begin with the notion of altruism. This life is a minor epic of altruism, altruism both in its benign and in its grotesque aspect. From as early as she or anyone else can remember, it seems that Mrs. Lauder has been exquisitely sensitive to the needs of others and was willing to put her pleasure in the service of theirs. This has made her a warm, caring, and life-giving presence in the lives of her parents, her children, and countless others in between. It takes nothing away from the virtue of this to say that it sometimes goes wrong. There can be a sense of strain, an unwillingness to take anything in return, which makes the recipient uneasy and guilty. And at its worst her altruism becomes a vicious caricature: I will kill myself in order to spare others the misery of having to live with me.

She was born into a family that needed an altruist. Father was a man cut off from his own emotional roots and locked into a hateful business relation with his brother. Mother had, we suspect, swallowed her romantic hopes both about marriage and about her poetry and she found herself feeling more and more the need for another child to fill her life. Enter Little Mary Sunshine. At first there is a moment of despair: this baby does not resemble the lovely jewel that mother had in mind, and in fact there is the threat that this child brings with her a somber philosphical approach to life (an attitude that would demand that difficult realities be held and looked at, not lathered over with sugar frosting). But miraculously the mother's suffering in the birth process is rewarded. Janet changes in her mother's eyes and from this point on all descriptions of this child have an air of golden and glorious unreality. It is uncanny to listen to the two different descriptions of this world: the parents speak of warmth, gaiety, and kindness; the daughter speaks of tension and a chilly emptiness.

The personal costs of her altruistic role are apparent. It promotes a sense of inner emptiness in that her attention is so attuned to the needs of others that her ability to notice her own needs atrophies from disuse. The only way to be consistently "nice" and giving is to deny one's own more grasping and aggressive wishes. To enforce this rule on oneself requires an exhausting inner vigilance and a suffocating set of limits on what is allowed expression. Because of the impossible image of self-sacrifice that it holds up, this altruism is bound to provoke guilt. Thus we find Mrs. Lauder stricken with self-hatred for not being a good enough daughter, wife, and mother, though anyone else would say that she does more than could be reasonably expected, especially in view of the fact that both her mother and her husband, out of their own depression, could be extraordinarily demanding and guilt-provoking. But her standards are far from reasonable. And part of the dilemma of course is that the standard goes beyond doing what others want. It requires that she do it lovingly and with joy. She must *like* her work. Any stain of anger or resentment spoils the portrait. So she is haunted by the guilt of not being loving *enough,* not being caring *enough,* in fact of feeling a fraud at the base of her dedication.

An allied theme is that of being the victim. Her altruism shades into slavery. Mother's enema syringe makes it apparent that victimization *can* come at the hands of a woman, but for the most part Janet experiences it as something men do to her. Her father, her brother, the boy she befriended in kindergarten, her husband, her sons—they all make demands, sexual and otherwise, that evoke fearful obedience on her part. She desperately tries to please but ends up feeling she has failed, especially when the man she has been trying to placate

turns out to want something sexual from her. The underlying fear
must have many parts to it, but the evidence from her psychotherapy
suggested that an important part was the fear of being deserted, of
being abandoned if she did not obediently submit to these cruel and
demanding men. The images that would come to her mind when
talking about this were images of concentration camp guards, tortur-
ers, and the Gestapo.

In this Mrs. Lauder may be the carrier of those forgotten horrors
that happened to her father's family. In an eerie fashion she enacts
in her own life the experience of those who died in the camps and
this pays homage to them. From this perspective her painful life
pattern of victimization would represent a "return of the repressed"
within the context of several generations of this family. But we also
need to understand the role of the victim in her individual life: in
what way is there internal pleasure or benefit that shapes the suffering
into a stable system? In some people about whom we use the word
masochistic in its narrow sense there is evidence that the very experience of pain is gratifying. There is no such evidence here, so we must
look further. At the very least there must be some hope that suffering
will eventually be rewarded. This is in fact the pattern of her birth:
her mother's depression, physical pain, and initial agonizing doubt
about this child were rewarded with joy and the fulfillment of her
wish to have a beautiful and loving little girl. And a poem Janet wrote
while in her twenties contains the lines: "I'll gladly suffer all/for those
precious seconds of human touch." She believes that pain is the price
we pay for pleasure.

But in a life where the hoped-for rewards seem always to be
receding into the distance, there must be a more immediate gain.
One of the important qualities of being a victim is that the activity
is located elsewhere. The victim is the acted-upon, not the actor.
Janet's story is remarkable for the absence of any sense of aggressive
activity. Not that she isn't often quite busy, even productive, but
there are no memories of any aggressive or boisterous childhood play,
no sense of the pleasure to be had in sudden extension or contraction
of large muscles, and little feeling of the power of her own initiative.
She is never the source of any intrusion or disruption. Except, of
course, when she assaults her own body. Even here her experience
during an episode of beating and cutting herself was that "someone
was trying to do something to me in my head."

But even though she will not see her own hand as inflicting the injury, it is apparent that her aggression has undergone a peculiar transformation and that by now her main source of power, her main method of controlling others or having some influence over them, is through her depression and self-destructiveness. We should not underestimate the amount of control over others' lives and feelings that such stubborn despair and self-injury can provide. But the important point is that it is a disguised and readily disowned form of activity. To even suggest that it *is* her activity would feel like, and probably be taken as, a cruel attack. This can be an important internal dividend of being a victim. It avoids any sense of oneself as destructive, hateful, or dangerous. For someone in whom almost any form of aggression has taken on those connotations, the position of victim may be, for all its pains, the better bargain.

But the bargain is a tenuous one, subject to constant inner renegotiation. While aggressiveness can indeed be partially masked, to oneself and to others, by standing it on its head, yet the more assertive needs and wishes do not magically disappear. They remain inside, a constant source of uneasiness, guilt, and the feeling of being a pretender. This will help us understand the final theme I wish to point to. In Mrs. Lauder's story we hear again and again of the importance of her body boundary, of the difference between inside and outside. This boundary has become highly charged in her imagination and any traffic across it is freighted with anxiety. For the most part the boundary is guarded, the border sealed. Very little goes in or out. This is the common meaning of various separate symptoms: constipation, amenorrhea, silence, and "frigidity." She remarks that on her wedding night it was "like a zipper closing up." This experience of closing up is frequent and very characteristic of Janet. It is rather like pulling up the drawbridge and attempting to transform her body into a secure fortress. She has come to expect aggressive forays, intrusive thrusts that will violate the integrity of her body. This is certainly her experience of sex and earlier must have been her experience of the enemas mother forced on her.

Unfortunately the enemy is already established within the fortress. For while she tries to bar the doors of her body, she also treats what's inside her with distrust and even loathing. The danger of not keeping her mouth shut is not only what might go in (for example, she fears overeating and becoming fat) but also what might come out: anger or a dirty secret. She experiences the invitation to explore her feelings as an invitation to become a murderer, says she has a vague memory that she might have pushed another child out a window when she was young (there is no reason to think that this actually happened), and she dreams of a pretty arsenic birthday cake for a child. She speaks of a constant sense of being dirty and ugly, and refers darkly to her insides as "a horror chamber." Her therapist is warned "if you play in a sewer you'll get dirty." Likewise pleasurable sexual fantasies are felt to be something that must be held in check for fear of drowning in them. Passions are thought of as mud or quicksand. She does allow herself some inner substance in the form of empathy and of artistic talents, but memory and thinking often seem to have fallen under the ban on dangerous inner contents. Her mind is frequently blank, her head experienced as empty.

In all this the metaphor of the enema keeps suggesting itself. Whether the forced removal of her feces happened for a year or several, it seems to have become one of the organizing fantasies of her life. She thinks of her own insides as a dirty and dangerous substance that must be contained, held back. She fears that someone will poke into her to remove it, yet hopes they *will* do it so that she might become clean inside.

Another piece of evidence for the importance of this fantasy came up in the course of her therapy. A complicated series of circumstances led to her inviting her husband to hit her. To her great shock and surprise he complied. During the next several hours she experienced a vivid and painful set of memories from about age nine (the year of the enemas according to mother): she was in a hospital, lying in a bed, and watching a set of tubes that were attached to her body. The tubes had "stuff going around" and she thought that their purpose was to take something bad out of her. With anger and frustration she wondered "how much dirtiness can there be, why do they keep doing it?" She felt she was being cleaned out but was angry that she had been told nothing about it. She lay there uncomplaining and bitterly listened to one nurse telling another about a date she had that evening. This epitomized the callous neglect in the whole situation, and worst of all "they never said they were sorry." As she related this memory she thought of the enemas and her confusion at the time: "I didn't know which hole they were working on."

No matter how much of this was "real" and how much later elaboration in fantasy, it states even more clearly the themes we have been discussing. And there is an important new element: the linking of this anal assault with sexuality (symbolized in the memory itself by the nurses' conversation about romance). The anatomical closeness of the anus and the vagina promotes the carry-over of the feelings of invasion and dirtyness. And although it is quite likely that a child of that age would already be inclined to think of her feces as dangerous, the helpless rage experienced in having them taken out will greatly reinforce the felt destructiveness of those body contents. And, we must add, midst the fear and anger will be some pleasurable stimulation, which will tend to invest this passive and helpless position with a kind of satisfaction.

The contrast between the inside and the outside is striking. Imagine the effort required to be so lovely, charming, and clean on the outside while feeling so ugly, dirty, and dangerous on the inside. And what a precarious effort that must be, constantly on guard against something bad slipping out. Much of Mrs. Lauder's life became an exhausting effort to get positive answers to the questions: am I pretty, am I clean, am I pleasing? These were the questions that her pregnant mother had about the child-to-be, and the change that the mother saw in her newborn, the change from dark philosopher to bright princess, is the first paradigm for Janet's efforts to please. All darkness—passion, feces, the family memory of mass murder—must be put away and replaced with happy, clean, and loving qualities. As we have seen, this impossible task involves a horrified recoiling from her own inner life and an attempt to project all anger or aggressiveness onto others. Only a hollow doll, beautiful on the outside but empty inside, could fulfill this ideal.

While talking about Mr. Langly we paid some attention to the probable vicissitudes of the Oedipal situation. We find that question more complex in the case of Mrs. Lauder. In part it is complicated in the way in which the female Oedipal development is always more complicated: the woman must shift her sensual and loving feelings from their original object, the mother, to that more strange and distant other parent. The transition seems to have been a troubled and incomplete one for Janet, at least in the sense that we see none of the affectionate tie with father that is so important in bridging childhood pleasure and adult sexuality. It would seem that there was both more holding her back and less drawing her on. Janet's father does not seem to have been very inviting, what with his own brittleness and the fact that he was an old and preoccupied father. And on the other hand Janet's mother was not one to loosen her grasp easily. She seems to have bound her daughter to her quite closely ("love will be our bond") with a combination of her own intense neediness and a very controlling and even intrusive stance.

Janet's brother was the only available male at home and he does seem to have been the focus of her romantic feelings within the family. She married a man who first knew her through her brother, was her brother's age, and whom the brother continues to treat as a rival. And her ambivalence (to put it mildly) about sex in her marriage is prefigured by her actual sexual experience with her brother. Brothers are not adequate substitutes for fathers, not least because they cannot be counted on as often to inhibit their own sexual wishes and keep the relationship on the level of sensual and affectionate teasing and play. The fact that the sexual feelings were acted upon only reinforced Janet's sense of sex as overwhelming and shameful.

Yet she was not so fearful or hopeless about it all as to prevent her trying to find a less forbidden version of her brother and, over many difficult years, come to find some pleasure in sexuality (her sons must have been important in this, particularly in the sense of being the first males from whom she did not have to fear sexual attack). She has peopled her world, both inner and outer, with men. But the erotic feeling that could make these relationships interesting even in their difficulties has been replaced or invaded by aspects of cruelty: seduction has become torture. In the background is an image which we sense more than see directly: this vivid and complicated mother who offers endless and total love in a relationship where even control of one's own bowels must be surrendered.

Aside from her periodic depression and her partial inhibition of sensuality, Janet Lauder would certainly be seen as feminine, as womanly. In fact she presents us with a rather extreme example of traditionally feminine traits and values: kindness, the willingness to put others first, an investment in care-giving, aesthetic interests, a penchant for responding rather than initiating, and so forth. She takes these traits far enough to become at times a mockery and a living indictment of this sexual stereotype. She paints quite clearly the horrors of total dedication to others, including the fact that the assertiveness thus denied will seep through and spoil the attempts to make others happy. And she shows us the short and straight path from submissiveness and self-denial to suicide.

Mrs. Lauder's life involves a struggle to make something livable out of hatred and potential destructiveness.

One of the unmistakable contrasts between Jonathan Langly and Janet Lauder is their orientation toward activity. Though both people suffer from a constriction of their capacity for successful and satisfying action, there is a considerable difference in their relation to mental and physical activity. Mr. Langly's life is full of extremes of action. He swings between vigorous mental and muscular motion on the one hand and a defeated paralysis on the other. It is often his own energetic outbursts that lead to exhaustion or actual injury. It is in the way that the world meets his own action that the fantasied danger lies. With Mrs. Lauder we see instead an astonishingly complete renunciation of any experience of initiative or self-generated movement. Her world is more a series of constricted and desperate responses to others' activity. While we can see much evidence of a sadly contorted assertion at work, on the level of her experience the predominant fantasied danger is what others may do to her.

Jonathan's story is one of attempted extensions, both physical and verbal, into the outer world. It has none of the focus on the *inside*, on bodily contents, which we see so vividly with Mrs. Lauder. She, on the other hand, is involved in a much richer and more complicated web of human relationships. Jonathan is obsessed with achievement in the external world and he is undone both by the fear of not achieving enough and, paradoxically, by the anxiety of having taken a successful step. Janet is much more concerned with the quality of her dealings with people. Her human ties are more at the center of things and rather than being ruined by external success she seems most distressed by a progressive inability to love as she thinks she should.

# Chapter IV

◐◆◑

# The Patterns of
# Pride and Caring

We have now traced the same patterns in three quite different types of material. If we had only fantasy stories, or only life histories, or only myths, we would have to feel very keenly the limitations of the evidence. But in fact our explorations have covered a wide area: from products of a single imagination to products of a whole culture over hundreds of years; from detailed investigation of one life to the comparison of large groups of people; from an empirical method using numbers and objective scoring systems to a more literary analysis. Each of the three modes can stand alone, but the most convincing notions will be those that find support in more than one place. This chapter is devoted to elaborating the areas of overlap in our three methods. This will give us both a final summary and a refinement of the meaning of the male and female fantasy patterns.

Taking first the male fantasy pattern, we see that both Phaethon and Jonathan Langly live in a world cut off from women. To the extent that either of them is involved in important relationships with anyone it is with other men. They seem to have little ability or inclination to imagine how women think or feel. We get the sense that their most comfortable relationships are with young men and that their most important emotional tie is with an older man. Similarly, we know from one of the empirical studies that men with a more extreme fantasy pattern tend to separate themselves from women both by envying them and by assuming that men should be "the boss" in their relations with women.

Both the research subjects and Jonathan have a firm notion of the standards men are supposed to live up to, and both feel uneasy about their ability to fulfill this self-imposed demand for a properly masculine performance. In our culture these qualities of staggering along under the weight of one's own imitation of manhood, and of living largely in a world of men, are most typical of the beginning and early phases of adolescence. Here the well-established and relatively comfortable sex segregation of the earlier school years has begun to be both intensified and shaken by an upsurge of physical growth and sexual feeling. The band of male companions becomes even more important both as a source of guidance about how to act and as a protection against those intriguing but intimidating female creatures across the room. But the bonds within this male group are threatened by a new concern with competitive "masculinity." How is it possible to remain friends with someone when you also want to defeat him and prove that you're a better man? There is a lurking recognition that while you and your brothers engage in a rough-and-tumble affection and wish to impress each other, yet all eyes are furtively on the female audience in the distance. There is a dawning awareness that the most loyal of the brotherhood may end up finding themselves deserted and left behind in favor of the enemy.

In the midst of this complicated transition it is common to feel lonely even while surrounded with friends, and here we remember the curious finding that more extreme fantasy patterns, for both men and women, are associated with reports of having felt isolated and cut off from others during the early adolescent years. And there is also Cramer's suggestion that Deprivation/Enhancement patterns may in fact reach their peak somewhere between ages eleven and thirteen. So a number of different indicators point toward the early adolescent years as being a critical period for these sex-linked fantasy patterns.

Jonathan Langly and Phaethon share the experience of an absent father. This is undoubtedly one source of their concern with lineage and of the idealized image they have of their fathers, since it is both more possible and more comforting to construct an heroic representation of a father who is not there (Phaethon's longer period of deprivation is balanced by the myth's assertion that his father really *is* a god). The same relationship appears in the research data. Men with more extreme male fantasy patterns view their fathers with admiration and awe. And while we have no reason to think that these research subjects actually had fathers who were away for long periods of time, they did grow up in a society where it is typical for fathers to be relatively invisible and for the young boy to have most of his experience with women. In any case, a repetitive element in the male fantasy pattern is the investing of one's father with great competence and power.

Pride is the most striking common quality associated with the male fantasy pattern. It is here that we come closest to the core of motivation, the engine that sets the plot in motion. Pride is the word that best describes a cluster of attitudes and wishes that includes an inflated view of oneself, a touchy vulnerability to feelings of shame and inadequacy, a worship of will and willpower, and a restless urge to achieve something outstanding. This pride is blatant in the story of Phaethon. It is less so with Jonathan Langly, but it is still easily discernable as the backdrop to his struggles. In the research data we saw that the male fantasy pattern is associated with an overblown estimate of one's chances of success, and with the strength of the motive to achieve. Added evidence comes from the compulsively brave denial of all fear or hesitation and the vision of masculine toughness and determination that emerged in the interviews with men whose fantasy patterns are strongly in the male direction.

This overweening pride is rooted in an attempt to *become* the idealized and powerful father. This is an impossible project on many levels. Not the least of its flaws are the wish to repeal one's childhood and the confusion of a fantasy image with real possibilities. The impossibility of the task is one source of the hopeless and fearful undertones of this pride. For in speaking of "pride" here we must take notice of the fact that its underside is unusually obvious. This species of pride is far from an entirely sleek and confident beast. The fear of failure or death, the echoes of past shame and humiliation—these are barely, if at all, concealed by the arrogant sheen of ambition. Phaethon is striving to erase a defeat, and his braggadocio shatters as soon as he runs into difficulty. With the Langlys there is a virtual tradition of men who feel themselves to have failed in the midst of success. Jonathan is no exception, as shown most poignantly by his fears of humiliation midst the social and athletic accomplishments of grade school. There is further confirmation in the research studies. The extreme men speak of similar bad times still vivid in their memories: having been beaten up, spurned by girls, or thought of as "queer." Bramante's study showed that such men, when aroused, reveal fantasy patterns full of foreboding and the prospect of disaster. So we are speaking of a brittle sort of pride, a pride that resorts to whistling in the dark. It is a pride fortelling its own collapse.

Phaethon's glory is posthumous. The notion of a fatal victory is one of the ways in which this pride carries defeat with it. The Phaethon saga argues, especially through the epitaph, that the glory is worth the price. Taken this way the prospect of a splendid death may only fuel the fires of pride. In the Langly case we see another variant of the link between pride and death. Death is still a presence, but the emphasis is more on a fear of death than on death as part of the final glorious act. With the Langlys, death acts more like a punishment. The threat is of being cut down in one's prime, of having time suddenly called before you have achieved all you want to, or in fact of courting death through the very exertions required to placate one's pride. It is this theme that Jonathan finally comes to be ruled by: the anxious restriction of activity in hopes of avoiding the fatal end that is implicit in this immoderate pride.

Pride provokes action. In fact these two elements are so intertwined that we are often hard put to distinguish them at all. It is as if pride immediately transforms itself into muscular action, and successful movement in turn encourages pride. I have already touched on the importance of physical activity for both Jonathan and Phaethon. In each instance activity is highly valued but also known to be dangerous. A constant question is whether action can be successfully modulated or controlled. In each instance we see the ills of activity run wild.

The empirical evidence is, I believe, consistent with these themes though it is on a different level (it had not occurred to me at the time to ask about physical activity, and since the research methods all involved sitting and talking, action was not given much space to show itself). The image of masculinity constructed by the men with high scores is made up of words that point directly toward action: father is a fighter, efficient, competent; men should be aggressive, in control, and always ready to prove their ability. More important yet is Cramer's study of defense mechanisms. The defensive strategy most associated with the male fantasy pattern is projection. This strategy is based on externalizing, on finding someone else to blame and hold responsible. It can be seen in clear contrast to the response of blaming oneself ("turning against the self"), which is in fact negatively related to the male fantasy pattern. Projection in its extreme form is of course associated with paranoid states, which carry the constant threat of actual assault. But even in the milder, essentially "normal," character type it represents an habitual channeling of anger toward the outside world. This anger is justified by imagining that there is someone out there with the power and the wish to do me ill. Thus what may seem from the outside to be an unprovoked attack will seem to me to be mere self-defense, or at least fair revenge for a previous injury. This stance toward the world naturally makes the question of modulation and control a critical one: will I act on what I feel, and if so how? Such people often experience themselves as hemmed in or constrained against their will, and the constant danger is a bursting out of unmodulated anger or assertion.

It has typically been the male members of society who have concerned themselves with erecting and maintaining that structure of laws and abstract principle that serves as an external prop for the unreliable inner controls of other men. Perhaps we have a glimpse of the same process in Cramer's finding that men with *less* extreme male fantasy patterns distinguish themselves from the other men by their use of the defense of "principalization," that is, the handling of conflict by resorting to intellect and to abstract rules. This is one of the more adaptive solutions to the male's internal dilemma: assert the rule of law over the temptation to blame others and to act on one's anger. Once such a system is functioning smoothly and autonomously it represents a considerable gain in psychic efficiency: no longer does one have to examine each incident carefully to determine whether to unleash the counterattack. For the men who have not established a trustworthy inner judiciary, the situation has all the draining aspects of a perpetual mobilization. This strain of constantly deciding which way to move may lie behind the high scoring male's envious perception of women as more free to be followers.

The last common factor in the male pattern also has relevance to the question of control, though it reaches much further. There is a level of social control that is essentially retaliative: laws saying that if you injure another you yourself will be injured, or the belief that hubris will be punished by the gods. But a more subtle and pervasive restraint on unmodulated assertion is the network of emotional ties we have to other people. Growing up in the emotionally intense and mutually dependent atmosphere of a family teaches us to attend to the pain of hurting someone we love. With luck this feeling spreads and makes us at least intermittently responsive to the call to be "our brother's keeper" in a much wider group. The capacity to imagine the needs and wishes of others puts a check on our aggression, whether it be in the stark terms of holding back from physical assault or in the gentler guise of restraining worldly ambition when it is at the expense of relationships we care about.

In the male fantasy pattern these ties are tenuous. The highly "male" research subjects have a wistful admiration for what they see as the woman's greater capacity for warmth and humanity. Both Phaethon and Jonathan show a striking absence of emotional bonds to others. We hear of no important friendships or loves in Jonathan's life. They may well be there, but their voice is soft indeed and there is no evidence that his interest ever strays far beyond his own anxious struggles. Phaethon as usual displays the extreme: a rampant self-interest in which all relationships are so attenuated or invaded by pride that they can no longer serve as useful checks on his destructive ambition.

Common to the three portrayals of the female fantasy pattern is an approach to human relationships quite different from that of the male pattern. Issues of caring and attachment are very much at the center of things. The myth of Demeter and Persephone is a long and moving testament to the fact that relationships matter. It organizes itself around ideas of caring, giving, and altruism. In the research data, we found that nursing—that very concrete situation of giving, which is such an important metaphor in the myth—actually does increase the frequency of female fantasy patterns. While in a group of younger women, the strength of their wish to nurture was the best predictor of their fantasy scores.

In our case study of Mrs. Lauder we see much the same thing. From a young age her life has centered on altruism and caretaking, both in its benign and malignant aspects. Her own birth is portrayed by her mother as a vivid example of a mother's willingness to take risks and undergo pain. One of the greatest sources of pain in her adult life is her constant guilt over not being as loving a mother or as warm and kind a person as she feels she ought. In her imaginative universe hell is represented by isolation and coldness. It is the lack of human warmth that is so horrible in her memories of early childhood (note the contrast with the warm, food-giving grandmother who cannot be mourned) and this continues to be a theme that haunts her, as in her explanation for returning home from college. This vision of the worst is quite different from Phaethon or Jonathan, for whom the ultimate disaster has more to do with failure and humiliation. But it is at one with the agonies of separation and isolated depicted in the story of Demeter. Both Demeter and Mrs. Lauder display the destructive power of the despair that can flow from such a cold and lonely state: both inner and outer worlds are soon blighted and barren.

The bond between mother and daughter stands out as a special example of the general concern for human ties in the female pattern. In each of our examples this relationship is particularly strong, active, and alive. Demeter and Persephone seem to matter more to each other than anyone else matters to either of them. Their feelings for each other appear entirely positive. In the research data the mother-daughter bond is still highly charged, as seen in the fact that it is aspects of *this* relation and not any other that are correlated with female fantasy patterns. But here the quality of the bond is not so entirely positive: the daughter views her mother as a source of unwanted pressure and unpleasant expectation.

The situation is the same with Mrs. Lauder—her mother's vivid presence in her life is experienced as demanding or even persecutory. One of the major areas of demand is the same one the research subjects complain about: pressure in the direction of being well-mannered, loving, ladylike, and generally "nice." In return the mother offers a special sort of love. Both Persephone and Janet

Lauder are especially lovely and valuable in their mother's eyes: a
jewel, a princess, a flower. The intense mother-daughter relationship
associated with a female fantasy pattern is characterized by a transaction in which the daughter is asked to give up any aggression or
nastiness; in so far as she does this, her mother will cherish and love
her beyond criticism. We must also note a clause in the contract that
identifies any sexual interest in men as one of those nastinesses that
would blemish the daughter's beauty and jeopardize the adulation she
receives from her mother.

We have already spoken of the importance of the concept of the
"inside" for Mrs. Lauder. In her case we noticed a heightened awareness of her body boundary and of the transition between inside and
outside. We also noticed a constant troubled wondering about what
was inside her, a wondering that oscillated between two painful poles:
I am empty and lifeless, there is really nothing inside; or, I am full
of dirty, ugly stuff, which people find revolting and offensive. The
theme of the inside is also prominent in the Demeter myth, though
here it is much more positive and not so suffused with conflict. The
myth's concern with fecundity illuminates the alternatives of full
versus empty. Goodness means full bellies, either from pregnancy or
from food. Taking in has the most profound results, whether it be
"taking in" a young girl by means of a beautiful flower, taking a
sorrowing old woman into one's home, or taking in a pomegranate
seed.

The crucial events of this myth are emotional, inner. It is a story
about carrying feelings, about holding them inside. This variant of
the theme provides the link with the research data. The female
fantasy pattern goes along with a set of psychological strategies
involving the containment of feeling inside oneself. This is in contrast to the more typically male strategy of immediately, so to speak,
spitting it out. Once held inside, the troublesome feeling can either
be neutralized and put away (repression), in which case the danger
is that one's inner experience is both impoverished and increasingly
threatened by the return of that which has been put away. Alterna-
tively, there can be the more favorable outcome dramatized by Demeter: through being held and accepted the pain is transformed into
something more positive and hopeful.

Something must be borne. This theme of endurance appears in

each of the three perspectives on the female fantasy pattern. I have already described the several ways in which the story of Demeter is a study of creative endurance. It counsels the acknowledgment of pain and the maintenance of hope. In fact it suggests that hope, and joy, come *through* the acceptance of suffering. On a quite different level we have the empirical link between female fantasy patterns and an objectively measured trait of endurance. The interviews revealed that a highly female fantasy pattern is accompanied by the sense of having to endure both maternal coercion and the tension of holding back in relations with men. Women are supposed to bear the burden of waiting for what they want. In Bramante's study the experimental intensification of sexual awareness led women to create fantasies with even more than the usual amount of trial and tribulation in the opening chapter. Finally, we have noted the way in which the female fantasy pattern is linked with the preliminary pessimism of expecting to do poorly.

All these pieces of evidence are consistent with the theme of endurance. So is the special affinity between an extreme female fantasy pattern and a so-called hysterical character structure. Curiously enough, Persephone is in many ways the model hysteric: beautiful, narcissistic, childlike, coy, and firmly tied to her mother. She has the quintessential hysterical experience of being overwhelmed and victimized. She is helpless in the hands of Hades, the plaything of his urges and able herself only to endure as best she can, to play Beauty to his Beast. Mrs. Lauder demonstrates this relationship even more clearly. Diagnostically she is one of the "hysterical character" group and she reveals a life in which endurance, holding on in the face of suffering, has become a central motif. Her brand of endurance is often indistinguishable from victimization. This quality of her imaginative world is epitomized by the fantasy of being at the mercy of a sadistic concentration camp guard.

In trying to understand Mrs. Lauder's repetitive experience of being victimized, I related it to her equally extensive inhibition of her own anger. Now we are in a position to recognize this as a more general truth about the female fantasy pattern. It is not just Mrs. Lauder and Persephone who show this curtailment of aggression or assertion. The research data suggest that the female fantasy pattern is linked to psychological strategies that attempt to transform anger, or at least work against the anger being focused on another person. Thus, as we have seen, women with highly female fantasy patterns rely on defenses that transform and contain, while women with minimally female patterns are remarkable for their use of "turning against the other." At a different point on the scale, we find that men whose fantasy patterns tend in the female direction are unusual in their reliance on the inhibiting defenses of "principalization" and "turning against the self." This would seem to be part of what our research subjects are complaining of when they speak about having to stifle their own initiative and aggression. It is likely that these matters of mental style include cognitive as well as more "emotional" factors. We have seen that women with highly female patterns are less likely to show that assertive and dissecting perceptual style known as "field-independence." So even here, far afield from matters of feeling, we can pick up the thread of an inhibited or at least restrained aggressiveness.

The notion that the female pattern, at least in its more extreme version, is related to an inhibition of aggression helps to clarify what the underlying danger of endurance is: taken too far it becomes helplessness and total vulnerability. Then the person seems to exist only as the potential victim of either literal or psychological rape and to be defined, to themselves as well as others, only by the designs and actions of their latest victimizer. Persephone on her own is a sad and limp creature indeed. She represents an extreme endurance without the leavening of toughness and competence that make it hopeful and creative. If this condition of hopelessness and helplessness continues, then the ultimate goal may be lost sight of and the process of suffering becomes its own reward. When the suffering starts to be invested with an erotic pleasure, we have arrived at something which can properly be called masochism. Mrs. Lauder veers in that direction, but never for long; we suspect it more in her mother, whose dwelling on the bloody pains of giving birth definitely has an excited quality.

One of the underlying fears associated with the female pattern must be the fear of being abused and victimized. But there is another, more apparent in the stories of Demeter and Mrs. Lauder. It is the fear that the waiting will have been in vain, that nothing good will come out of enduring after all. The waiting was not supposed to be for its own sake but rather it was necessary in order to protect, and honor, an important relationship of caring. If the dilemma of the Pride pattern is how to modulate and control self-assertion, the difficulty of this pattern is how to keep alive a fertile yet realistic hope and how to make sure that the enduring is in the service of caring rather than vice-versa. When the hope is momentarily lost, then in creep images of endless and barren emptiness. It can happen that attempts to master the first of these fears will result in exacerbating the second. A case in point is Mrs. Lauder's ban on sexual pleasure. This particular inhibition comes about because of fears of being abused and invaded. It is a way of putting her "insides" in protective cold storage. But it also has the result of making her feel even more dead, frigid, and empty.

You will have noticed that in these first chapters I have used several different names for the fantasy patterns. "Deprivation/Enhancement" is the term most directly tied to the scoring system and the empirical studies of chapter II. It has the advantage of keeping us mindful of the sort of events that comprise a particular score; yet it can be cumbersome when we want to distinguish between "Deprivation leading to Enhancement" and "Enhancement leading to Deprivation." Its closeness to the actual measurement scheme is at the expense of carrying any broader meaning or connotation. It is a rather neutral and lifeless title.

On other occasions I've referred to "male" and "female" fantasy patterns. This is simpler, and justified by the empirical results. But it is overly general and may also trouble those who are unwilling to accept the evidence that these fantasy patterns are indeed linked with sex. Even for those who do accept the evidence, the labels "male" and "female" tempt one to slide into the unjustified assumption that all men show the "male" pattern and all women the "female."

After looking at the areas in which our three different kinds of evidence agree, we can choose words closer to the core meanings of the fantasy patterns. "Pride" does very well for the male case. But the female pattern is more complex and various. It is harder here to find one word that will be adequate. "Endurance" was one candidate, but it has the drawback of focusing on a single and sometimes painful, piece of the pattern, and of elevating a means to an end. "Caring" risks being vague but it does more justice to the web of relationships that is so characteristic of the female pattern. And it speaks more directly to the hopes and wishes that lie at the center of the pattern.

We are now at the verge of an even larger question. Why should these patterns of Pride and Caring be typically male and female? Where do they fit in terms of the other things we know about man and woman and their development? I might as well say now that I don't think these questions are answerable in any ultimate way. But there are a number of possible connections well worth looking at. To do this we must start with the general issue of sex differences.

*Chapter V*

❧✦❧

# The Case for Sex Differences

In the United States a *real* boy climbs trees, disdains girls, dirties his knees, plays with soldiers, and takes blue for his favorite color. A real girl dresses dolls, jumps rope, plays hopscotch, and takes pink for her favorite color. When they go to school, real girls like English and music and "auditorium"; real boys prefer manual training, gym and arithmetic. In college the boys smoke pipes, drink beer, and major in engineering or physics; the girls chew Juicy Fruit gum, drink cherry cokes, and major in fine arts. The real boy matures into a "man's man" who plays poker, goes hunting, drinks brandy, and dies in the war; the real girl becomes a "feminine" woman who loves children, embroiders handkerchiefs, drinks weak tea, and "succumbs" to consumption.[1]

This grotesque tongue-in-cheek description was meant to seem quaintly old-fashioned even when it was written. Now it is likely to strike us as downright archaic. But it would really not require many changes to turn it into a serviceable contemporary comment. We would need to alter a few brand names, and perhaps to interpret "consumption" as meaning not tuberculosis but rather the equally wasting process of endless buying.

The question we will be exploring in this chapter is whether there are, underneath this amusing but perishable level of detail, persistent and important differences between the sexes. More fundamentally, is there reason to think that psychological differences between the sexes are not entirely the result of social conditioning and cultural convention? I will argue that there is, that justice can be done to the evidence *only* with a theory that honors the body as well as culture.

The empirical literature on sex differences is massive, and complex enough to lend itself to many interpretations. We shall have to enter that thicket a bit later, but first a more general look at the landscape. Bardwick and Douvan summarize the research on the early years:

> Comparisons between boys and girls in infancy and the earliest school years reveal modal differences between the sexes. Boys have higher activity levels, are more physically impulsive, are prone to act out aggression, are genitally sexual earlier, and appear to have cognitive and perceptual skills less well-developed than girls of the same age. Generally speaking, girls are less active physically, display less overt physical aggression, are more sensitive to physical pain, have significantly less genital sexuality, and display greater verbal, perceptual and cognitive skill than boys.[2]

Girls learn to speak earlier than boys do, and they remain more verbally fluent. They are typically better at perceiving details. Boys soon begin to show a greater spatial and mechanical ability. Their cognitive style tends to be more "analytic," and in the later school years they show more skill in mathematical and abstract reasoning. After reviewing considerable research, Julian Silverman argues that there is a general sex difference in cognitive style:

> The prototypical female attentional style is characterized by: (a) sensitivity to subtle social and nonsocial cues; (b) distractibility; (c) a "yielding" nonanalytic, nonrestructuring perceptual attitude; (d) a receptivity to emotional and intuitive stimuli; and (e) a disposition to reduce the experienced intensity of strong stimulation. The prototypical male attentional style is characterized by (a) a relative lack of sensitivity to subtle social and nonsocial cues; (b) minimal distractibility; (c) a "counteracting" analytic, restructuring perceptual attitude; (d) an inhibition of response to emotional and nonrational inner stimuli; and (e) a disposition to augment the experienced intensity of strong stimulation.[3]

There are many links between cognitive style and more purely emotional, or even "physical," characteristics. Intellectual ability and mastery is associated with an inhibition of physical impulsiveness and aggressive daring in boys, while in girls a relatively greater degree of boldness and aggression is linked to achievement and intellectual mastery later in life.[4] It is as if there is an optimum level of aggressiveness, a level that many men are too far above and many women too far below (the idea of a certain balance, of the maladaptive quality of an extremely "male" or "female" stance, is an appealing one—we will meet it again).

The overwhelming bulk of the evidence shows the male, both young and mature, to be the more aggressive sex.[5] "Aggressive" is a broad and slippery term, but in fact we are talking about a broad range of behavior: from actual fighting and dominance by means of force and threat, through general physical activity and impulsiveness, to the above-mentioned cognitive style that relies on the ability to fragment or dissect. Females, young and old, are more likely to show nurturance and a preoccupation with other people, which is variously referred to as "affiliation," "conformity," or "dependence." These general tendencies have been shown in actual behavior, in choices of games or hobbies, and in fantasy. Jerome Kagan points out that when boys and girls act in these ways they are acting in accord with what their parents expect from little boys and girls respectively. He notes some evidence that parents are more likely to punish a girl for expressions of aggression and sexuality and more likely to punish a boy for signs of dependence or fear (though this does not seem necessarily true of later adult authority, such as primary school teachers—they are more likely to discourage aggression in boys).[6]

An extensive longitudinal study by Kagan and Moss[7] found that traits of relative "passivity" and dependence are stable for women from childhood to adult life, whereas the degree of aggression and sexuality are not. The results for men are the reverse, with a positive correlation between childhood aggression and sexuality and those qualities in adulthood; for men dependence and passivity are not stable traits over the years. Kagan and Moss take this as evidence for the effects of social influence and training: those characteristics that fit with the parental and cultural expectations for one's sex will be encouraged while those that clash or deviate will be punished and thereby be either extinguished or transformed.

Kagan and Moss's argument accords with our day-to-day observations of social relations and the existence of stereotyped sets of expectations for men and women. It is necessary to note, however, that their conclusion does not inevitably flow from the results. The fact that a trait is more stable over time does not require us to conclude that its stability is due to cultural pressure. If the forces at work, for instance, are the punishment of timidity and the encouragement of aggression in boys, wouldn't this result in those boys who are initially timid becoming considerably bolder, thus *decreasing* the stability of the overall aggression ratings in the male group? It appears that we could just as well use Kagan's data to argue that the stable traits are the ones most deeply rooted and resistant to tutelage.[8]

Adolescent boys are more concerned than girls with the question of establishing independent control over their own impulses. They are more likely to resent any outside authority and at the same time to be deeply involved in an anxious struggle to gain a reliable inner sense of control over their own aggression. The importance of this struggle is shown by the research finding that the extent to which the boy has succeeded in this particular task is a good indicator of general achievement, energy level, and self-confidence ("ego strength"). For the adolescent girl this relationship does not hold. Instead there is a relationship between ego strength and interpersonal development (defined as mature attitudes and skills in the area of friendship).[9] And in adulthood, to pick another example of a typical result, "males represent experiences of self, others, space, and time in individualistic, objective, and distant ways, while females represent experiences in relatively interpersonal, subjective, immediate ways."[10]

Young men tend to describe themselves as cool, deliberate, foresighted, individualistic, industrious, outspoken, self-confident, and shrewd. Or, to take a less flattering selection: aggressive, arrogant, conceited, cruel, opportunistic, reckless, and vindictive. Young women by contrast see themselves as more cheerful, civilized, friendly, generous, reliable, sensitive, sympathetic, and warm; and on the darker side—complaining, fearful, meek, self-pitying, submissive, timid, and worrying.[11] These self-perceptions come from people chosen as likely to display sex differences most clearly, and in that sense they represent extremes. These were young people of the sixties; no doubt some of the words would be different were we to repeat the process now. Nonetheless, it would not be hard to find many other examples in the research literature of male and female self-descriptions that order themselves along similar dimensions.

But rather than plowing ahead through a detailed summary of research results, a task that others have already done with greater verve than I would be able to muster, I want to mention two more general attempts to describe the underlying dimensions on which men and women may differ. Talcott Parsons and Robert Bales speak from backgrounds in sociology and social psychology. They have developed a complex framework within which to understand the different roles or functions that evolve in the family or in a small working group, and to understand how this role differentiation both responds to and promotes the needs of a broader social system. They use the terms "expressive" and "instrumental" to identify the typical female and male roles in the family, in small groups, and in the society as a whole. The fact that the woman bears and nurses the child establishes "a strong presumptive primacy of the relation of mother to the small child"[12] and makes it likely that she will specialize in managing the inner workings of the family while the man will specialize in managing the relations of the family to the surrounding environment. Thus the expressive role is concerned with internal integration and function and has a particular focus on ensuring amicable and gratifying relationships within the group. The instrumental role focuses more on "external goal objects" (at the simplest level—food, shelter, and so forth).

Through a process of further specialization and elaboration of these roles, we arrive at the more complex contemporary situation. The instrumental function tends toward the technical, executive, and judicial. It stresses achievement, rationality, and a striving for success. It focuses on the active manipulation of objects and often requires the denial of emotion. The expressive function tends to be integrative, supportive, and personal. Its goals have more to do with gratification and cooperation and it takes emotion seriously. Any group, or individual, needs to have some access to each of these two modes of function. Although our culture puts higher value on the instrumental role, Parsons and Bales point out that both are vital for the continued constructive functioning of a group. Valuing one above the other has more to do with politics and prejudice than with understanding.

David Bakan's intriguing book *The Duality of Human Existence* ranges over psychology, theology, and the history of science. To let him summarize:

> I have adopted the terms "agency" and "communion" to characterize two fundamental modalities in the existence of living forms, agency for the existence of an organism as an individual, and communion for the participation of the individual in some larger organism of which the individual is a part. Agency manifests itself in self-protection, self-assertion, and self-expansion; communion manifests itself in the sense of being at one with other organisms. Agency manifests itself in the formation of separations; communion in the lack of separations. Agency manifests itself in isolation, alienation, and aloneness; communion in contact, openness, and union. Agency manifests itself in the urge to master; communion in noncontractual cooperation. Agency manifests itself in the repression of thought, feeling, and impulse; communion in the lack and removal of repression.[13]

Bakan takes these rather general "modalities" and exemplifies them over an impressively broad spectrum of situations: from cellular differentiation, through the legend of Satan, to the rise of modern science. The separation and assertion that characterize Agency make it stand out against the background of Communion; thus Agency is easier for Bakan to describe in detail, and it is also rather the villain of the piece. Bakan points to the "agentic" qualities of pride, manipulation, fragmentation, scientific rationality, and the urge to master or conquer. As he says, his main interest is in showing the forms and interactions of these principles in "all living substance." No person or organism is all Agency or all Communion. But the balance is critical. Our sense that these two modalities have an implicit link with gender is confirmed: Bakan draws on research into sex differences to support his claim that while every individual shows both, Agency as he defines it is greater in men and Communion in women.

After reading much of the research literature on sex differences (if you'd like to follow that path yourself I'd recommend starting with the cited books by Bardwick, Hutt, and Maccoby),[14] I find it useful to organize the unruly mass of data around three clusters of traits or concerns. The more typically male areas of these clusters have to do with vulnerability, action, and detachment.

Women are more resilient and physiologically viable. They are born more mature than males and continue to be more adaptable in the sense of having available a wider range of physiological fluctuation (the male being more constantly geared up for maximum muscular output). Thus men are physiologically more vulnerable than women. From the moment of conception onwards, the male is more likely to die or be defective. Spontaneous abortion, stillbirth, irritability in early infancy, infant and childhood diseases, difficulties of maturation and learning, alcoholism, suicide, early and sudden death—all these come more often to the male. And in terms of life expectancy, male vulnerability is *not* just due to the stresses and dangers of the male role, since the sex difference in longevity also holds amongst cloistered religious orders.

Men specialize in *doing something to* an object, a person, a perception, or an idea. The forms of this activity are many and may include actual violence, an impulsive bravado, or inability to just let things be, or an inventive and productive reshaping. Women are more likely to excel at responsiveness and caretaking: the ability to notice what is there and to take care either by providing something that is needed or simply by respecting the context enough to forgo "manhandling" it. Included here is the ability to evoke responses rather than forcing them (only if taken too far or distorted does this become a stance that could merit that tired epithet "passive").

Males more often operate in a detached and isolated fashion. Solitary work to master a skill is a common characteristic of male life, and men are more quick to dismiss the claims of other people and even of their own emotions. This approach tends to make things (machines, ideas) at least as important as people in the man's inner life. Words such as rational, independent, and objective describe positive aspects of this tendency; cold, detached, and unfeeling are words for the more destructive aspects. In contrast, women's lives are more likely to embody the theme of connection—both connection between people and connection between the emotional and intellectual parts of oneself. Women have less of a penchant for deciding things independent of the relevant network of connections. In most instances people matter more to them than things and they will put a faithfulness to human ties above dedication to "principle" or pure "independence" of judgment. It is a testament to the male bias of our society that such qualities are often referred to with the demeaning names of "dependence" or "conformity."

## The Roots of the Controversy

It would be easy to quarrel with any particular finding in the voluminous work on sex differences or, even more likely, to quarrel with the summary terms offered by Parsons, Bakan, or myself. But to do that would be to evade what I think are the real issues of contention. The debate about sex differences has of late become quite heated in American psychology. The skirmishing often takes place on the terrain of research, where positions are won or lost on empirical technique, but it is apparent that the fight itself has little to do with these particulars. Basic assumptions are at stake, one being whether it is allowable to speak of sex differences in the first place. To do so strikes some as at the least undemocratic and at worst downright malicious. In part this is a peculiarly American sentiment, flowing from our estimable concern with equality and individualism. But as Tocqueville noted, the American democratic valuing of the individual runs the risk of defining equality as sameness. There is bound to be a tension between our twin ideals of liberty and equality: absolute equality is only attainable if we assume that all people when truly "free" will want the same things, act the same way, and have the same abilities.

The crux of the argument comes at a more sophisticated level. Assuming we do find psychological differences between the sexes, do they mean anything? The voice that says "no" to this does so by asserting that the differences we see are merely the result of social training, that they are outcomes of the imposition on the individual of cultural rules and roles. Thus such differences in behavior, attitude, or feeling are seen as arbitrary manifestations of a particular social arrangement at a particular point in history.

Kate Millett's *Sexual Politics* is still the most engagingly written and forcefully argued example of this position: "For the sexes are inherently in everything alike, save reproductive systems, secondary sexual characteristics, orgasmic capacity, and genetic and morphological structure."[15] Granted, the list that follows "save" is rather a long one. But the way Millett phrases it makes the acknowledged differences seem insignificant—the list is an appendage to be put aside and forgotten. The items on her list are all facts of the body. Not surprisingly, the attempt to dismiss sex differences requires, first, a radical split between "self" (behavior, feelings, ways of thought—in short our "personality") and the body. Once that separation has been accomplished then the body can be elbowed to the back of the stage.

The word "inherently" is both the most powerful and the most ambiguous in Millett's sentence. It makes a distinction between phenomena that are basic, persistent, universal, and generally to be reckoned with, versus phenomena that are superficial, fleeting, temporary, or changeable. This argument then aims at depositing all psychological sex differences in the latter bin. Unfortunately this intriguing venture often ends up stumbling along the rutted path of nature versus nurture. "Inherently" is implicitly interpreted as "hereditary" and is contrasted with the supposedly less inherent effects of environment. Indeed this is one of the reasons the body is given short shrift: it has overtones of immutable biological inheritance.

But this bald dichotomy is deeply misleading. Significant human traits are almost inevitably the outcome of a complex interaction between genetic inheritance and subsequent experience. The trick is one of sorting out the relative influences, the mechanisms at work, and the relevant "critical periods" during which the interaction is most delicate. To ask whether the human ability to use language, or a person's height, or various aspects of temperament, are due either to heredity or environment is about as enlightening as asking whether steam is the result of water or of heat. It is possible to say, for instance, that the genetic influence on height is major while on language it is probably minor, but not to completely dismiss either our chromosomes or our experience.

Human genes rarely carry immutable behavior patterns. While on the other hand, cultural influences are not all that ephemeral. The "cultural" arrangement, for instance, of a relatively long and helpless childhood in the presence of at least minimally caring adults who will serve as models for learning language—this is an absolute necessity for human development. It is only by contrast with a fantasy of inexorable heredity that we can manage to overlook the pervasive and tenacious effects of our own personal histories. Any practicing psychotherapist, or novelist for that matter, will quickly disabuse us of the notion that because something has been "learned" or experienced in early life it is therefore easily unlearned or forgotten.

Another sign that we are lost in the thickets of "innate" versus "merely cultural" is the implication that only universal and invariant traits could possibly have significant biological or genetic roots. If it is "innate" it must appear identically in all cases—so goes this mistaken premise. This variety of totalism underlies the technique of argument by misleading exception. We will see a few examples further on. The basic notion is to find a species, or a culture, or an individual who does not reveal the sex difference in question. *Therefore,* this particular trait in which the sexes are supposed to differ must be only the result of accidental external circumstance. Hardly. The interaction of heredity and environment means that we expect a wide range of results. The effect of a genetic or physiological common ground will show itself as a "central tendency," as a propensity rather than a strict requirement.

The argument by misleading exception does not ordinarily stand alone. It is usually accompanied by evidence that the culture *does* in fact have rules and expectations that could shape its members. That's fair enough, and important to know about. However, there is a difficulty. The simple fact, for instance, that parents generally expect their sons to be more aggressive than their daughters does not prove that the sons are turning out more aggressive *because* of their parents' expectations. This is yet another question that we will be revisiting later. For now we will note a paper by Lawrence Kohlberg.[16] He presents evidence that the child's set of "sex role stereotypes" is typically *more* rigid than that of the parents and that the child's conception is not directly related to either the parents' actual behavior or to parental attempts to teach and reinforce "appropriate sex typing." Parental expectations may be a *reaction to* the child, or the distillation of the whole culture's past experience in the ways of children.

Naomi Weisstein[17] and Miriam Rosenberg[18] have each recently raised the anti-sex-differences call. Their articles are quite similar in tendency and tone and they represent an attempt to carry the Millettian argument into psychology and use it as a critique of sex differences research. Both authors are quite selective in their surveys—feeling, for example, that the field of anthrophology is adequately represented by some allusions to early Margaret Mead and some passes at late Lionel Tiger. Weisstein even manages the mid-air trick of first saying that the study of primates is a waste of time, but then grabbing a few choice bits from such studies to support her own case.* Both argue from the assumption that all the important influences on personality come from the outside: social expectation, cultural prohibition, and so forth. And when the evidence threatens to go against them, both are quick to lay about them with blanket accusations of bias. Thus Rosenberg ends up in the quaint position of saying that 1) "as a scientist I am in favor of open-minded investigation" but that 2) she is "suspicious of the intentions" of research that include the possibility of biological causes (and in fact she dismisses most such work as biased), while 3) it is apparent to her that research *disproving* the role of biology "will be merely disregarded by the power elite."

Rosenberg's ultimate argument echoes Weisstein: in the current climate of social inequality it is not possible to find any worthwhile answers to the question of how men and women may differ. This position runs a serious risk of being self-serving and tendentious. It can be an invitation to give up the attempt to understand, to dismiss evidence that does not suit us, and instead to fall back on moralistic and political tenets (what we call "bias" when the other side does it). So we will decline for the moment the advice to close our eyes until after the revolution.

Having so resolved, a complicated question now presents itself. If we're wondering whether some psychological sex differences might be more than just cultural products, how might we find out? How could we begin to untangle the relative effects of heredity and environment? One traditional, and logically neat, method goes as follows: locate a large number of twins, find out whether they are identical (monozygotic) or fraternal (dizygotic), and classify the pairs as to whether or not both twins show the trait you are investigating (blue eyes, schizophrenia, "nurturance", etc.). If this "concordance ratio" is higher among monozygotic than dizygotic twins, we take that as evidence for a genetic effect. The neatness of the method depends

---

*Sad to say, Weisstein's piece is a good example of a familiar paradox. Though she speaks in the cause of "liberation," against the forces of oppression and such, her intellectual stance verges on authoritarianism. She has no doubts about who is good and who bad. Work she agrees with is praised to the skies ("brilliant"), while whole professions are dismissed out of hand (psychiatry and psychotherapy are "worse than useless") and even entire zoological orders are thrown on the trash heap if they won't serve her purposes (primates are "too stupid" to be worth study).

on the assumption that environmental influences are roughly the same within each pair of twins, or at least that they are as equal within dizygotic as monozygotic pairs, whereas the major difference is that monozygotic twins have exactly the same genetic constitution. To the extent that identicals are more similar to each other than fraternals, to that extent do we see the hand of their closer genetic makeup. This approach is ingenious but obviously useless for our purposes. Nature has unkindly neglected to provide identical twins of the opposite sex.

But all is not lost, assuming we are willing to settle for less than the impossible dream of absolute proof. There are a number of kinds of evidence that, taken together, increase the likelihood that a particular sex difference is more than cultural artifice or convention. Firstly, there is the study of a wide range of other animal species, especially those relatively near to us. The reasoning here is that if primates, for instance, show sex differences similar to those in humans, those differences are more likely to be a result of common evolutionary heritage (including such factors as sexual dimorphism, reproduction, and mammalian birth) than a result of similar "culture" and socialization amongst the monkeys.

One can reject this reasoning, as Weisstein does, and maintain that primates aren't people. True, but it's hard to believe that this objection is sincerely meant. If it were, it would mean also rejecting much of the research into the functioning of the brain since it relies heavily on experiments with animals, most testing of drugs, and sundry other fields such as ethology. At heart the objection rests, again, on a false split between body and mind: we will accept the physiological parallel between our species and others, but we reject any parallels that smack of "personality" or psychology.

Another useful source of information is the study of hormonal effects. Gender makes itself felt physiologically by means of hormones. If we find clear links between sex hormones and various psychological traits, again culture recedes a bit. Or, we might study neonates, infants in the first days of life. Here it can be argued that the culture hasn't had time to mold the infant yet, and that neonates are hardly very responsive to socializing influences anyway. Or, we could survey different cultures. If certain sex differences remain relatively constant across many societies with differing customs, differing economies and differing social structure, then we either have to believe in a gigantic global coincidence, or look elsewhere than the details of culture for the explanation of these differences between men and women. Finally, we may also be persuaded by evidence that the sexes differ in seemingly insignificant or unnoticed things—traits that are on the face of it very unlikely targets for social tuition but yet fit logically with bodily sex differences. So, let us see what the evidence is like in each of these areas.

## Other Species

Across a wide range of mammalian species the male is typically larger and more aggressive. Focusing on primates, the general rule is that the male is more the specialist in the arena of physical force, whether it be defending against external threat or comfortably holding a high position within the dominance hierarchy of the group. Of course there is variation among various primate species in the degree to which overt aggression is important, in the degree of differentiation between male and female, in the extent of male participation in the rearing of young, and so forth. It is usually the case that a mother defending her infant will be able to face down any male in the group. But it is one thing to acknowledge this variation, quite another to imply, as Weisstein does for instance, that the variation is so large as to be random or uninterpretable. On reading the text on which she draws[19] it becomes clear that we are in the presence of the technique of the misleading exception. She picks out the one and only case in over twenty-five examples that shows the female to be more aggressive and the male to be more involved in rearing the infant. She also cites two or three other instances (all of them also tree-dwelling, New World monkeys) in which the father carries the infant, referring to these fathers as "male mothers." By selecting such examples a quite misleading impression is given of the overall trend of the data (example mongering is indeed fun, and for my contribution I will note that Mitchell's series of more than twenty-five species includes seven for whom there are field reports of males killing infants, but no such instances of females killing infants).

When we visit the chimpanzee and the gorilla, the most terrestrial of the anthropoid apes and generally thought the most similar to man,[20] we again find the males to be more dominant and to be the main practitioners of aggression and threat. They also are the more solitary members of the species, and this stands in contrast to the consistent impression we have of the strength, durability, and importance of the tie between mother and infant—this bond is far and away the strongest in the entire group.

Observation of infant monkeys in captivity has shown that male infants are more likely than females to be highly active and to engage in "rough-and-tumble" play. Females are more likely to draw back from such boisterous occupations and to spend more time in the intimate contact of "grooming."[21] However, it seems that mother monkeys engage in more "nonpunitive" physical contact with their daughters: they are more likely to embrace, restrain, and protect a young female infant, while being more likely to physically withdraw from a male infant.[22] So even here we face the question of whether the sex difference in the young is due to maternal influence. Does the mother monkey promote "dependence" in her female offspring? There may well be something to this idea, but it loses part of its appeal in the face of the fact that being reared by a "surrogate mother" constructed of wire and terry cloth not only fails to decrease these sex differences in young monkeys but if anything enhances them.[23] The same intriguing evidence for a complex interaction between mother and infant will show itself when we come to talk of humans.

## HORMONES

The first sex difference is genetic. We are male or female from conception according to whether the sperm that fertilized the ovum was carrying an X chromosome or a Y. From that moment on, every cell in our body has a chromosomal gender. The direct effect of genetic gender is brief but far-reaching: during the seventh week after conception, if there is a Y chromosome present the embryonic gonad will differentiate into a testis. In the absence of an effective male chromosome, differentiation proceeds in the direction of ovaries and female development. From this point on sexual differentiation is by means of the sex hormones, androgens and estrogens. Androgen produces development in the male direction, its absence leads to development in the female direction. The hormones are secreted by the gonads and are under the ultimate control of yet another set of hormones called gonadotrophins. These controlling hormones are secreted by the pituitary gland and are in turn regulated by the region of the brain called the hypothalmus. It is this complex system that carries the timetable for the changes of puberty and menopause.

We now turn to the question of whether these hormones have effects beyond fostering the unfolding and function of the genitalia and the development of secondary sexual characteristics. As we do so it is good to keep in mind that the hormonal system is both intricate and time-bound. Things happen according to the balance and sequence of hormones and at least early on the timing and sequence is crucial. There is a hormone-induced sensitization of the brain during the first twenty weeks of life that then determines which set of hormones the system will be most responsive to in later life. The two periods of greatest hormonal activity are during the prenatal differentiation and again at puberty, and intervention or accident will have different consequences at each of these times. And the hormonal difference is not a categorical one—women naturally secrete small amounts of androgen.

The presence of testosterone, the primary androgen, not only determines whether the genitalia will begin to develop in a male direction. It also has an important direct effect on the fetal brain. If testosterone is present, the hypothalamus is permanently and irreversibly altered so that the future hormonal pattern will be noncyclical (male) rather than cyclical (female). At the same time the presence of testosterone desensitizes the brain to later doses of female hormone while the absence of testosterone at this stage of differentiation leaves both genetic males and genetic females sensitive to later female hormones. We do not yet know all the ramifications of this sexual differentiation of the hypothalamus. It is apparent that the effects of testosterone, which we will outline in a moment, are dependent on this preliminary organization of the central nervous system. Some researchers have argued that certain sex differences in cognitive abilities are due to the effects of the sex hormones on neural structure and processes.[24]

Testosterone is an anabolic steroid. It promotes protein synthesis, the retention of calcium, and ultimately the growth and repair of muscle and bone. By contrast, estrogens and progesterone seem to promote the breakdown of proteins and to have a slowing effect on growth. Those fond of poetic justice, or of the metaphor of the male body as a machine capable of high speed but likely to burn itself out in the process, will appreciate the fact that these slowing, "weakening" estrogens seem also to have a life-protecting quality: they decrease fatty substances in the blood and probably account for premenopausal women's lower cholesterol, and thus coronary disease, level.

Robert Rose provides a careful and detailed review of the animal research on the behavioral effects of testosterone. His particular interest is in whether there is any link between testosterone and aggression, and especially whether such a link can be proven in primates (this being a more demanding question than with rodents, since the simple and automatic hormonal control of behavior decreases as one ascends the evolutionary scale). The final conclusion: "As an overview it is highly likely that androgens do play some role in the expression of aggressive behavior in various primate groups. Perhaps this effect is only permissive; perhaps hormones function to establish some behavioral propensity, which may be modified or overshadowed by the influence of life experiences."[25] He is referring primarily to a propensity for active physical contact play in the youngster and then for competition in the dominance hierarchy as an adult. But the extent to which this propensity shows itself depends on many things.

The first critical period in primates (and humans) is prenatal, so that on the one hand castration of males at birth does not erase the sex-linked differences in behavior and, on the other hand, the later administration of androgens has little effect if prenatal differentiation has been female. Sexual differentiation is brought to its full flower by the hormonal surge at puberty. Thus, studies show that the effect of injecting testosterone into a castrated primate depends in part whether the castration occurred before puberty, in which case testosterone replacement does not lead to more successful dominance behavior, or after puberty when the full repertoire of dominance has already been developed. Then subsequent castration and testosterone replacement does affect the position in the dominance hierarchy. As the final argument against simple, one-way causality, Rose describes some work of his own showing that a resounding defeat in the struggle for dominance leads to a drop in the level of testosterone. So the body acknowledges overwhelming odds by reducing the hormonal urge to struggle and compete.

Of course the radical surgical and chemical techniques used with animals can not in good conscience be used with humans. So the experimental evidence is much more limited. But Persky[26] has reported that a psychological test measure of aggression and hostility is significantly correlated with both testosterone production and the level of testosterone in the blood (interestingly, this is true for young men but not for men in their forties). It is also evident that androgen is "the libido hormone"[27] in humans as well as primates and lower animals. Sexual excitement, interest, and receptiveness are importantly affected by androgen, and this holds true for both sexes. That is to say, even in females the level of sexual energy and excitement is more under the influence of small amounts of circulating androgens than it is under the influence of estrogens.

Testosterone in larger, "abnormal," dosages has effects on the female that are quite important for our understanding of its possible role in sex differences. Given the natural order of things, in which androgen is the active and initiating factor in sexual differentiation, it is possible to administer testosterone to a genetic female fetus and produce a "masculined" female. Since differentiation into a female is the strongest tendency of the organism, in the sense of its doing that *unless* a specific something else (androgen) happens, it is considerably harder to produce a "feminized male" by early chemical or surgical intervention. Both the accidental experiments that Nature, and the medical profession, visit on humans, and more deliberate tampering with primates, suggest that genetic females who are exposed to unusual amounts of androgens at a critical time in development will later show behaviors more typical of, or in the direction of, the male sex.

For instance, when pregnant rhesus monkeys are treated with androgen their female offspring show behaviors more characteristic of young males: they initiate and engage in rough-and-tumble play, threaten other monkeys more frequently, are less likely to withdraw when another monkey approaches, and show more sexual mounting behavior than normal females. On all these measures androgenized females are intermediate between the untreated females and normal males. There is little doubt that the *prenatal* period of sexual differentiation is the critical one for these particular sex-linked behaviors: the injection of testosterone into six-month-old female monkeys has marked effects on the rate of growth and on their dominance status but it does not change the frequency of aggressive play, threat, or mounting.

In parallel with this information about monkeys, we have instances of women who were "masculinized" (that is, exposed to large amounts of androgen) in utero. This happens in a naturally occurring abnormality called the adrenogenital syndrome and was also an unintended and initially unsuspected side effect of a now discarded treatment to forestall miscarriage. John Money and Anke Ehrhardt have studied groups of adolescent women so androgenized. They remark that their subjects all had early corrective surgery or hormonal therapy if necessary, so that there were no obvious external or hormonal abnormalities in later childhood. All were raised without qualm as girls—neither they nor their parents doubted which sex they were. There turned out to be a number of significant differences between these young women and a matched group of nonandrogenized females. They were more likely to see themselves, and be seen by their mothers, as "tomboys." They preferred more athletic activities, especially group sports with boys, preferred boys as playmates, and preferred what are traditionally more "male" toys (for example, cars and guns rather than dolls). They were successful competitors with boys in the childhood dominance hierarchy, although they did not try for the very top of the pile; if necessary they were willing to fight (but impulsive aggressiveness was not a characteristic trait). They showed less interest than their nonandrogenized counterparts in self-adornment and were less moved by "maternalism" in the form of doll play or caring for other children. As for their sense of the future, they expressed little enthusiasm for motherhood and gave greater preference to career achievements as opposed to romance and marriage.

Thus in both human and rhesus females it appears that fetal exposure to androgen leads to a type of physical activity and assertion that is more often characteristic of males. Although we have not touched on the animal studies of "maternalism," Money and Ehrhardt comment that the results with androgenized females are again similar: "In mammalian species, one may infer that the release of maternal or caretaking behavior in adulthood is to some degree a function of prenatal hormonal history. Regardless of genetic sex, prenatal or neonatal presence of male hormones, whether endogenous or exogenous, has an inhibiting effect on the neural mechanisms that otherwise would later mediate maternal behavior."[28]

At the risk of becoming tedious, I would like to emphasize again that this argument for the behavioral effects of "masculinization" of the fetal brain does *not* imply that certain assertive, or maternal, acts are automatically and unfailingly determined by which hormones bathe us in the womb. The sexual differentiation of the brain, given the right timing and dosages, makes some behaviors more likely and others less. But this predisposition is part of a growing and experiencing organism. Money and Ehrhardt are quite clear that such inclinations are shaped, and on occasion even overridden, by later events.

## OTHER CULTURES

I would like to pull back now from inspecting at close range the inner workings of the body to a wide-angle view of the expanse of different human societies. The argument that sex differences are only social products, and in that sense arbitrary, depends in part on seeing the range of human societies as infinitely and randomly variable. In this view anything is possible and the particular roles of the sexes are rooted in each culture's peculiar combination of geography, history, and economic structure. This argument would run into difficulty should there seem to be universal sex differences across greatly dissimilar cultures.

This is an area ripe for the use of the misleading example. If we accept the absolutist assumption that any "inherent" sex difference must show itself in the same fashion in *every* human society, then we need find only one negative example and we're home free. The commonest example seized for this purpose is Margaret Mead's Tchambuli:

We found a genuine reversal of the sex-attitudes of our own culture, with the woman the dominant, impersonal, managing partner, the man the less responsible and the emotionally dependent person. . . . If those temperamental attitudes which we have traditionally regarded as feminine—such as passivity, responsiveness, and a willingness to cherish children—can so easily be set up as the masculine pattern in one tribe, and in another be outlawed for the majority of men, we no longer have any basis for regarding such aspects of behavior as sex-linked.[29]

We can pass over quibbles about the facts of the case (one report has it that these mild-mannered Tchambuli men are expected to kill and behead an enemy as part of their initiation into adulthood),[30] or that Mead herself doesn't seem to agree with the use which is made of this early work,[31] or that more recent anthropological investigation suggests that the "female dominance" that Mead saw was a momentary aberration in a sexually quite traditional society.[32] The important response is to realize that, even if it were true, such an example is persuasive only if we are laboring under an overly simple conception of "inherent" versus social.

The proper question to ask of the cross-cultural data is what regularities, if any, there are in the roles of the sexes. Are there common tendencies or features, appearing in many different societies, that would suggest an underlying predisposition for men and women to act and feel differently? The first thing we notice is that every society we know about does distinguish between men and women. The sex-linked division of labor is virtually a cross-cultural constant. The usual explanation for this universal tendency to divide the world into men's work and women's work draws upon the body: women have an advantage in childbearing and rearing, men in activities calling for strong arms and back.[33] Thus the sexual division of labor tends to cluster around female specialization in child care, feeding and instruction, and male specialization in hunting, tending livestock, or heavy agricultural work. And to the extent that the culture deals in violence, this too will be a male specialty. There is a strong tendency for this allocation of tasks to establish itself even in a society such as the kibbutz where the ideology urges sexual equality in labor.[34] It is also the cross-cultural norm for the man to be seen as the initiator of sexual activity and for the culture to place more restrictions on female sexuality than on male.

Along with the sex-linked division of labor is another striking regularity: men wield more authority. There are many ways of measuring this, all leading to the same result. If we look at whether societal residence rules give preference to the paternal or the maternal kinship line, in a worldwide ethnographic sample of 565 societies, 376 are predominantly patrilocal while 84 are matrilocal. In a more detailed study of 31 societies, 21 give more authority to the male within the family while only 4 (one of which was are our friends the Tchambuli) give more familial authority to the woman. If we consider authority and leadership roles beyond the family, it is safe to say that every known society has been controlled by men.[35]

Morris Zelditch took the Parsons and Bales categories of "instrumental" and "expressive" and used them to classify the family roles in a heterogeneous group of between fifty and sixty societies. He found that the role categories were borne out by the cross-cultural data, though more clearly for the mother than for the father. That is "the initial relation of mother and child is sufficiently important so that the mother's expressive role in the family is largely not problematical," whereas the instrumental leadership role is effected by the kinship system and may be filled by another male, such as the mother's brother, rather than the father.[36]

One of the problems that plagues anthropology is the wide variation in the quality of the information: surveys that aim to include hundreds of different societies of necessity end up equating the observations of a meticulous anthropologist who lived a whole year in a certain culture with the hundred-year-old outrage of a missionary who happens to have been the only visitor to a particular group of "savages." The so-called Six Culture Study[37] was a large-scale and serious attempt to use trained observers and get accurate, and equivalent, information on child development in six communities: Kenyan, Okinawan, Indian, Filipino, Mexican, and American. This study resulted in a mass of material, which could be analyzed in varying ways. An early summary of some of the results went as follows:

> We have behavioral observations on boys and girls in six different
> societies up to the age of six, and in each of these societies a factor

analysis of [the girls'] behavior shows three things: dominance,* nurturance and responsibility, and this combination is essentially the definition of what a mother is to her children. She must be dominant, she nurtures and does the care taking, she is responsible. We find that girls show these types of behavior in each of the six cultures which are located in six parts of the world entirely unrelated to another. Girls exhibit this at an earlier age and more than boys do. Conversely, in each of these six cultures, boys are characterized by more physical attack, more physical aggression, than are girls. This seems to me to indicate an underlying difference in the physiological wiring of the two sexes.[38]

More recently, a report has appeared that offers detailed data from this study and stresses the parts of the data that support the social training hypothesis.[39] (It seems that the debate about ultimate causes was present even within this one research group. There must have been a few rather lively prepublication conferences.) Across the six cultures, and looking separately at younger (age three to six) and older (age seven to eleven) children, there are the following significant sex differences: in the younger group, girls are more likely to seek help, to seek physical contact, and to be "responsible" in the sense of standing up for social rules and the maintenance of standards. Younger boys show more "egoistic dominance" and are more given to insult and aggressive physical play (the familiar "rough-and-tumble"). In the older group, girls are more supportive and helpful, whereas boys are more boastful, more likely to reply to aggression in kind, and again more fond of insulting others and engaging in rough physical play. All told, fifteen such categories of behavior were evaluated. All were chosen as representing aspects of traditional Western sex role "stereotypes." Statistical criteria for significance aside, it is interesting to note that of these thirty comparisons (fifteen categories, each scored for both younger and older children), twenty-eight reveal a difference that is in agreement with our popular stereotype.

---

*The word "dominance" as used here by Whiting is a good example of the need to keep clear about what we mean. It refers to responsible care-taking and to invoking the power of social rules ("don't do that, it's not nice"). What we will later see called "egoistic dominance," the bald assertion of individual strength which has victory as its own reward, is the more *male* form of dominance. Although these are both modes of trying to determine what someone else does, they draw on very different areas of personality and have different consequences for the social group. They deserve to be kept separate.

The Six Culture Study is useful in that it shows us a range of sex differences. Whiting and Edwards make a sensible distinction between the basic intent of behavior, which may be the same for both sexes, and the style or outward manifestation, which may be quite different. Thus we can understand both the girls' direct request for help and the boys' showing-off as "dependent" behaviors directed at eliciting a response from an adult. Or we may understand the boys' addiction to wrestling matches as their way of getting the physical contact that girls feel more free to ask for directly.

But Whiting and Edward's summary and interpretation of these findings gives the feeling of an as yet unresolved struggle with the data. They remark on the apparent "universal sex differences" but go on to say that the differences are "not consistent" (which seems to mean not absolute and automatic in every culture) "nor as great as the studies of American and Western European children would suggest." It is not immediately obvious in what ways they think their results show sex differences "not as great" as in previous studies of American children. It would be wrong to infer from their comment that our culture is an extreme instance of differences between the sexes: among these six cultures, the American children show the smallest overall sex difference; American girls offer less help and support than in any of the other societies and they are one of the two instances of younger girls who are more involved in rough-and-tumble play than younger boys.

Whiting and Edwards say that "aggression, perhaps especially rough and tumble play, and touching behavior seem the best candidates for biophysical genesis." As for the rest of the differences between boys and girls, Whiting and Edwards wish to argue for the influence of "socialization pressure in the form of task assignment." They remind us that if girls are typically kept around the home and expected to care for younger siblings, or for the aged, that they are apt to become skilled in "nurturance." They show that the female specialization in offering help and support increases significantly from the younger to the older girls (this age effect is not true for male aggression). Reference is also made to examples of African communities where circumstances require some boys to act as nurses and domestic caretakers: these boys show less typically male irresponsibility, aggression, and egotistical behavior. So it seems reasonable to conclude that the particular sexual division of labor affects the nature and extent of sex differences in behavior. However, the mechanism appears to be more complicated than simple training: we are told that the most detailed study of "domestic" African boys shows not an increase in the nurturant qualities of offering help and support but rather a decrease in characteristically "masculine" behavior. Rather than a direct training effect, learning to be nurturant through being a nurse, we see some more complicated process of masculinity being modulated and tempered through more contact with affairs of the home. And if it is true that the largest sex differences in the Six Cultures data appear in the *younger* group,[40] this does not fit well with a social training explanation.

The tension shows itself in Whiting and Edwards's summary: "all of the behaviors that are characteristic of males and females seem to be remarkably malleable under the impact of socialization pressures, which seem to be remarkably consistent from one society to another." So the "universal sex differences" with which we began are now to be understood as the result of universal "socialization pressures." But this only moves the question back one step: why should these various societies be so consistent in the way they delineate sexual roles?

A larger, less finely focused, view of some eighty different societies confirms that boys are most often trained to be self-reliant and to achieve, while girls are trained to be responsible, obedient, and nurturant. The authors, like Whiting and Edwards, find evidence of:

> universal tendencies in the differentiation of the adult role. In the economic sphere, men are more frequently allotted tasks that involve leaving home and engaging in activities where a high level of skill yields important returns: hunting is a prime example. Emphasis on training in self-reliance and achievement for boys would function as preparation for such an economic role. Women, on the other hand, are more frequently allotted tasks at or near home that minister most immediately to the needs of others (such as cooking and water carrying); and in their pursuit a responsible carrying out of established routines is likely to be more important than the development of an especially high order of skill. Thus training in nurturance, responsibility, and less clearly, obedience, may contribute to preparation for this economic role . . . the biological differences between the sexes strongly predispose the distinction of role, if made, to be in a uniform direction.[41]

The article goes on to show that the greatest distinctions between the way boys and girls are raised occur in societies where the economy requires male strength (in hunting, animal husbandry, or large-scale agriculture) and in societies having a large or extended family unit that allows considerable specialization of tasks.

The question remains whether social training, which in turn is tied to economic and political structure, is a sufficient explanation. It is indeed valuable to know which factors influence the variations within these "universal tendencies in the differentiation of the adult role." But once more we bump up against the question of why there should be such a universal tendency in the first place. It is here that the socialization argument runs into difficulty. Why this persistent predisposition for women to be the caretakers and men the more aggressive wielders of power? As Kate Millett has taken the social argument to its furthest extreme, so she also shows most accurately its ultimate dilemma. Ultimately her explanation is founded on the notion that men are beasts and that a male conspiracy is responsible for this troublesome historical and cross-cultural continuity.[42] It is often here that the discredited idea of a prehistoric "matriarchy," including Amazons and such, is brought in to buffer the implication that the regularities in human society stem from an ancient sexual coup d'état. As we shall see later, the idea of matriarchy may have an important meaning in the life history of the individual, but as history or anthropology it is a largely fruitless attempt to escape a conceptual blind alley.

Even within its proper sphere, there are limits to the power of training and socialization. The kibbutz culture deliberately aimed at minimizing sex differences in its children, but even here girls were reported to be more "integrative" (helpful, affectionate, and coopera- tive) and boys more "disintegrative" (disobedient, aggressive, and imperious).[43] These sex differences would seem to exist in spite of, rather than because of, the social ideology and goals.

Socialization, after all, does not write on a blank page. The creature to be "socialized" already has nascent urges, abilities, and tendencies that socialization can only shape. The next topic we will take up is that of sex differences in newborn and very young children. What of the basic material upon which socialization begins to work? Is there evidence for sex differences here, at the beginning of human life?

## EARLY INFANCY

Human infants come into the world in a quite disorganized and immature state. No other self-respecting species would put up with such a protracted period of chaotic dependence in its young. The extremely simple and limited repertoire of the newborn lends even more weight and interest to whatever sex differences do exist in the first weeks and months of life. On the purely physical side, males tend to be larger and heavier from the beginning, and from the second month on they have a larger caloric intake. The female is born more mature (four to six weeks ahead at birth) and will sit up, crawl, walk, and talk sooner than the male. The newborn female is also more sensitive and receptive to tactile stimulation.

As early as a few days after birth it becomes apparent that males and females have different types of spontaneous activity. The male's tends to be gross and vigorous, involving the whole body. The female's is more centered in the muscles and skin of the face and shows itself in rhythmic mouthing and spontaneous smiling. This oral focus is also shown in the female's greater response to sweet-tasting things.

> While there is cumulative evidence in the literature that males and females are treated differently from the start, a review of the sex differences found among neonates clearly points to innate sex differences as well. The newborn female tentatively emerges as more receptive to certain stimuli, particularly of the oral and cutaneous type. At the same time, she is in no way less active or expressive, as no significant differences have been found in activity level or crying. There is suggestive evidence that the male newborn is endowed with greater muscular strength. Since the literature on adult sex differences suggests persistence, either in direct or derivative form of the sex differences found in newborns, an explanation of these differences on maturational grounds is not the most cogent. More plausibly, the hormones responsible for sexual differentiation *in utero* may account for the sex differences at birth through sensitization of the organism's CNS [central nervous system] which will facilitate sex-linked behaviors to emerge at a later time. Possibly the androgens circulating during foetal life, which are required for the foetus to become male, may be responsible for the male's greater muscular strength and may also serve to suppress his responsiveness and sensitivity of both mouth and skin.[44]

At three weeks of age males are stronger and more vigorous, as shown by the infant's ability to lift its head. Males also sleep less and are more given to crying and irritability. This is still true at three to four months, and in addition we now find males more responsive to visual than auditory reinforcement, while the opposite is true of females (this visual preference holds with male monkeys and rats also, and it continues to be a sex difference in adult men and women). Female infants continue to show more spontaneous movements of the mouth. By six months we find that females show a particular interest in human faces, or other social stimuli, and that they are more interested and attentive in general: "If one assumes that sustained attention and a preference for deviation from the familiar are *mature* attentional habits, it appears that girls are developmentally advanced over boys as early as six months of age. These data support the general belief that there are basic biological differences between boys and girls in the rate of psychological development during the opening year of life."[45]

By the end of the first year of life there are important differences in infants' spontaneous play. Girls are more likely to remain close to their mothers, to touch, look, and babble at her; boy infants wander farther away, and show more vigorous muscular activity in their play. But might this just be an outcome of the fact that even earlier, at six months, these mothers touched, talked to, and handled their daughters more than their sons?[46] Here we are reminded of the rhesus monkeys, who showed the same heightened physical closeness between mother and daughter. But here with humans the question is even more pressing: is this just the opening wedge of the mother's program to foster greater "dependence" in daughters? Is it mother or daughter who is most responsible for this greater intimate bond? Of course if we view what goes on between mother and child as an *interaction*, then the search for the first term is meaningless—since long before birth this child and mother have been *influencing each other*. But because there is a tendency to overlook the infant's active participation in this complex mutual shaping process, we will try to follow the interaction one step further back.

Howard Moss studied thirty first-born children and their mothers; detailed observations were made when the infants were about three weeks old and again at three months.[47] Overall he found that there were larger sex differences, both in infant behavior and in maternal response, for the younger babies. For instance, at three weeks mothers of male infants do significantly more cuddling and attending than do mothers of females. But by three months the amount that mothers hold and pay attention to their male infants has declined so much that there is no longer a significant sex difference (and as we saw a minute ago, by six months the trend has reversed, with girl babies being held more). The most likely explanation for this lies in the fact that male babies are more restless and irritable. Early on this will lead the mother to pay more attention, to hold the baby in hopes of pacifying it. But male babies, being physiologically less mature and less sensitive to physical contact, are considerably more frustrating to try to comfort. Gradually the mother gives up on cuddling this recalcitrant creature, while she does not give up on her more rewarding contact with her daughter. The two differences that remain even after making allowance for the greater male restlessness and irritability are: mothers imitate the sounds of girl babies more, and mothers stimulate, arouse, and physically exercise male babies more.

This example of the amount of physical contact between mother and child helps to show how complicated the interaction is. The closer one looks, the less clear it is who is influencing whom. So often it is assumed that any correlation between the behaviors of the parent and those of the child is evidence for parental influence. Because of the infant's lesser power and experience in these matters, it is easy to assume that all the influence flows from parent to child. Under the sway of our American ideology, we are especially prone to believe that everything can be taught and that children are almost entirely the products of their surroundings. This environmentalist bias is in part a reaction against an earlier and just as fruitless belief in a crude version of Social Darwinism. But the counteracting swing to an overemphasis on the effects of socialization has been just as constricting in terms of theory and research in child development.[48]

There are many ways in which the mother is controlled by the infant. The fact that such a statement could even begin to be surprising or controversial suggests that we should have been doing more listening to the experiences of mothers of young children—they could have told us this years ago. The most obvious example is the infant's crying, which has an immediate and powerful effect on any responsible adults in the neighborhood. We have seen how what might appear to be a maternal decision to pamper or restrict little girls is just as likely to have arisen as a frustrated reaction to the crying and irritability of little boys.

A similar example can be sketched out about female talk. At thirteen months girls talk to their mothers more than boys do. At six months mothers talk more to their daughters than to their sons. Still pursuing the roots of this conversation back in time, at three months we find that mothers have different ways of pacifying boys and girls: they tend to hold or offer a distraction to the boys, while the girls they talk to. At this same age the mothers are doing more imitating of the sounds their daughters make. But at three weeks mothers are if anything talking more to boy babies, though the females make more sounds and the mothers imitate them more often (none of these differences are large enough to be statistically significant).

There is one study that found that mothers are talking more to their girls as early as forty-eight hours after birth. This same study mentions talking *and* smiling at the infant, and this deserves attention. Female infants do more spontaneous smiling from birth onwards. A small but powerful gesture, it is the single most rewarding and exhilarating thing that a baby can do for its mother. And what more natural response than to smile back, and to talk a bit? It may well be out of this pleasant moment, initiated as much by the infant as by the mother, that the later conversations between mother and daughter emerge. The mother finds that talk works with girls, that it soothes, whereas boys require something more physical, something that engages more of their bodies. It is necessary to distinguish between different kinds of talk, since some of the seeming contradictions in the research results originate here. At three months of age there is no overall difference in the amount of verbal noise mothers direct at sons and daughters, but mothers are *imitating* their daughters more.

The notion of imitation is important. We are quite used to noticing the ways in which children imitate adults. A parent speaks, with guilty pride, of "tricking" an unwilling child into eating by opening his own mouth and then popping the unwanted food into the child's mouth when the child unwittingly imitates him. Observation of young children being fed indeed shows that the person doing the feeding will open his or her own mouth with each spoonful they offer. But typically they open their mouth *after* the child opens his. Who is imitating whom? The mother, or caretaker, responds by imitating, by playing back to the child what the child has done—but playing it back in a way that is shaped into a more "adult" version of the act.

Being a good teacher, the mother starts where the child is. It is more a matter of gradually transforming by a process of exchanges back and forth than it is a matter of imposition or command. By focusing responses on the girl's mouth (smiles, babbling, talk) and on the boy's large muscle systems (holding, jouncing, stretching) the caretaker is responding to that part of the infant most salient and pressing. It is an agreement to play the game in the infant's strong suit.*

## THE UNNOTICED

There remains one more area in which we might look for evidence that the differences between men and women are more than cultural in origin. This is the area of the unnoticed, the area of the insignificant detail. Here we lack any sharp definition of content or method. The idea is simply that no matter how strong the hand of culture may be in some matters, its grasp must have limits. The culture, as expressed through the fallible instrument of the parents, is neither so energetic nor so uniform as to supervise every fragment of behavior. So there may be occasions when we look at a particular sex difference and feel that the cultural explanation just isn't very plausible. Of course this is a matter of judgment and opinion. The example I've chosen will make this element of interpretation apparent since it consists of some work that has meant different things to different people even before it first reached print.

In the years just prior to the Second World War, Erik Erikson was

*Related to this is D.W. Winnicott's idea that one of the mother's crucial functions is to reflect back to the infant what is already there. From this "mirroring" grows the child's consciousness, creativity, and ability to have human relationships. See *The Maturational Processes and the Facilitating Environment* (London: Hogarth Press, 1965); or "Mirror-Role of Mother and Family in Child Development," in *Playing and Reality* (London: Tavistock Publications, 1971).

one of many psychoanalytic refugees newly working in America. In Vienna he had trained in child analysis with Anna Freud, and this interest led to his being involved in a longitudinal study of normal development, which was being done in Berkeley, California. Erikson was fascinated by the ways in which children use play both to express and to master their central concerns or conflicts. He also had a particular eye for the spatial configurations in which themes are embodied. Erikson asked a large number of boys and girls, ages eleven through thirteen, to construct a dramatic scene with play materials. His report on the resulting rich data gives some examples of the particular individual meanings that the play construction had in each child's individual life history, but goes on to focus on the typical male and female forms.[49] The article deserves reading in the original, but for our purposes it can be summarized as follows: in spatial terms the boys' constructions are characterized by the erection of structures, buildings and towers, and by forms that channel activity or move- ment (roads, sidewalks, tunnels). The girls' constructions concern themselves more with simple enclosures (often with ornamented entrances) and what happens inside these spaces. In terms of themes, the boys distinguish themselves by their focus on height and the imminent possibility of collapse (the depicting of ruins is a male specialty) and on the control or arrest of motion (the policeman is their favorite human figure). Girls tend more toward interior family scenes, scenes where the pleasant goings on are periodically threat- ened by an intrusion from the outside.

Erikson describes these common themes as "caution outdoors" versus "goodness indoors." He goes on to consider the possibility that these differences reflect only sex differences in training for future roles, but finds that explanation inadequate. He then puts forth the idea that one aspect of the raw material with which culture must work is "the ground plan of the human body" and comments that "the spatial tendencies governing these constructions closely parallel the morphology of the sex organs: in the male, *external* organs, *erectible* and *intrusive* in character, serving highly *mobile* sperm cells; *internal* organs in the female, with vestibular *access,* leading to *statically expectant* ova."[50]

That puts the matter bluntly indeed, and it is not surprising that it has recently incited considerable outrage.[51] Interestingly enough, there seems to have been disagreement, or at least an alternative emphasis, even within the original probject. In the same year as Erikson's paper, Marjorie Honzik published another perspective on some of the same material.[52] She looked at a more limited aspect— what materials the children chose to use in their constructions—and found that boys inclined toward blocks, vehicles, and people in uniform, while girls more often used furniture and people in ordinary dress. She holds that these differences flow from the fact that the sexes pick different sites for their dramas (factories, filling stations, etc., for the boys, and the home or school interiors for the girls), and that this in turn is a function of differing cultural roles. She does allow that the greater energy and variety of the male constructions might be "physiobiological" in origin.

One reason I have chosen this example of play constructions is that we have the fortune, rare in psychology, to have had this work carefully repeated by another investigator. Thirty years and a continent's breadth removed from the original study, Phebe Cramer has expanded and clarified Erikson's work.[53] Cramer's approach is more systematic concerning rating categories and statistical treatment of the data. She also used two groups of children, five-and-a-half year olds and eleven-and-a-half year olds, so as to see whether the approach of puberty makes any difference in these matters. All in all her results are a solid confirmation of the original study. The choice of play materials followed Honzik. And what was done with the materials followed Erikson to a large extent. When boys use blocks they use them to build horizontal channels for movement or to build vertical structures; when girls use blocks they use them more often to construct ornamented entrances into houses. Boys place their scenes outdoors and focus on external activity; girls place their scenes indoors and concentrate on interior happenings. The themes of the dramas have to do with danger, violence, and arrested motion for boys and with peaceful family scenes for girls.

These sex differences are by and large true for both older and younger children. But there are also some interesting effects of age. The older children, the ones on the verge of adolescence (and closest in age to those Erikson studied), show a greater number of vertical structures, for the boys, and gates and archways for the girls. There is also a shift in the themes. Both sexes show more active themes in the older group, but the type of activity differs. For the girls the increase in activity comes by way of agitated and excited activity within the interior (for example, an animal comes to life and races around in the house) or by way of a fantasied male intrusion (a burglar comes into the house). For the boys the increased activity shows itself in an increase in the "high/low" theme: concern with rising and falling, erection and collapse.

I don't doubt that with enough dedication and ingenuity one could construct a purely social-training explanation for these sexual variations in play. But it wouldn't be easy once we pass beyond the simple levels of what materials are chosen or why boys show more themes of aggression and destruction and girls more themes of family life.[54] It sorely strains the imagination to think of a cultural purpose behind the full detail of what Erikson and Cramer show us. Are girls encouraged to be interested in entrances and boys in towers? Are boys taught that activity occurs outside and girls that it occurs inside? And are they taught these things with increasing intensity as puberty approaches? Cramer and Hogan conclude:

> While it is likely that social and cultural factors help shape the child's adoption of sex-related behaviors and his preference for sex-related play materials, it does not seem likely that such external factors can be entirely responsible for the results of the present study. The verbal and spatial fantasies of these children—the configurations that are created and the themes that emerge—seem unlikely to be a function only of such conditioning. Rather, we suggest that these fantasy creations of children reflect basic differences in their inner feelings of sexual identity, which in turn derive in significant part from biological differences.[55]

*Chapter VI*

⟨⬥⟩

# Male and Female
# Development

Culture is, at least in part, that which we make of our biology.[1]

No true role concept would ignore the fact that functioning roles, if ever so flamboyant, are tied to certain conditions: a role can only provide leeway within the limits of what bodily constitution can sustain, social structures make workable, and personality formation integrate.[2]

Cultures, after all, elaborate upon the biologically given and at least attempt to arrive at a division of labor between the sexes which is, simultaneously, workable within the body's scheme and life cycle, useful to the particular culture, and manageable for the individual ego.[3]

These statements are all first steps in an important direction: the attempt to integrate culture and biology. But even to phrase it this way puts us in immediate difficulty. One only "integrates" things that are already separate or distinct. A distinction between "culture" and "biology" can exist only in our way of thinking, not in reality. We have already seen how misleading it can be to make a split between the categories of "biological," meaning innate, and "cultural," meaning external and changeable. The discussion of differences between men and women is absolutely plagued by this polarity. It is quite humbling to see how nearly impossible it is to have such a conversation without the speakers sliding off to one side or the other and ending up in two equally indefensible camps: those who talk as if they believe *all* is due to biology and those who talk as if *they* believe with equal fervor that all is due to culture. There are, of course, more sophisticated versions of the dichotomy: internal versus external, past versus present, individual psychic history versus collective social history. All are equally futile.

So it would be better to speak of the task as describing the ways in which culture and biology, inner and outer, interact and intertwine in the course of human development. We must speak in terms of *and,* not *or.* It is a daunting enough task. In a somewhat more specialized sense it shows itself in that unfinished chapter of modern thought: the yet-to-be-accomplished marriage of Marxism and psychoanalysis. There has been no lack of eager matchmakers, no lack of effort toward consummation. Perhaps the task is indeed impossible. The very ideal may be a Faustian fantasy of knowing everything, a dream of omniscience. In any case, such a grand goal is well beyond the scope of *this* work.

But even to begin to talk about sex differences requires an implicit position on these broader issues, and that position is best acknowledged. As you have undoubtedly have noticed by now, I start from the psychoanalytic end of the ideological continuum. And I have a particular appreciation for the work of Erik Erikson.[4] He has made a serious attempt to move psychoanalytic understanding in the direction of a greater respect for social, cultural, and historical factors, and thus two of the opening statements in this section are his.

I would also like to make a brief gesture towards the rehabilitation of the image of Sigmund Freud. In many discussions of sex differences his appearance is greeted with all the reverence and acclaim accorded an unrepentant boozer at a temperance meeting. The socialization-is-all approach often includes a raid on Freud, Millett's *Sexual Politics* again being the prime example. The point is not that some of his comments about women don't sound demeaning to our ears, especially when plucked out of context, or that there aren't still important modifications to be made in the psychoanalytic understanding of women.[5] The point is that the polemic urge constructs a caricature, which is then duly derided and dismissed. The complexity, tentativeness, and evolution in Freud's thought are ignored. The cultural enthusiast's extreme position on one end of the seesaw must be balanced by building an effigy of Freud at the other end. So Freud comes to be described as the archadvocate of biological determinism and of rigid and categorical sex roles. This is doubly unfortunate because in fact his theory, taken on its own terms, reaches toward a way of integrating the impossible polarities of body and society.

The centerpiece of the caricature of Freud is often his supposed belief that "anatomy is destiny." This quotation may be used in such a context as to suggest that he thought women were inevitably inferior and should reconcile themselves to their limited role. But let's look at an example of how Freud actually used the phrase. It is in a paper that talks of the difficulties that *men,* and less frequently women, have in managing their erotic impulses.[6] Toward the end of this paper Freud is letting his mind wander out from consideration of a specific type of inhibited sexual relation, that which requires the degradation of the sexual object, to a more general musing about whether "something in the nature of the sexual instinct itself is unfavorable to the achievement of absolute gratification." He considers those aspects of family and cultural life that militate against sexual expression: for instance, the incest taboo or Christian asceticism. Then he moves to the thought that some of our persistent sexual inhibition might also be related to a fact of our body's geography: "The excremental is all too intimately and inseparably bound up with the sexual; the position of the genital organs—*inter urinas et faeces* —remains the decisive and unchangeable factor. One might say, modifying a well-known saying of the great Napoleon, 'Anatomy is destiny.'" A paragraph later he ends the paper by saying, "But I myself am quite ready to admit that such far-reaching conclusions as those I have drawn should be built on a broader foundation, and that perhaps developments in other directions may enable mankind to correct the results of the developments I have here been considering in isolation."[7]

Whatever you may think of Freud's line of thought, I trust you will agree that it would be a considerable distortion to read this passage as involving either an invidious distinction between the sexes or an assertion that anatomy determines everything. But it *is* characteristic of psychoanalytic thought to insist that the body is indeed *one* of the important places to look in trying to understand human life. This insistence is enough to make Freud a lightning rod for those who see biological thinking as a mask for social oppression. The most valuable aspects of psychoanalysis are indeed those concepts and concerns that attempt to bridge some of these dichotomies and to operate across the borderline between two realms of thought. For instance, "instinct" (or better translated, "drive") as Freud uses it refers to the psychological representation of a physical tension or need—thus it is a concept that connects body and mind.

The evolution of Freud's thought shows a continuous puzzling over the proper roles of "inner" and "outer" experience. In the beginning he thought that his hysterical patients were suffering from reality: that as children they had in fact been sexually seduced. Continued experience as a therapist, and more importantly his exploration of his own inner life, led to the initially shattering realization that what he had taken for a memory of a real event was better understood as a fantasy. The debate continues: there are those who feel that Freud's transforming insights took him too far in the opposite direction, away from social reality. But this is a dispute about balance, not about whether we could completely dispense with either one of the terms. Much of analytic theory is dedicated to studying the interchange between inner and outer: how does childhood experience shape psychic reality and thus effect later experience; how do our wishes transform our perceptions and memories; how is social reality, as embodied in the family, "internalized" by the individual; to what extent, or under what conditions, do we come both to imagine ourselves as others have treated us and to treat others as we imagine ourselves?

The vision of Freud as the ultimate male chauvinist also leaves out the fact that the notion of psychological bisexuality has always been important in psychoanalysis. In 1899 Freud wrote: "I am accustoming myself to the idea of regarding every sexual act as a process in which four persons are involved."[8] Aside from parental ghosts in the bed, he is referring here to a male and female part of each of us. Again in 1905, ". . . pure masculinity or femininity is not to be found either in a psychological or a biological sense. Every individual on the contrary displays a mixture of the character-traits belonging to his own and to the opposite sex; and he shows a combination of activity and passivity whether or not these last character-traits tally with his biological ones."[9] Again the analytic concern is about the internal balance and how these aspects of the person get on with one another (and notice that the final sentence explicitly leaves open the question of biological influence). In one of his last papers[10] Freud ends by emphasizing our repression of our wish to be the other sex—this is the "bedrock" in our character that most resists therapeutic change.

In short, I hope these examples will at least suggest that the psychoanalytic tradition is not as simple as some of its critics would have you believe. In fact, it is not a bad place from which to begin an exploration of sexual differences and development.

Two fundamental facts out of which psychological sex differences may arise are first the fact that men and women have different bodies and secondly that in most ordinary instances female infants are cared for and raised primarily by someone of the same sex while males are initially cared for by someone of the opposite sex.* It is here that an explanation needs to begin, with these minimal yet universal terms. In thinking about male and female bodies we need to keep in mind the wide spectrum of hormonal effects: the "priming" of the hypothalamus to respond differently to certain hormones later on, the probable sensitizing of various perceptual modes (for example, touch versus sight), internal and external sexual anatomy, metabolic function, secondary sexual characteristics (muscle, hair, etc.), and the various timetables that are laid down for the later events of puberty, menopause, and death.

The second factor is simpler on the face of it, but its effects may be just as far-reaching. There is an asymmetry in the life of boys and girls. Girls are born into the hands of a similar creature, boys are not. The infant forms an intense and complex relation with the person who cares for it in the early months and years. Regardless of whether the child is born into an extended family in a tribal society or into a modern "liberated" urban family where the father is adept with diapers, the likelihood is that the person with whom the first and strongest bond develops will be a woman. Even if the mother and

---

*Dorothy Dinnerstein's *The Mermaid and the Minotaur* (New York: Harper & Row, 1976) is a subtle and intriguing consideration of the effects of the second of these facts. Her neglect of the first fact, male and female bodies, leads her to suggest that sexual dilemmas could be solved if men shared equally in child rearing.

father were to devote equal time and energy to the care of the infant, the experience of breast feeding and, more important, the experience of having carried this creature inside one's body for nine months—these are bound to give a special quality to the relation between mother and child.

From the point of view of the young infant being nursed or cuddled, we may assume that he or she knows little and cares less about the gender of the person who is providing the milk or affection. As the world gradually becomes organized in the child's mind it is likely that categories such as large and small, or feels-good versus feels-bad, are initially more important than gender. Nonetheless a relationship has been growing with a particular person and when, in early childhood, the category of sex does become important, the girl discovers that the person who early on defined the world for her is in fact one of her own. The boy discovers that he owes his life to someone different, an Other. Meanwhile, of course, the mothering-one has been thinking of this child as like her (female) or unlike her (male).

In the rest of this chapter I wish to describe some important aspects of male and female development. I will do this in terms of three important segments of the life cycle, and two themes that cut across these different stages. We will look at the first stages of male and female development, up through early or middle childhood. Next we will consider the entry into adolescence, and then take up one of the more general themes: sexuality. Finally, we will focus on maturity or the second half of life, and on the other general issue: what are the pathological possibilities of male and female development. Throughout we will keep in mind the two fundamental sources of sex differences: our bodies and the gender asymmetry of the mothering relationship.

## EARLY DIFFERENTIATION: THE MALE PUSH

One fruitful way in which to think of male and female development is in terms of the degree of differentiation and separateness. Again and again male events partake of moving away from, of separating oneself from the context, of pushing off and out into space. Female events are more akin to being part of, staying in touch with, being embedded in.

These themes appear with the first players in the drama: the sperm and the ovum. The sperm specializes in movement. It leaves one body and enters another. Its task is to get there while it still lives, and in this race it competes with many others. The ovum has a more enduring function: it forgoes rapid mobility for the sake of carrying life-sustaining nutrients and having the ability to support life in transit. The next stage of differentiation depends on the genetic information carried by the sperm. If it is male, the embryo begins to develop in that direction. If the male chromosome is not present, or if anything goes wrong in the complicated process of differentiation, the embryo will revert to its original course: being female. To the extent it makes sense to talk of a "natural" or basic human form, it is female. Something, or rather a series of somethings, must happen to move the embryo in a male direction. This standing-out-from has its hazards. At every step, from the journey of the sperm onwards, the male is more liable to injury, deformity, or death.

The theme continues in the young infant. Maleness is associated with restlessness, irritability, and a style of physical movement that is vigorous, all-encompassing, and poorly organized. Already the focus is on large muscle systems and abrupt movement. Femaleness shows itself in more localized and controlled movement. The infant girl is more in touch, both in the sense of being more alive to physical contact and in the sense of using her mouth to be in touch with others by means of smiles and babbling. She is more able to sit still and watch. She can learn and take things in without disrupting everything within reach.

The parents come to the child with a vast collection of hopes, fears, and wishes. Some of these preconceptions would be recognized by most people in a similar social position in the same society: how an infant should behave, what is a good life and what is a bad one, what to expect of a little girl, and so forth. Other thoughts about this child will be much more personal and idiosyncratic: leftover bits of the parent's own childhood, attempts to either emulate or disown one's own parents, family traditions, and mythologies, and the particularly loved or feared parts of one's own self.

As we have seen in the previous chapter, the infant is far from being a passive receptacle waiting to be filled up with parental urgings and fantasies. Infants are quite capable of holding up their own end of a complex process of mutual influence. But there is a systematic sex difference here: the girl is generally more reachable, more accessible to influence, than the boy. Throughout the period of physical and psychological growth, the girl is more willing, and able, to be shaped by social forces. She is simply more susceptible to being civilized and much of what we know suggests that a frequent danger in female development is that this process will be *too* successful and thus lead to a stifling of initiative, autonomy, and assertion. The clash between the male child and his culture is much harsher and the threat for him is that the civilizing process will be incomplete and inadequate.

It is in the interrelation of the child and the mothering-one that the first steps are taken in learning to distinguish between "me" and "not-me," and in becoming able to modulate or regulate the urges of the "me" out of consideration for the effect it will have on that surrounding world of "not-me." The girl spends more time in this formative relation and is more responsive to it. She stays physically closer to the mother and is more attuned to her. The male's greater restlessness and impulsive urge to move away make him more often a difficult foreigner in the mother's arms. This may start a spiral of decreasing contact: the less reachable he is the less she is able to use tender contact to help him guide his own activity. Her awareness of his otherness also means he will likely come to represent to her the parts of her which are hidden or buried. A male child is a screen onto which the mother can project her disowned or suppressed "maleness." Thus the mother is more prone to give her male child a license to be different, a license that at the extremes can promote either productive innovation or abrasive egotism.

Any set of cultural categories as pervasive as that of sex roles must have an adaptive core. It must work, it must provide some important benefits to the members of the society, in order to survive as a living part of the cultural pattern. The minimum requirement is that the role definitions be consistent with a family structure that can insure the survival and training of new members of the society. This in turn requires a family system that has the stability to provide the long period of caretaking prerequisite for such human characteristics as the learning of language, abstract thought, and the ability to be intensely attached to others. Stability in a human group is facilitated by a certain division of labor, a degree of specialization that allows cooperation but also promotes development of individual skills and limits the areas of direct competition within the group. Whatever the division is, and there is considerable latitude here, it must be an arrangement that does not violate the bodily capacities and predispositions of the individuals involved.

The most sensible and successful tactic for a society is to begin with the raw material available, to shape rather than to ignore or oppose those qualities that are already latent in the infant. Much of the evidence presented in the previous chapter suggests that this is in fact what happens. Thus the society takes the female aptitude for tender contact and builds on it. The parents respond to the girl infant's sensitivity to touch, her readiness to smile and talk, her attention to human faces. These abilities are then drawn out, encouraged, and practiced over the months and years. Our cultural ideal expands this picture into a female role conception involving gentleness, the ability to care for others, an intense and complex involvement with human relationships and emotion, and a valuable conservatism that is willing to hold on to those people who matter in one's life.

The boy's original thrust is in another direction. He is more likely to present his parents with the challenge of both fostering and helping to direct his random muscular excursions, his propensity for outward movement. The mother is more likely to stimulate and exercise this baby, and as he grows the parents begin to emphasize control and to use coercion when necessary. He is encouraged to practice his strength, but always with the issue of limits in the foreground: can his activity be channeled in a direction that will benefit rather than damage the group? The cultural stereotype at the end of this line of development is the independent man whose considerable aggressive potential is held in check and channeled well enough so that it expresses itself in ambition, competitiveness, and pride.

It is an exceedingly long road from the initial sex-linked potentiality to the final culturally approved vision of maleness and femaleness. We need only take a few steps along that path before it becomes impossible to separate the respective contributions of the child, of the parents as people with their own life histories, and of the parents as representatives of the wider society. The problem with cultural visions of maleness and femaleness is that they become solidified and detached from the details of experience. Their very value as guideposts for social arrangements and for our thinking about others leads them to become caricatures—too simple and too starkly depicted to be accurate about any individual person. They also become invested with emotion, become enshrined not just as what's usually most workable within certain limits, but rather as what *ought* to be, what's proper and good. Thus these images of male and female often become constricting, and unresponsive to changes in social conditions. Freud pointed out that our ideals tend not to be modeled so much on our parents' actual behavior as on how they secretly feel they should be or wish they were. We take on their less than conscious ideals and install them as our own fantasy images. Thus there can be a continuous line of aspiration or ideals passed from generation to generation without being much touched by reality or by changing life experience.

But we have gotten considerably ahead of ourselves here. It is time to return to the events of childhood.

By age four or five the child is aware that the world is divided into male and female. He or she is very curious about all the differences between the two and is intent on becoming even more skillful at classifying. This scientific effort is closely linked to that more basic question: where do babies come from? Curiosity is also fueled by the beginning awareness that males and females have different genitals. This fact is mastered more slowly than the other aspects of sex difference. The genital equipment of the other sex provokes a twinge of the uncanny—it's fascinating but at the same time odd and just not *right*. It is a puzzle that demands repeated attention and thought, thought both about one's own body and that of those Others.

It was this discovery of anatomical differences that Freud thought to be the trigger of that most crucial period of childhood: the Oedipal crisis. Until then the child is happily spinning out his or her imperial designs: just a little time, a little more preparation, a little more growth, and I shall achieve that wished for exclusive domination of the mother as a source of pleasure. But, according to Freud, the discovery of genital differences raises the terrifying possibility that these lustful aspirations might be dangerous. Fears of bodily damage and the recognition of superior parental power become focused on the matter of penises and vaginas: the boy, having decided that penises aren't as firmly rooted as he had assumed, fears that his continued attempt to get a monopoly over all pleasure will provoke his father to punish him by taking away that very instrument of pleasure, his penis. So he evolves an indirect strategy: he will give up his cruder ambitions and instead ally himself with his father in hopes that if he can become like this man he will eventually have access to adult powers. For the girl the story is more complicated, and, as Freud told it, less convincing. She feels herself to have already suffered the punishment of castration. She comes to see women as deficient and blames her mother for not having equipped her adequately. Thus the daughter turns away from her mother and begins to pursue father in hopes that by way of a loving relation with him she may remedy the lack she feels.

The strategies of boy and girl both serve to protect the fantasy of an exclusive sexual and emotional relationship with the parent of the opposite sex: the boy will take the place of the father in relation to his mother and the girl will displace her mother and capture father's affections. In this sense each is bound to fail, and the slow and painful lesson is that one has to look outside the family for such satisfactions. Freud puts it poignantly:

> The early efflorescence of infantile sexual life is doomed to extinction because its wishes are incompatible with reality and with the inadequate stage of development which the child has reached. That efflorescence comes to an end in the most distressing circumstances and to the accompaniment of the most painful feelings. . . . The tie of affection, which binds the child as a rule to the parent of the opposite sex, succumbs to disappointment, to a vain expectation of satisfaction or to jealousy over the birth of a new baby—unmistakable proof of the infidelity of the object of the child's affections. His own attempt to make a baby himself, carried out with tragic seriousness, fails shamefully. The lessening amount of affection he receives, the increasing demands of education, hard words and an occasional punishment—these show him at last the full extent to which he has been scorned.[11]

The Oedipal project for both boy and girl is in part a futile attempt to breach the barrier between generations, an attempt on the child's part to rush into adulthood. The unbridgeable age gap between generations is a constant reminder that growth is irreversible and ultimately leads to death. Whether thoughts of death are part of the motive force behind the child's Oedipal project, they are almost always involved in the parent's willingness to play his or her own part in the drama. Through allowing a flirtation with a child of the opposite sex the parent can try to keep his or her own youthful side alive, and through opposing a child of the same sex the parent can try to deny his or her own aging and eventual demise. After all, the Greek fable that Freud chose as the paradigm begins with a father's attempt to murder his infant son in order to prolong his own life.

Along with a denial of mortality, the Oedipal project is also a partial denial of the difference between the sexes. The fantasy of having a child by one of our parents includes the notion of becoming our own parent. To think of making my mother pregnant amounts to being my own father. Buried in here is the primitive wish to be totally self-sufficient, to be able to make babies without anyone else's assistance. The fact that reproduction needs two, one man and one woman, is an affront to our childlike narcissism. As Freud suggests, the inability to make a baby on one's own is more painful for the boy than for the girl, but a lingering fascination with the possibility of androgyny remains in both men and women (see chapter VII).

In describing the Oedipal process Freud is trying to construct an explanation for the asymmetry we see in the development of boys and girls: in the typical instance both start out with their primary attachment to the mother, but the ultimate outcome is that the boy takes the father as his model, while retaining his mother's kind as sexual partner, while the girl keeps her mother as model and switches her sexual interest to father's kind.

Whether we see the developmental process as more arduous for the boy or the girl depends on whether we place greater importance on identification or on "object choice." These are two qualitatively different sorts of imaginative relationship. In the first you take someone else as the image of what you would like to be, and use them as a template for your own behavior and beliefs. In the second you do not wish to *be* them but rather to *have* them as a source of sexual and emotional gratification. Freud's interest in the distortions and difficulties of sexual wishes led him to emphasize the latter and therefore to see female development as more arduous: the girl must shift her sexual desires from mother to father (and Freud posited a parallel shift in the main erotic zone from clitoris to vagina).

The trend of psychoanalytic work since Freud has been away from his primary focus on object choice. There has been a recognition that the two types of relationship cannot be easily separated. When we construct an important identification with someone it is likely to include our ideas about their romantic successes, so that when we imagine ourselves carrying on as we think they do we have already included an object choice in the identification ("I want a girl just like the girl that married dear old Dad"). Similarly, a serious erotic relationship includes moments of imagining what our partner is experiencing and of coveting certain qualities they have, so bits of identification play a part here too. Much of recent analytic thinking has moved toward the notion that psychological development proceeds by the internalization of *relationships.* The images that we carry inside us as guides and ideals are images of people doing things with other people. Thus each imagined relationship carries both poles at once and we can emphasize our participation either as the actor or the object—typically we alternate between the two.

There has also been a recognition that, whatever value distinctions between types of imagined relationships may have in adulthood, the life of the child is much less finely structured. As far as we can tell, the child begins in a state of primitive fusion with the mother. The ability to internalize is a sophisticated one: it requires the capacity to hold on to and manipulate memory images, and it requires a reliable distinction between "inside" and "outside." This ability develops slowly, out of the diffuse state of identity with the mother and the world.

Even once the first stages of differentiation have been accomplished, we can assume that identification and object choice are not finely distinguished. The young child feels that *being* someone and *having* them are much the same. Both are included in the intense attachment to the mothering person.

This point of view throws a quite different light on the early development of male and female. Freud's sense of the hardships of the female path gives way to the realization that the girl at least can maintain a continuity of identification with the mother, whereas the boy must pull himself free of that and shift toward his father. The shattering of the matrix of mother and child is more severe for the boy. The boy learns, to his considerable pain, that he can never be that most important of figures in his early life, a mom. Parents who are sensitive to the signs of this failed career aspiration will regale the young boy with the joys and significance of being a father. But this is small compensation for the sense of alienation from the maternal body that once defined his world, and for the feeling of being far removed from the process of creating babies. Here the boy's sense of disappointment outstrips the girl's. His fervent turn towards an allegiance to his father, and against all things feminine, has strong traces of making a virtue out of necessity.

The view of sexual development that gives identification an equal role with object choice helps to explain some matters that are puzzling within the classical framework. The idea that the woman's development is more complex and precarious because of the required shift both in the object of her affections and in the part of her sexual anatomy that she sees as most important fits well with the clinical fact, in Freud's day and in ours, that sexual pleasure is more variable, erratic, and subject to blighting in women than in men. For instance, it is quite rare to find a mature male who is unable to masturbate to orgasm; it is not unusual in women. In this narrow sense male sexuality may indeed be more straightforward. But what of the fact that so-called perversions, those alterations of sexuality in which pleasure becomes dependent on items of clothing, parts of bodies, or intricate rituals, what of the fact that these are much more prevalent in men? This hardly suggests a direct and unperturbed line of sexual development. And what of male braggadocio? The boasting, pretense, and scalp-hunting attitude that is so often a part of male sexuality would seem to bespeak an inner unease. In our culture the greater rigidity and constriction of the male role is apparent. There is no male equivalent of that acceptable part of female development, the "tomboy" period. And fear and loathing of homosexuality is also a largely male preoccupation.

The same theme appears on a broader scale in the exaggeration of male domination that characterizes most cultures. From tribal societies in which men make an exquisite fuss over their secret rituals, to our own long history of legal and social attempts to limit and diminish the role of women, we must wonder whether such energetic, and periodically brutal, efforts to assert male superiority don't stem from insecurity. There is such an insistence that the man is the source of all power and goodness. Thus the Napoleonic Code (and similar examples could be found in most societies) holds that the father is lord and owner of both woman and child. Or, to take an example where the need to make the point is so intense that rationality crumbles, Aeschylus's *Oresteia* has Apollo asserting that the father is the only real parent and the womb only a temporary storage area for his child. Our religious heritage is full of the fantasy that men can give birth on their own—Zeus does so from his forehead, and the Biblical God single-handedly creates a woman out of the body of a man.

The examples could be multiplied endlessly. The point is that it is hard to overlook the consistent note of protesting-too-much in all thismale swaggering about. It helps if we understand how far a boy travels in separating himself from his mother. It is not innate and unruffled pride, or a confident sense of social entitlement that we hear. It is more the shrill voice of someone who is not at all sure that he has established a reliable and worthwhile notion of himself in relation to women. He wonders whether they don't have the more significant role after all, and his envy and wish to return to that earlier state of warm, ambiguous union are on occasion strong enough to touch off all manner of defensive demeaning of women.

It is on this level that the persistent idea of a prehistoric matriarchy makes sense. Many religious and cultural traditions give hints of a prehistory in which a great goddess was the dominant figure. It has been tempting to assume that the original form of society was a matriarchy. By now this theory is out of favor as historical or anthropological fact,[12] though it is likely that many ancient societies (for instance, the Minoans) did imagine their deities as women. But in terms of *individual* history, we all begin in a matriarchy. In all but extraordinary instances the infant lives in a world where a woman (or women) holds sway. It may be that the ubiquitous myths of the transition from matriarchy to patriarchy are reflections of the common human experience of maturation and movement away from the mother.

In sum, the movement away from the maternal environment is more dramatic and pronounced for men. It is fed from at least three directions. First there is the greater physical restlessness and muscular expansiveness of the boy. Then there is the asymmetry in childrearing, the fact that boys have their first crucial relation with someone of the other sex and must therefore make a psychological leap out of that context. Thirdly, this movement on the boy's part is reinforced by cultural values that put a premium on male power and encourage his beginning efforts to "be a man."

## THE BEGINNINGS OF ADOLESCENCE

The singling out of separate "stages" of development is bound to be a bit misleading. It fragments the organic continuity of the growth process, in which each moment is a function of all the moments that have gone before. Attaching specific ages to each stage runs the risk of insensitivity to the tremendous individual differences in the pace of growth. But the fact remains that bodily maturation and social structure conspire to arrange a series of critical periods during which certain issues come to the fore. Although each of these issues has roots in earlier life, and though it will continue to be of concern later, nonetheless it makes sense to speak of a stage in which a critical confrontation and crystallization occurs. Adolescence is such a stage.

The research data cited in chapter II gave hints that adolescence may be a particularly important time for the formation of Deprivation/Enhancement fantasy patterns. Phebe Cramer's work points towards the time around ages ten to twelve as a time when the fantasy patterns become most differentiated and extreme. Interviews of young adults with extreme fantasy patterns showed that one of the unexpected factors that set them off from people with less extreme patterns was their recollection of having felt isolated and cut off from their peers in the years around puberty. So this adds to the already considerable attention that this time of life deserves in any study of the development of male and female.

The advent of adolescence is marked by an unmistakable and important event: the bodily changes of puberty. Aside from the direct effects these changes have on the individual in whom they are taking place, they are also a sign to which the society must respond. Depending on whether sexual fertility and the ability to be an adult member of the society are welcomed or feared, the response will differ in tone. But response there will be. Once again we see a complex cycle of interaction between body and culture.

The years around puberty are socially defined as a transitional time. In some societies sexual maturity means adulthood. In the more intricate sort of industrial society we live in, puberty is more likely to signal the beginning of a long period of training, and waiting, to be a full member of society. In either case a threshold has been crossed and the person is now seen against the background of what they will soon become rather than what they recently were. It is no accident that most adults' conscious sense of themselves feels as if it began during this time: there is usually a continuous notion of "me" stretching forward from these transitional years, whereas before that the memories are vaguer, more external, relegated to being "a child," and lacking in that inner experience of "I." In an important sense self-consciousness begins here. The self-consciousness of adolescence includes that acute anxiousness about one's appearance and performance, which is part of the popular caricature of these awkward years. More importantly, it also includes the burgeoning of awareness of the wider world and intense speculation about one's proper moral and personal position toward that world. Most important, it includes the first steps toward a unified and workable internal definition of "I."

There are three streams that feed this new current of self-definition. The first is the social expectation, which by now has also become an inner need, that one should shape a conception of one's vocation and future life. This demand now has a force that was lacking in the childhood invitations to imagine "what you want to be when you grow up." Impressionistic and exciting fantasies about being a fireman or the queen of Bohemia will no longer do. There is a new awareness of the realities of social structure and status, played out in miniature, but with deadly seriousness, in the early adolescent peer group. The young person's sense of his or her own maturing capabilities reaches out to the society for an acknowledgment that there is indeed a satisfying and useful part to be played.

The second force is sexual maturation. Our memories tend to blur these events so that in retrospect we may overlook just how tumultuous the bodily changes of puberty can be. During childhood we have become accustomed to our body as an instrument with certain strengths and certain limitations. While we are not likely to be totally content with it, at least we have a workable knowledge of its nature and shape. During puberty this is radically disrupted. Things are happening to us, totally unbidden. Though the changes may have been long wished for in some fantasy of adulthood, the actuality is strange as well as exciting. Our body is no longer ours. It becomes larger, hairier, differently shaped. The onset of menstruation and of ejaculation calls attention to a part of the body interior that was poorly, if at all, imagined before, and gives new energy to sexual fantasies and exploration. Pride over these developments is mixed with unease and regret. The boy's joy in his nascent muscles or body hair is balanced by the horrors of an erratic voice and the new social problem of how to conceal an erection. The girl's pride over her growing breasts may be colored by the resentful feeling that she is loosing her competitive physical edge over her male friends.

As the body changes so must the conception of self. One of the developmental demands of this period is that work begin on a notion of self that can include this new sexuality and new awareness of mature maleness or femaleness. An important source of information for this revaluation is at the same time the third factor pushing for change: a dramatic increase in the wish, and ability, to imagine what someone else thinks and feels. This is partly a cognitive achievement, an aspect of the adolescent flowering of abstract and hypothetical thinking. It is also the next step in the gradual development of social relations that has gone on since birth.

In the period before puberty there is an evolution in the nature of friendship. Up to this point the focus of friendship is likely to have been activity: what can I *do* with (or to) this other person? This sort of mutual play required only a minimal grasp of the other's inner experience. But as puberty approaches there is a growing concern with what one's friends think or feel. Empathy shows itself more strongly. There are the beginnings of an ability to imagine the other, and the wish to share thoughts, opinions, and fantasies. This opens up a whole new landscape of self-definition. It is now possible to find out what someone else thinks, including what they think of you, and to see how your own thoughts are like or unlike those of a particular other about whom you care. Intense and relatively intimate relations may develop, as they often do in the early adolescent years. Typically these are friendships with someone of the same sex. It is by way of this intimacy, whether it is overtly sexual for a while or not, that genital sexuality is woven into the context of a human relationship. The transition to heterosexuality is usually by way of the sharing of sensuality, bits of sexual play, and fantasied sexual dramas with this close friend.

The concept of "identity," which Erik Erikson brought into the center of the study of adolescence, has become tattered and torn from indiscriminate use. But it remains important. It was a rather fickle word to begin with, and Erikson chose it in part because of its ambiguity, its refusal to be tied to any one meaning. In one of its several guises Erikson defines a sense of ego identity as "the accrued confidence that one's ability to maintain inner sameness and continuity (one's ego in the psychological sense) is matched by the sameness and continuity of one's meaning for others."[13] We notice two things in this statement. The first is Erikson's acknowledgment of the social: this sense of identity depends as much on the response of others as it does on internal changes in the individual. And then there is his central emphasis, that the major issue of adolescence is in fact that of finding a stable, valued, and socially supported definition of oneself.

Erikson describes the stage just prior to adolescence as a time when the youngster is working to establish a sense of "industry" as opposed to "inferiority." The learning of skills, ways of doing and knowing, becomes most important. If all goes well the person brings into adolescence the notion that he or she can be a good and productive worker. But in adolescence this fragment of a self-concept must be integrated with all the other fragments brought forward from childhood and with all the new elements of puberty. Adolescence is a "normative crisis" and offers the opportunity to construct a unique and coherent identity that both synthesizes the self-images of childhood and integrates the sexual and assertive impulses of puberty— and does all this in concordance and connection with a larger social group.*

---

*Lest you detect the sound of violins in the background here, I hasten to say that Erikson is clear that this wonderous achievement is not easy or automatic and is not something accomplished for good-and-all at this stage, but rather is the first episode of a continuing life drama.

Harry Stack Sullivan is another well-known theorist of adolescence and his ideas provide an interesting contrast to Erikson. Every theory has its Eden, its idea of when and where the pinnacle of human living is reached. For Freud it was the second or third year in the life of the male child—before any rivals for mother's affection have come on the scene. For Erikson it is probably that period in late adolescence when the air is so full of energy, idealism, and identity possibilities. For Sullivan it is in the years just before puberty. He speaks of "the quiet miracle of preadolescence" and comments: "I believe that for a great majority of our people preadolescence is the nearest that they come to untroubled human life—that from then on the stresses of life distort them to inferior caricatures of what they might have been."[14]

What makes this period so idyllic in Sullivan's eyes is the first appearance of an ability to love. In his view the need for intimacy, an innately human characteristic, matures at this time. Up to this point the child's relationships with peers reach as far as cooperation, learning to adjust one's behavior to another's in order to reap more pleasures for oneself in the end. But now, under the impetus of the need for intimacy, the youngster moves toward collaboration. This is a relationship of an importantly different character. It involves coming to feel that someone else's satisfaction and happiness is fully as important as one's own. If all goes well there develops a bond with a "chum," an intimate friend of the same sex with whom one feels sympathy, "affectional rapport," and "uncomplicated love." This obviously would be an important experience in its own right, being the first blush of one of the saving graces of our species. But Sullivan sees its value as considerably more than just the first experience of the human ability to care deeply about someone else. The value lies in what he calls "consensual validation." The chum offers an opportunity to see yourself through someone else's eyes. This is crucial because it can correct and heal all sorts of distorted and fantastic notions about oneself that have been built up during childhood. Through open and intimate talks with this special friend, we may have our first glimpse of an honest and reliable picture of ourselves.

The demon that disrupts this Eden is Lust. Sullivan is not very sanguine about sex. With luck we may survive its onslaught, but something valuable has been lost. Love is no longer "uncomplicated."

The early adolescent transition is difficult. Lust impels one toward someone *different* from oneself. Thus it disrupts the chumship, and also impels one into situations that are intensely anxiety provoking and fraught with potential humiliation. But, again with luck, the intimate chum relationship may in fact be a bridge. If it is not damaged by the onset of puberty, as it may be if one member matures considerably earlier than the other or if the threat of sexuality in a same sex relationship is too great, then there will be the opportunity to explore one's growing sexuality within a relatively safe and caring context. The intimate same sex relationship can expand to include the sharing of sexual fantasies, the playing out of bits of romantic drama, and the experience of genital pleasure with another person. In this way the new part of the self, sexuality, may be more easily accepted and integrated as "me." This facilitates enormously the main task of adolescence proper, which is to arrive at a pattern of durable relationships that can satisfy both lustful urges and the need for intimacy.

The classical psychoanalytic approach to adolescence, as exemplified by the writings of Peter Blos,[15] emphasizes the pubertal rush of sexual and aggressive energy. The adolescent dilemma, in this view, has to do with finding ways to manage and express these new urges. More specifically, the onset of puberty revives childhood feelings about one's parents. Adolescence is seen as a recapitulation of certain parts of childhood, but a recapitulation with a new urgency and reality. Incestuous fantasies are if anything more troubling, now that it would be physically possible. The developmental task of adolescence, in this view, is to renounce childhood ties to parents and to make the transition to successful relationships outside the family, relationships in which sexual and affectionate wishes can find real expression. Blos refers to this as the "second individuation," the first being the awareness of separateness that occurs in infancy.

As Blos points out in considerable detail, this shift away from parents is preceeded, and facilitated, by a complex series of internal alterations. In the period just before the physical changes of puberty, the already increasing "instinctual energy" threatens to revive the now dormant infantile tie to the mother. The prepubertal child struggles against the temptation to sink back into an all-encompassing relationship with the remembered mother of early childhood.

Thus there is often an intensification at this time of the turn to the father, in both boy and girl, as a protection against this temptation and as an avenue away from childlike gratification. The whole Oedipal transition is repeated in early adolescence, impelled and made more final by physical maturation.

The several stages of all this need not concern us here, except to say that the person goes through alternate identifications with both mother and father. This shift in identifications involves a period of imagining oneself as a member of the other sex and this is one of the factors that make for a crisis of sexual self-definition at this stage of life. Other factors are the confused childhood notions of sexual anatomy, which are again brought to the fore, and the rerecognition of the difference between the sexes, which calls up all the old envious and anxious obstacles to accepting one's own body. Early adolescence raises the question of sexual identity with a keenness and persistence that it hasn't had since the first awareness of sexual differences. The answer is more important now, since it is likely to lead toward an actual sexual relationship.

As a final source of information about this time of life it is worth looking at Elizabeth Douvan and Joseph Adelson's *The Adolescent Experience*. [16] They report on information gained from interviews, in the mid-1950s, with a representative group of several thousand Americans between eleven and eighteen. The picture is more conservative and conforming than the popular stereotype of adolescence (even in the fifties) would have suggested, with the much bemoaned peer group appearing more as a force for restraint than for excess or rebellion. Two primary adolescent concerns emerge. The first lies in achieving a degree of autonomy. This has both an internal and external aspect. The adolescent must develop a comfortable sense of being able to control and direct his or her own behavior, so as not to be prey to impulse, and must gradually construct a reliable set of values or standards that he or she is then willing to follow and work for regardless of what parents or other outside authorities may say. These values, which include notions of a proper life's work, will owe much to the parents' beliefs. But the point is that through a process of experiment and confrontation they are internalized to the point of feeling "mine" and being relatively independent of the vicissitudes of any particular relationship.

The second concern is social success. On the surface this shows itself as the scramble for popularity and the often cruel caste system of adolescent society. But there is also a quieter and ultimately more significant level on which people are learning the skills of intimacy, friendship, and love. The aim is a feeling of "interpersonal competence." This would include both an idea of what sorts of persons and relationships one wants in one's life and also a hopeful impression of one's ability to be liked by the people one likes.

Douvan and Adelson were surprised by the extent of the differences they found between the sexes. They had expected both these areas of concern to be prominent for men and women. While it is true that neither sex has a total monopoly, they came to feel that "the adolescent crisis for boys and girls differs in almost every regard." Autonomy is primarily a male concern and interpersonal competence primarily female. Their summary deserves to be quoted at length:

> The key terms in adolescent development for the boy in our culture are the erotic, autonomy (assertiveness, independence, achievement), and identity. For the girl the comparable terms are the erotic, the interpersonal, and identity. Differences between the two sets of problems are larger and more complex than a single discrepancy implies; for this discrepancy is so central that it reverberates through the entire complex. For the girl the development of interpersonal ties—the sensitivities, skills, ethics, and values of object ties—forms the core of identity, and it gives expression to much of developing feminine eroticism. Feminine sexuality, consciously inhibited from active and direct expression, seeks more subtle, limited and covert expression. The search for popularity, the effort to charm, all of the many and varied interpersonal ties which are the setting for the girl's practice in winning and maintaining love—these engagements filter and express a good deal of the girl's erotic need. We have noted the greater intensity and importance of girls' like-sexed friendships when compared to their friendships with boys or to boys' like-sexed friendships. And we have held that the intimate friendship between girls serves a number of functions, all tied to the girl's need to explore and understand her sexual nature as well as her individuality. It is primarily through these serial, episodic, intimate twosomes that the girl comes to terms with her sexual nature and gradually sorts elements of identification from aspects of individuality to form an identity. The tie to objects is both the key to her erotic

realization and also the mechanism through which she arrives at an individuated personal identity.

For the boy, on the other hand, the integrated capacity for erotic ties and the solution of the identity challenge demand separation and autonomy. What the girl achieves through intimate connection with others, the boy must manage by disconnecting, by separating himself and asserting his right to be distinct. His biological sexual nature is more explicitly and individually stated than the girl's. It has less compelling interpersonal features, depends less on the existence of a fully developed object relation and it insists on the resolution of certain authority problems in order to gain expression. The boy can know gratification outside a full or fully developed love relationship, but his sexual realization depends on severing infantile ties and asserting his independence of them. Without autonomy, the boy's sexual realization suffers the constant hazard of crippling castration fears. To achieve full status as a sexual adult, the boy must clarify the difference between himself and his father and assume the status of the father's independent peer. The girl's adult sexuality, on the other hand, depends on an intricate and little understood process of consolidating a satisfactory identification with her own mother.

The identity problem is also phrased differently for boys and girls in our culture, and the distinction again revolves around their different requirements for object love and for autonomy. We have noted that feminine identity forms more closely about capacity and practice in the personal arts, and we have seen in our findings evidence that the girl's ego-integration co-varies with her interpersonal development. Masculine identity, in contrast, focuses about the capacity to handle and master nonsocial reality, to design and win for oneself an independent area of work which fits one's individual talents and taste and permits achievement of at least some central personal goals. The boy's ego development at adolescence already bears the mark of this formulation and reflects his progress in mastering it. Identity is for the boy a matter of individuating internal bases for action and defending these against domination by others. For the girl it is a process of finding and defining the internal and individual through attachments to others.[17]

The point of reviewing these approaches to adolescence has been partly to clarify the particular concepts they use, but even more to demonstrate that they all include the notion of sexual self-definition as an issue at this stage. The years just before and just after puberty are a time when physical maturation and social expectation combine to require the first steps in feeling oneself to be, and in acting like, a mature man or woman.

In this broad perspective it would not be surprising to find that adolescence is a time in which sex-linked fantasy patterns reach a peak. Here we are assuming that fantasy runs on ahead of experience and that experience has if anything a moderating effect on fantasy. A person who is just crossing the threshold of puberty is energetically concerned with maleness and femaleness but has little experience of his or her new body or social position. Their thinking is heavily influenced by a less than conscious fantasy process that speaks in a language of extremes and magical concreteness. These individual imaginings are also influenced by the idealized and absolute images of male and female that are the stuff of group and collective fantasy. So it is at this point that we might find the most heroic, exclusive, and one-sided expressions of what it is to be male or female. Later, when the transition to genital sexuality has been made successfully and when there has been a degree of intimate experience with the other sex, then one can begin to moderate and revise these unreal images.

Let us now see in more detail how these notions of male and female are influenced by both body and culture.

In our society the model of femininity held out to the young girl is replete with contradiction. In relations with men she is supposed to learn to interest, attract, and intrigue them, without being too openly enticing. She must act by restraining herself—learning the art of making others come to her. She must learn to invite without either then always slamming the door (being a tease, a bitch) or always letting in (being loose, a whore). She must learn a whole set of complicated maneuvers that take place on the threshold. It is the art of being sexy without being sexual. Until recently, and often still, the thinly veiled assumption is that her vagina is her bargaining card: she must withhold the final sexual step until the man agrees to marry her (the self-degradation this implies, treating oneself as a commodity, is well-captured in that cautionary mother-to-daughter aphorism, "why should he buy the cow when he gets the milk free?"). All this practice in holding back, hinting, and promising more than one is ready to deliver is obviously destructive to later sexual pleasure. The main skills learned here are first to suppress and control erotic feelings and second to dissemble. Neither skill is helpful when the social ban on sexuality is finally lifted, and by then the obstacles are well internalized.

The traditional definition has seen a woman as shaping large parts of her life through a man. *His* job will determine where they live, and *how* they live, in terms of social and economic status. Thus her identity is dependent on someone else. As Douvan and Adelson point out, this means that a young girl's idea of the future is heavily loaded with fantasy. So much of it is out of her control and she can take little practical action beyond putting herself in the way of meeting the right man. Needless to say, this particular absurd notion of femaleness has shifted considerably in recent years. But a fragment of the same conflict remains in that many women feel they must choose between a life's work *or* children, a choice that our culture has not typically demanded of men.

Women are thought of as being more kind, empathic, and concerned with their ties to others. From doll play through careers in nursing, girls are given opportunities to be caring and caretaking. The opposite side of this coin is the inhibition and modulation of aggression. While this has been a theme through childhood, the girl typically feels it keenly around puberty: it is no longer right to be a "tomboy," to wrestle and fight and physically contest with boys. Words are the only weapons allowed a woman, and even here there is an expectation of restraint from all-out assault. A fine line divides this allowable female aggression from its common sins: deviousness, bitchiness, and studied helplessness.

While the social portrait of a proper woman focuses on qualities of being—kindness, attractiveness—the portrait of manhood emphasizes doing. A young man is supposed to build his conception of the future around what he can accomplish with exertion of body or mind and to dedicate himself to doing and making. He is to rely on his own resources and thus must learn to make practical plans. Activity and strength are welcomed, holding back or timidity scorned. The aggression allowed is greater in quantity and blunter in quality than with women. The basic minimum is the willingness to fight if challenged. The maximum is harder to define and this is one of the troublesome aspects of the male role in our culture. Once aggression is encouraged, how can it be contained? Thus rules and limits become crucial.

There must be agreement about the rules of a fair fight, a sportsman-like game, or an ethical pursuit of self-interest in business. But this is a constant dynamic struggle. The rules are always being tested, subverted, enforced, and revised. The dangers here are that maleness will degenerate into juvenile bullying or calculated sadism.

The popular prescription for male sexuality is also heavily invested with assertion and activity. The man is supposed to be constantly on the move and on the make. The image of the tireless seducer differs only in style and degree from that of the rapist. The main difference is that it is supposed to be overwhelming attractiveness and skillful technique, rather than raw force, that persuades the woman to give in. The similarities are more impressive: the location of all the activity in the man, the sense of a predatory chase, the overtones of victory, and the lack of emotional recognition of the woman's real experience or wishes. Short of these extreme positions, men are still likely to experience a burdensome feeling of having to prove one's competitive prowess in bed, over and over. Men often conspire to deny them-selves a very important freedom: the freedom to say no, the freedom to be uninterested in the sexual possibilities of a particular relation-ship or moment.

The aggressive coloration of the male role is heightened by an emphasis on independence and lack of attachment to others. The idea of being able to stand on one's own two feet shades over into stoic solitude or a trained incapacity to enter into the emotional complexities of a serious relationship. A real man would not be "tied down" by such human webs, would always put his honor, his free-dom, his achievements, first. What could be a valuable trait of inde-pendence threatens to become indifference. If it does, then one of the prime forces that limit individual assertiveness—the sympathetic ability to imagine how my acts will affect someone else—becomes dangerously ineffectual.*

---

*A few remarks for the reader who may be feeling that this picture of the male role has been exaggerated and overly harsh. Leslie Fiedler's *Love and Death in the American Novel* (New York: Stein and Day, 1966) traces in detail the theme of pathological male independence in our literature. As for what I refer to as juvenile bullying or calculated sadism, it's all too present around us. I hesitate to use topi-cal examples, since they invoke all our political and aesthetic prejudices, and they age very quickly. However, two come to mind. Clint Eastwood is a film star of much note these days who seems to have built a successful career on a total ina-

One of the unfortunate facts about our culture is that its general values are much closer to the image of maleness than of femaleness. When it comes to a choice we will almost always grant greater merit to independence over attachment, assertiveness over responsiveness. To *make* and to *do*—these are our prime virtues. Such vital human traits as the ability to promote someone else's growth and development are relegated to the sidelines—it's all very nice but it's not really *work*. This cultural bias obviously compounds the girl's identity dilemma by building in, as a likely part of the traditional female identity, a secret disdain for oneself.

There are aspects of these cultural stereotypes, exaggerated as they are, that are congruent with physical differences between the sexes. As I suggested earlier, societies do not simply invent arbitrary role distinctions but are more likely to build on and shape something already immanent. For example, the emphasis on autonomy and the management of aggression for men and the emphasis on caring and contact for women: we have seen that these themes have analogues, or foundations, in the bodily equipment and tendencies of male and female children. Thus the adolescent crisis in sexual differentiation is continuous with the childhood developments that we looked at in the previous section.

---

bility to act (in the sense of conveying any emotion or inner life). This is just the point. The character he enacts over and over again, a character to whom millions respond by laying down their money, is made of equal parts of total isolation and detachment on the one hand and casual brutality on the other. And on a somewhat, some would say barely, higher plane, the foreign policy of our country has in recent years often been that of the big, nasty kid on the playground. We need only remember a newspaper photograph of a few years ago: the secretary of state and the president sit in the latter's office, grinning with all the proud glee of middle-aged coaches whose team has won a crucial game. What they are celebrating is that our Navy and Marine Corps had succeeded in recapturing a ship that had been detained in some confused fashion by what must have been at that point one of the weakest and most disorganized countries in the world. This valiant rescue cost more American lives than there were "hostages" to begin with. That this squalid business was celebrated as a victory makes it clear that the basic motive had to do with pride and throwing one's weight around.

## SEXUALITY

But it is now necessary to ask whether there are psychological consequences of that physical difference that we associate most immediately with male and female: genital anatomy. This discussion will take
us beyond the bounds of adolescence. Many of the concerns we will
be touching on have been present years before puberty, and continue
to be important in adulthood. It is in adolescence, however, with the
onset of sexual maturation, that awareness of sexual anatomy is most
acute and pressing.

Erikson's article on "inner space" will be familiar to many. It is
worth reading along with his response to feminist criticisms of the
original article.[18] I won't summarize his discussion of the ramifications of woman's "productive inner space," though the views to
follow are influenced thereby. I share his basic assumption: the
"ground plan" of our bodies has important effects on our character
and behavior; it is in fact one of the cornerstones of our picture of
ourselves. The genital area is one of the more important parts of this
ground plan, both because it is invested with intensely pleasurable
feelings and because the processes of conception and birth are of
great interest to the child and to the society.

How is the young man's sexuality and picture of himself shaped
by having testicles and a penis? In the first place it gives sexual
feelings an external and clearly defined focus. What probably began
as a more diffuse experience of arousal or pleasure comes to be located
in the penis. Sensations experienced in the penis, and its tumescence
and detumescence, become the barometer of sexual interest. Because
it is visible, accessible, and sensitive the penis rapidly becomes the
primary bodily focus of attempts to heighten and then resolve sexual
tension. The same characteristics make it likely to be a lightning rod,
as it were, for tensions not strictly sexual. It is characteristic in young
men that the penis is also invested with aggressive fantasies. The
penis lends itself to thoughts of penetration and attack and in early
adolescence is likely to play a role in all manner of sadistic fantasy.[19]
It is only through eventual sexual experience within an intimate
relationship that this aggression is tamed.

Its outward and mobile quality also makes the penis (and testicles)
a vehicle for exhibitionistic pride. It can be shown off and made to

perform. But this same outwardness makes it vulnerable. Concern about the intactness and functioning of the genitals is a convenient metaphor for a variety of fears about physical intactness. Likewise there is a difficult business about willpower and control that gets involved. Pride over the activity of the penis is counterbalanced by the eerie recognition that these movements are not under one's conscious control. Hear St. Augustine: "Justly, too, these members [the "organs of generation"] themselves, being moved and restrained not at our will, but by a certain independent autocracy, so to speak, are called 'shameful.' "[20] This statement captures well both the feeling of helplessness (in the grip of a powerful and foreign "autocracy") and the resulting shame. Augustine goes on to describe an ideal state, before the Fall, in which the penis was at the command of man's will rather than being "disobedient" and "a shameless novelty which made nakedness indecent."

Out of this awkward dilemma, that of an important part of one's body that seems to have a mind of its own, comes a whole range of male strategies to assert one's will over the rebellious organ: abstinence in thought and action in order to keep it down, extensive masturbation in part to learn what thoughts and touches it responds to, or meditating on baseball averages during intercourse in hopes of keeping it up longer. Simone de Beauvoir comments that "whereas the woman . . . identifies herself with the total image of her body from childhood on, the little boy sees his penis as an alter ego; it is in his penis that his whole life as a man finds its image, and it is here that he feels himself in peril. The narcissistic trauma that he dreads is the failure of his sexual organ—the impossibility of reaching an erection, of maintaining it, and of satisfying his partner."[21]

Put simply, the male genitals function to embody and delineate the themes of external focus, motion, aggressive extension outward, and prideful control versus shameful failure.

By their nature the female genitals are less easily knowable. They do not stand out to be seen. They are more likely to be experienced as part of a vital but ambiguous "inside." While the male genitals pretend to be all outside, for the female the distinction, the threshold, between inside and outside, is crucial. She has both an external genital (vulva and clitoris), which becomes a site of curious manipulation and of pleasure, and also a passageway to a more latently present, dimly imagined space. This latter inner area cannot be directly explored by the child and thus it remains mysterious to a degree. The accidents of anatomy mean that the girl is likely to go through a stage in which there is no clear differentiation, in sensation or in her mind, between the vagina and the anus or bowels. The vagina can certainly be explored indirectly, by inserting things in it, and it makes itself known as the center of repeated experiences of excitation. But the knowledge gained this way is fragmentary. The notion of the internal genitals continues to be laden with fantasy and it is vulnerable to later repression and denial.[22]

Judith Kestenberg[23] distinguishes between inner and external genital experiences in both sexes. The external genital experience, typified by stimulation of the penis or clitoris, is active, focused, and consists of repeated episodes each of which has a definite beginning and end. The inner genital experience involves the rhythmic spread of arousal and pleasure through the pelvic and abdominal area. Thus one sees in young children a wavelike writhing and an opening and closing of the thighs that does not have the characteristics of focal masturbation and is not necessarily associated with it. Kestenberg holds that the inner genital experience has troubling qualities, since it can be a pervasive and uncontrollable feeling of tension, irritability, and generally being all in turmoil. Both men and women struggle to bring this feeling under control by externalizing and localizing it. But this shift is easier to accomplish with male genitals (as we will see when we discuss adult sexuality, it is not really an advantage to shift entirely). Female sexuality stays closer to the inner genital experience.

The difference in sexual anatomy gives the woman more opportunity and incentive to pay attention to and puzzle about what goes on inside her. Her sexuality is likely to remain more in tune with other cyclic internal processes, processes with a repetitive and continuous quality quite different from the more discrete male experience of a rapid rise and then sharp drop in excitement. In this sense a woman's sexuality is less detached from the regular events of the rest of her body.

Possessing a vagina and womb requires imagining, and experiencing, various transactions across that threshold. Menstruation, intercourse, and childbirth are all events in which the boundary is crossed —something goes in or comes out. The common theme of incorporation, of taking in, favors a psychological continuity for the woman between sexuality and the issues of trust and dependence, which first became crucial in the oral phase of infancy. A growing fetus is a vivid example of something being inside yet feeling independent and thus outside: eventually it becomes a piece of the inside that *is* now outside. Female sexuality calls for a greater degree of flexibility and openness to interchange, a less rigid sense of inviolability and assertion of absolute control than men oftimes retain. The girl's imaginative world must also find some comfortable space for the notion of being penetrated, for the likelihood of discomfort and even pain in the course of her sexual life, for the realities of blood and physical damage. Fortunately, it is true that these pains can lead to pleasure (for instance, childbearing typically increases the physiological capacity for sexual gratification), so acceptance has something to be said for it.

In the ordinary course of events a woman's growing awareness of her own sexual anatomy will tend to highlight the themes of internal focus, taking in, enclosing and holding, and the need for a faith that things will come out all right.

What are the important differences between the sexual experiences of men and women? In talking about this it will be best to put out of our minds that fascinating but impossible question, a rashly honest answer to which brought Tiresias so much grief: which sex has more fun? Let us take for granted that sexuality is one of the most persistent and intense sources of pleasure for both sexes.

Starting with the central moment of pleasure, the orgasm, there is a different patterning for men and for women. Here the term "orgasm" must be understood broadly since it is often used in a way that takes the characteristic male experience as the model. For a man orgasm is relatively predictable and uniform. It is an event with a definite sequence and an imperative momentum that tends to override distractions or obstacles. Once a certain level of excitement is reached, it is typified by rapid arousal to a peak of tension, which then resolves itself in intense discharge, followed by an equally rapid decline in interest and activity. There is then a "refractory period," of variable but significant length, during which the man is literally incapable of further sexual arousal.

Women may have this experience on occasion but it is not so

characteristic. In the first place there is likely to be more variation
in a woman's orgasmic experience. It is more subject to external
influences, such as the time, place, and person involved, and more
vulnerable to distractions and interruptions. But beyond that, the
typical rhythm differs. In most cases the woman experiences something repetitive, undulating, or wavelike in pattern: a peak of excitement followed by a subsidence to a level of less intense arousal
followed by a rise to yet another peak, and so forth. The trend of
the whole series may be upwards, so that each peak is higher than
the previous one, but the ascent is typically not as steep as with
men and the end not so decisive. The physiology of the female
orgasm is such that each spasm of resolution can be rapidly followed by the reinstatement of the previous level of pelvic congestion (this congestion is the basis of felt sexual tension in the genitals). In theory only physical exhaustion would put an end to the
repeated waves of arousal.*

I have already argued that the penis serves as a focal point in the
development of male sexuality, and that the availability of such a
focus has various consequences. Sexual feeling in men is much more
exclusively located in the area of the penis, whereas women more
often experience sexual sensations over a wider area of their bodies.
Many parts of the body become centers of pleasure in their own right
and not just, as they would likely be in the male, brief steps along the
way to the genital. Undoubtedly the greater skin sensitivity of women
also contributes to this. An increased erotization of the whole body

*See William Masters and Virginia Johnson, *Human Sexual Response*, (Boston:
Little, Brown and Co., 1966); and Mary Jane Sherfey, "The Evolution and Nature
of Female Sexuality in Relation to Psychoanalytic Theory," *Journal of the American
Psychoanalytic Association* 14 (1966):28–128.

I have deliberately avoided entering into the debate about whether there are two
distinct types of orgasm for women, the clitoral and the vaginal. I do want to say that
any such discussion has to include, for instance, the laboratory conditions under which
Masters and Johnson made their physiological observations. It was a situation that
would tend to call forth a variety of orgasm more impersonal, heedless of the human
context, and more masturbatory than anything else. And it is easy to lose track of the
fact that two sexual experiences may be physiologically quite similar and yet psychologically very distinct. (There are orgasms and then there are orgasms.)

For anyone who wishes to pursue this, I would recommend: Natalie Shainess's
article in *Sexuality of Women*, volume ten of *Science and Psychoanalysis*, edited by
Jules Masserman, (New York: Grune and Stratton, 1966); and Leslie Farber's "I'm
Sorry, Dear," in *The Ways of the Will* (New York: Basic Books, 1966).

lends more possibilities to sexuality than is the case when the genitals are the monopolistic masters of all excitement.

In like fashion the phallic focus can serve as a distraction from a whole host of internal bodily sensations. Here we turn to Judith Kestenberg again. She describes the woman's orgasm as follows: ". . . gradually ascending and descending waves of deep sensuous tension in the vagina merge with spasms and sensations from all over the body, ending in dimming of consciousness."[24] This is an experience that may seem to involve the whole inside of the body; the usual distinctions between regions—here the genitals, here the lower intestine and anus, here the heart, etc.—these distinctions become blurred and submerged in an overall sense of inner tumult. This inner mixed-upness can be both pleasurable and frightening in its abolishing of the usual boundaries and its implication of loss of control over bodily function.

This sort of experience is less frequent, briefer, and generally less salient in the man. He is able to organize, externalize, and thus attempt to control, such feelings by centering them in his penis. The woman may of course move in the same direction by trying to make her clitoris the beginning and end of all her sexual feelings or by persistently thinking of her sexuality in external and phallic terms (for instance, with that curious word "horny"). But this shift is tenuous, involving as it does a studied ignorance of important areas of her sexual anatomy. A more severe defensive step is to begin to deny one's own active sexual feelings completely and instead to focus all one's attention on the intruding, phallic man. Thus inhibition of sexual pleasure in women often is associated with two complementary themes. The first is a fear of loss of control over the insides of one's body, a fear that orgasm might lead to defecation or inner disintegration or some such disaster. The second theme is an anxious and obsessive concern with men as cruel intruders or rapists. (Mrs. Lauder, in chapter III, exemplifies both themes.)

There is also an important difference between men and women in the extent to which sexuality asks to be embedded in the context of a significant human relation. A type of arousal, totally independent of any particular relationship either in fact or fantasy, is painfully familiar to most young men. Leslie Farber refers to it as "undifferentiated lust" and describes it thusly:

By undifferentiated lust I mean the surgings of sexual excitement—usually chronic, often acute—that first begin to possess the young man in his adolescence. In terms of the world about him, this excitement seems to come from everywhere and nowhere, and to be directed at everyone and no one, as it presses for bodily release. Obviously there is pleasure, or at least the possibility of pleasure, in this lust, but just as often it is experienced as an affliction in its obsessive claims on both the body and the imagination. In time the nonspecific, unfocused nature of this lust may give way to differentiation, as actual relations with actual women develop, the attendant discriminations depending critically on real talk in these relations. But such a passage is a shaky one, for undifferentiated lust can never be wholly banished; it may be transcended, or more often, deliberately withstood. Every man knows he can be subject, if he so chooses, to undifferentiated sexual arousal, and it should be noted that there is a pornography industry dedicated to the arousal of this undifferentiated impulse.[25]

The young man's urgent sexual wishes quickly submerge the subtleties of getting to know another person. Meanwhile, he is likely to have been masturbating regularly and thus training and developing his sexual responsiveness in an isolated situation where other people are creations of his imagination, characters in his own private blue movie. Often for the young man it is the sexual urge that initiates the relationship, and the sexual urge that provides the emotional capital to maintain it.

For the young woman it is more likely the case that she begins exploring her erotic feelings as an outgrowth of an intense emotional investment in another person; sexuality is more likely to emerge from an affectionate tie rather than vice versa. The woman's more ambiguous and various sense of the erotic lends itself to using a complex relationship, first with a same sex friend and later with boys, for the gradual definition of her sexuality. The interpersonal context remains more important than it typically is for men.[26]

In part we see the imprint of androgen in the young man's more isolated lust. But the greater male tendency to divorce lust and intimacy must also have to do with the boy's history of having to detach himself from his mother. In leaving her behind the boy is likely to wall off much of the tenderness and comfortable dependence which he felt in relation to his mother. All that becomes "childish" or "girls' stuff" and he struggles to build a sexual identity based on action, independence, and autonomy.

Male sexuality is vulnerable to being invaded by competitiveness and an anxious concern with performance. This too is best understood by keeping in mind that adult sexuality is one of the main inheritors of the ambivalent journey outward that the boy embarked upon years ago. The persistent need to separate from the original maternal matrix and the challenge of learning to master his own potential for energetic activity combine to make the issue of control a central one. Sex may become an extension of this struggle, since it offers the illusion of control on two levels. First is the sense of control over others that sexual conquest provides (and the focus may be fully as much on besting male friends and rivals as on the actual women "gotten"). But there is also the matter of control over oneself. We have already seen the way in which the phallus can become a symbol of control over one's own body. Its rise and fall provides a metaphor for success and failure. At the same time it is liable to be drawn into the psychic struggle to deny or abolish a wide range of feelings, which in the course of the male rush for autonomy and separateness have come to be classified as immature or "feminine." These feelings include: the bodily experiences that Kestenberg refers to as inner genital sensations, strong feelings of attachment, states of quiescence or responsiveness (to call it "passivity" is already to have taken the first step in the disowning process), and an awareness of weakness or fear.

What would in technical terms be called a "counterphobic" trend in male sexuality is more simply described in John Updike's comment "we want to fuck what we fear.[27] Our cultural and literary tradition is rich with indications of some of the fears against which phallic aggressiveness attempts to defend. One consistent theme is that the postorgasm state may be experienced as a sudden and frightening decline of activity and energy. Thus Aristotle's rather grim choice of words: "In most men and as a general rule the result of intercourse is exhaustion and weakness."[28] The loss of erection and the flowing away of what a moment before was an intensely energized state may evoke feelings of helplessness and even thoughts of death (Alexander the Great is reputed to have said "Sex and sleep alone make me conscious that I am mortal";[29] and Ovid's "all animals are sad after intercourse" is, I suspect, primarily a statement of male experience). In the midst of this apprehension it is sometimes possible to discern a more amorphous anxiety, which sounds as if it has to do with thoughts of being reabsorbed into that overwhelming, ever-waiting mother. A particularly vivid example occurs in John Osborne's *Look Back in Anger.* Jimmy Porter reveals one of the roots of the desperate viciousness he visits on the woman he lives with. Complaining of what he experiences as a lack of response to his sexual endeavors, he says:

> Oh, it's not that she hasn't her own kind of passion. She has the passion of a python. She just devours me whole every time, as if I were some over-large rabbit. That's me. That bulge around her navel—if you're wondering what it is—it's me. Me, buried alive down there, and going mad, smothered in that peaceful looking coil. Not a sound, not a flicker from her—she doesn't even rumble a little. You'd think that this indigestible mess would stir up some kind of tremor in those distended, overfed tripes—but not her! She'll go on sleeping and devouring until there's nothing left of me.[30]

A man may emphasize the aggressive and combative side of his sexuality as an attempt to master this sort of dread. To try to do so, however, lands him on a treadmill of endless repetition. Every sexual conquest leads him back to the scene of the crime, as it were, and subjects him to yet another experience of the ebbing of desire and potency. The phallus is not a reliable weapon for this sort of war of independence.

Certain kinds of male sadism spring directly from insecurity and envy. Take for instance, the case of a man whose greatest sexual excitement came when a woman would submit to being called "obscene" names and to suffering mild physical abuse (his fantasies meanwhile went further, involving tying her up and beating her). Following out the details of his experience clarified the emotional sequence behind this: it would begin when he noticed her sexual pleasure and became envious (it often seemed to him that she enjoyed lovemaking more than he); this envy brought with it the fear that his own sense of himself would be lost in the rush of his wish to be her; *then* came the sadistic urges, as a defensive attempt to assert his power.

Before leaving the field of sexuality I want to say again that we have *not* been speaking of categorical differences. On a psychological level none of these aspects of sexuality is the sole property of either women or men. We must think instead in terms of propensities and typical qualities, without losing sight either of the tremendous variation among individuals or of the fact of psychological bisexuality. We each carry within us a rich area of fantasy about what it would be like to be one of the other sex. Part of what makes sexual experience so compelling, and at times so troubling, is that it can be a means of testing and expanding these imaginings. The fullest sexual pleasure comes when we can accept and enjoy that part of ourselves that we identify with the other sex. Masturbation is usually the first situation in which we can, consciously or not, take both roles in an imaginary intercourse. Thus the man can shift back and forth from being the containing hand to being the penis, or can experience penetration in anal masturbation. Likewise the woman can invest herself in the arousing and intruding fingers as well as in clitoris or vagina. Once there has been enough good sexual experience with another person so that the initial anxieties wane, then it becomes more and more possible to empathize with the other's pleasure and bring to life that part of oneself. The man sacrifices pleasure if he is unwilling to enjoy being the recipient, or is unable to value the quiet and tender period after intercourse. The woman sacrifices pleasure if she is unable to freely mobilize her own physical activity and her assertive wish to *get* what she wants. In each case this is likely to require a comfortable working relation with our other sex inner twin.

## THE SECOND HALF OF LIFE

After reviewing the research data on fantasy patterns we were left with the tantalizing question of what might happen to these patterns in the years beyond young adulthood. They peak in early adolescence and perhaps, if Cramer's preliminary findings hold true, even reverse before reaching a more moderate position in the latter part of the college years. Do they then continue on as stable adult characteristics of the sexes? Isn't it likely that the events of adulthood and aging would have important effects? The question matters for us not only because of curiosity about the trajectory of these fantasy patterns over the life cycle, but also because the patterns themselves are probably influenced from childhood on by the individual's conception of what it will be like to grow up and grow old as a man or a woman. Thus the fantasy patterns of Pride and Caring themselves may embody expectations about the life cycle of each sex.

The myths with which we began tell us that parents show a much more complicated, differentiated, and mixed pattern than do their adolescent children. Persephone is almost a caricature of helpless attachment. She can only wait in hopes of ultimate rescue and reunion. Demeter, on the other hand, shows much more initiative, freedom of movement, and ability to make her anger felt. Phaethon is a specialist in heedless pride and defensive determination to prove his own strength. His father, while in fact more powerful, shows tenderness freely and does not hesitate to plead his love and concern. So the wisdom embedded in the myths suggests that maturity matters.

One of the most provocative and stimulating contributions to the study of the second half of life is Elliot Jacques's paper, "Death and the Mid-Life Crisis."[31] Jacques begins by noticing a typical crisis in, or alteration of, artistic creativity that happens around the age of thirty-five or forty. In early adulthood artistic work tends to be inspired, spontaneous, and lyrical; later, it is more "sculpted," carefully reworked, and tragic in tone. Using *The Divine Comedy* as a literary guide, Jacques considers what aspects of the life cycle might make for a potential crisis or transition in all of us around that age. The defining events for this time of life (and here we must add five or ten years to the ages he first mentioned) are that, in the ordinary case, one's parents have died, one's children are almost grown, and one's career is likely to be nearing its peak of achievement. These events demand an acknowledgment of limits—limits to one's powers and indeed limits to one's life. Before this time we can let ourselves be carried along by manic optimism and idealism. But the mid-life crisis, in Jacques's eyes, is the first real confrontation with death and human destructiveness. These unpleasant realities must be accepted and some new accomodation of good and evil arrived at.

Jacques quotes a thirty-six year old patient: "Up till now life has seemed an endless upward slope, with nothing but the distant horizon to view. Now suddenly I have reached the crest of the hill, and there stretching ahead is the downward slope with the end of the road in sight—far enough away it's true—but there's death observably at the end."[32] Note the trajectory in this image. It describes the male arc: a rise followed by a decline. Does the male fantasy pattern in fact grow out of some such awareness of death? A similar tantalizing clinical fragment occurs in Erikson's 1951 play construction study (see the end of chapter V). Erikson gives two examples of girls whose productions were quite "male": one was the only girl in the group to depict the male theme of collapsed ruins, the other a girl whose story involved an aviator falling from a high tower. Both these girls had potentially fatal illnesses—they lived under an imminent threat of death. Is such a threat part of the ordinary fabric of male life? Certainly the mortality tables show that men have a virtual monopoly on sudden and early death. A latent awareness of this may indeed be one of the factors contributing to the characteristic male fantasy pattern.[33]

Jacques holds that the notion of death is always present in the unconscious. The important question is whether and how this idea is denied or kept out of consciousness. In youth and early adulthood one of the most successful defenses is activity. The illusion of immortality can be maintained by a constant show of one's vigor, energy, and ability to produce. The idea that activity can ward off the destructive aspects of life is captured in the phrase "do or die." Jacques says that it is this defense of doing that is losing its effectiveness by the time of the mid-life crisis, so that there must be a confrontation with death and a new inner equilibrium established. If we follow Jacques, we could see the two parts of the male fantasy pattern as coming from two different levels: the first part of the story, with its success, achievement, happiness, and such, reveals the defense by means of activity; the second part, the collapse or decline, is the voice of the underlying anxiety breaking through the defense. This model would lead us to expect a less extreme pattern after a successful mid-life transition that has resulted in a greater integration of the idea of death. If such thoughts are no longer held at bay then the fantasy would have a more moderate quality throughout and not be a sequence of defensive assertion suddenly undermined by "the return of the repressed."

The role of activity is also central to David Gutmann's work on maturity and aging. He has defined, using fantasy material from the Thematic Apperception Test, three types of stance toward the world.[34] The first, "active mastery," is a vigorous, achievement-oriented stance. It relies on self-initiated action. Happiness results from overcoming obstacles in the external world, unhappiness from failure in competitive or productive activity. The second stance he names "passive mastery." Here the world is seen as too complex and unruly to be successfully changed by personal action—such attempts are given up in favor of "resigned accommodation." The emphasis shifts to one of managing the internal world, if need be by altering one's own perceptions. The third stance, "magical mastery," takes this trend even further. Here security and mental ease are bought at the price of distorting reality. Psychologically primitive mechanisms are used to magically redefine liabilities as assets and to ignore real sources of danger or pain.

Gutmann argues, with considerable empirical evidence, that as men get older they shift from a predominant pattern of active mastery to a combination of passive and magical mastery. Here we must note that he sees this shift happening considerably later than does Jacques: Gutmann finds that the active mastery style is typical until the early fifties. One of the things that makes this work most interesting is that by studying Mayan farmers in Mexico and traditional Navajo Indians, Gutmann has deflected the possible criticism that his results are a function of the particular demeaned and disregarded role that our society often allots to old people. The cross-cultural stability of his results leads him to see the shift away from activity as an intrinsic, developmental change.

A fortunate accident allows us to make a direct link between Gutmann's "active mastery" and our male fantasy pattern. In the Mayan study he used a TAT picture of a man climbing a rope, a picture that has also been successfully used to measure the sex-linked fantasy patterns of Pride and Caring (see studies by Phebe Cramer, appendix B). Over ninety percent of the younger (ages twenty-six through forty-nine) Mayans told a story of a man energetically climbing, but finally falling. There is little doubt that these stories would be scored in our scheme as clear examples of the male pattern. But with the Mayan men over fifty the stories changed. Fully half of the older group saw the man in the picture as playing or enjoying himself, a thought that occured to none of the younger men. Only about half the older men tell a story that ends in a fall.

So Gutmann's work lends some empirical weight to the expectation that the male fantasy pattern moderates with age. But his framework points to a different reason for this moderation than does Jacques's. Gutmann implies that the shift to passive and magical mastery involves a large element of denial and avoidance. He seems to view it as a defensive turning inward, a giving up on realistic efforts to influence the world and a move toward self-serving distortions and fabrications. If this is true we might find, for instance, that older men would still receive "male" scores with our scoring scheme but that they would be getting them in a different way than the younger men: with stories full of unrealistic bliss in the beginning and then a rather neutral end.

Jacques does not assume that the outcome of the mid-life crisis is necessarily in the hoped for direction of acceptance. If a person already relies heavily on manic defenses and if there has not been satisfying accomplishment in both work and relations with others, then the chances are high that the mid-life crises will provoke an intense flurry of attempts to deny the facts of bodily decline. Jacques mentions the possibilities of escape into an imitation of youth, into promiscuity, or into a superficially optimistic religion. These are all efforts to hold off time. Each is "a continuation on a false note of the early adult lyricism." And each involves a more and more fearful reaction to the real future, which, in contrast to one's grandiose aspirations, seems to offer only disaster.

A resolution of this normal crisis requires an ability to tolerate grief. Jacques says we must be able to mourn our future death, and relinquish our cherished hopes of becoming perfect some day. But given enough positive experience in earlier years this grief can be mitigated by love. We come to value our life *with*, not in spite of, its limitations. In describing this favorable outcome, Jacques uses the word "endurance." His metaphor for the resolution is from Virgil: the descent into hell and the reemergence with greater wisdom and strength. Once again the parallel with our fantasy patterns, this time with the female pattern, is unmistakable. Not only does Jacques use a familiar word, endurance, but he brings in an image that has the trajectory of going down (undergoing) and then returning. It is Persephone's journey, just as his earlier example of the preresolution phase was Phaethon's.

To translate Jacques into the terms of this book, the resolution of the male mid-life crisis involves a tempering of Pride with Caring. He describes the final stage as "resigned but not defeated," which has echoes in Gutmann's "resigned accommodation." Lest this sound overly grim or isolated we should remember that they both point to the importance of love and attachments to others. Gutmann elaborates this, pointing out that the shift from active to passive mastery in fact allows the older man much more space for tenderness, affection, attention to one's inner world, and expression of wishes to receive things from others.

It is an unfortunate characteristic of much of the writing on the second half of life that it takes male experience as the unacknowledged or sole model. Jacques does not mention the question of sex differences. But in fact every example he uses, whether clinical or artistic, is of a man. As we've seen, much of what he says sounds in our terms like an acute and plausible description of the *male* mid-life crisis. But we are left wondering to what extent it would apply to women. Certainly both sexes may be distressed by the physical effects of aging, may fear death, and may use the strategies Jacques mentions as attempts to stop time and to preserve a world in which all is perfectable. Yet there may be important differences in degree and in context. As I argued earlier, there is reason to see the fear of death as more persistent and disruptive in the life of men. The decline of physical strength and potency directly undermines one of the basic male techniques for managing the world. But is this any more troublesome than a woman growing old in a culture that puts such a premium on youthful beauty? For women who do not invest most of their lives in a career, is the departure of children and the advent of menopause an equivalent to the man's having touched the limit of his success at work? Both sexes must come to grieve the lives that have been unlived, but is it as hard a task for a woman to learn to mourn the loss of a fantasied future, and to moderate this grief with love?

Gutmann's recent publications have also focused on men. But his first paper, and some footnotes in the more recent ones, raise an interesting possibility about sex differences. In the early work Gutmann felt that the sequence of active to passive/magical mastery applied equally to the women he studied, the main difference being that with women the arena in which this shift was played out had to do with interpersonal relations and not with work. He was less sanguine about the change in men:

> Their commitment to logic and to impersonal perspective makes men vulnerable to objective estimates of their prospects as aging men. Attentitive to the stern demands of their superego, and to the remorseless logic of their situation, they seem to retrench, to withdraw interest from the world, and to prepare for death. Women, more deeply wedded to a continuing personal, affectional world may suspend some of their rationality and reality testing, and consider the loss a small price to pay for continued engagement in their chosen affectional milieu.[35]

He also noticed that the older women who used the magical mode were much more zestful and combative than the men. It was as if aging had liberated some of their wishes to assert themselves and to dominate others. In fact, the content of the stories suggested a movement of each sex toward what earlier had probably been considered the province of the other sex: the older men were more accepting of their tender attachments and their wishes to be caring and cared for, the older women were more accepting of their aggressive and egocentric urges. More recently Gutmann has noted evidence of a possible cross-cultural tendency for dominance to shift from men to women as both grow old. But this is really just a piece of that larger and more interesting hypothesis: that with increasing age men and women shift toward each other psychologically. Or, to put it more carefully, as people age they become more conversant with the parts of themselves that had been suppressed or underplayed previously. Having proved one can be an adequate man or woman, the second half of life may allow, or even require, the emergence of the other side.[36]

## THE PATHOLOGIES OF PRIDE AND CARING

One of the underlying themes in the preceeding pages has been that an extreme version of either the male or female fantasy pattern is not fit to live in. Pride and Caring both have their virtues and their hazards. Pride may show itself as a sustaining aspiration or as destructive willfulness. Caring may appear as a hopeful determination to conserve that which is dear, or as helpless self-abasement. But neither in isolation has the richness or complexity that we rightfully expect from life. Our discussions of adolescence, sexuality, and aging have all provided occasions to notice the importance of having a working relationship with the opposite sex both internally and externally. A split between the sexes, whether it be by way of a society that segregates men and women and thus creates the single sex world that typifies the myths of Phaethon and Persephone, or whether it be by an internal segregation and denial of our other sexed self—this separation exacts a price. We have already touched on many aspects of the price, but it is a question that deserves our exclusive attention for a while. We shall try, by looking at examples extreme enough to be called pathological, to get a clearer notion of the internal dynamics of Pride and Caring.

The characteristic pathology of the Pride pattern would involve elements with which we are by now familiar. The theme of outward movement will be important. Typically there would be both an emphasis on activity and a cluster of underlying fears of failure, fears of the catastrophic collapse of one's own initiative, fears of being reabsorbed into the "ground" against which one has been so vigorously trying to stand out. Along with this standing-out-and-away-from goes a certain isolation, a separateness, and detachment from complex relationships. The approach to the world will be a blend of the Technician and the Gladiator. The Technician values precision, clarity, and control above all else. He attempts to shape both the inner and outer worlds by the application of rules and procedures. He is constantly making and remaking. It is the style of Daedalus, the universal engineer and artificer.[37] It is the style that psychoanalytic terminology calls "obsessional." The Gladiator is less neutral and tightly controlled. Here the constant experience of being challenged and threatened is most prominent. The world is an arena in which it is necessary to overcome an endless series of adversaries. The ability to construe almost any situation in terms of combat brings this stance within the orbit of what we refer to as "paranoid."

Different combinations and balances of these themes lead of course to quite different clinical pictures. But there is one constellation in particular that seems very close to the core of the Pride pattern as we outlined it in chapter IV. In psychoanalytic language this character style is called "phallic narcissism." There are two pieces of work that will help us understand what this means.

Henry Murray's "American Icarus"[38] is a case study of a college student to whom he gives the pseudonym Grope. On the surface this young man was notable for his apathy and deliberate withdrawal from any activity, let alone competition, in the areas of work or sex. But upon closer investigation it appeared that Grope's inner life was equally notable in the opposite direction: he was filled with vivid and extravagant dreams of grandeur. As Grope himself put it: "I am just biding my time and waiting for the day when my 'soul' will ignite and this inner fire will send me hurtling, two rungs at a time, up the ladder of success." It is this kind of imagery that leads Murray to cite "ascensionism" as a primary component of the Icarian personality type. A detailed review of Grope's life and thoughts provided many instances of this wish to climb, to rise, to fly spectacularly through the air. Murray comments that "The precocious, importunate and extravagant character of Grope's ascensionism suggests that he belongs with the adolescent, overreaching, would-be solar heroes, Icarus and Phaethon—father-superseding enthusiasts with unstructured ego systems."[39]

The fantasy of spectacular rise involves the wish to be the compelling center of attention, the brightest star in the sky. Murray dubs this "cynosural narcissism" and gives numerous examples of Grope's craving for unsolicited attention and admiration. When he felt himself to be in the center of the stage he could then forsake apathy and show considerable activity and productivity. But such energy came only in spurts.

Grope's memories, fantasies, and dreams all suggested that both the ascensionism and the narcissism had phallic connotations. Experiences of erection and urination formed a vivid theme. His fantasy of flying over, and urinating on, a city made of women's bodies showed the excited fusion of urination, levitation, and sexuality. The burning ambition, the expectation that others will be spellbound by one's rise, and the unhappy awareness that rises are followed by declines, all these can be partially understood as analogues of a boy's experience with his penis. It is not that the phallic narcissist has invented something absolutely new and bizarre, but rather that through a particular combination of circumstances the threads of narcissism and intense interest in his penis, which occur in the development of every boy, here constitute the main design in the tapestry.[40]

The cycle of ascension followed by a fall shows itself in many areas of Grope's life. He speaks of having reached a pinnacle of physical, social, and academic success in fifth or sixth grade (the crucial years just before puberty), after which he experienced a "fall" into weakness and anonymity. There is a lifelong pattern of intense interests, as in a new toy or a new friend, quickly followed by an ebb and a return to a state of flat indifference. And then there are his fantasies. Again we are fortunate to have a story in response to the TAT picture of the rope climber. It is worth quoting Grope's story as Murray relates it:

The fourth World War ended, he said, when a nation of supermen overran the globe, and now, in each conquered country, the victors are trying by means of strength tests to select other possible supermen with whom to start a new race. He continues as follows: "In this case this person elected to climb a rope; he was quite strong. The bottom of the rope was made of an inflammable—soaked in potassium chloride, I guess. They would set fire to the bottom of it and the flames would go at a certain slightly increasing rate. If the person failed to reach the top before the flames did, of course he was killed. This person starts out like fury and by fifty yards the rope is burned only about five yards from the bottom. . . . About seventy-five yards up his arms are like lead-weight. He doesn't feel that he can go any further. . . . He goes another five or ten yards and suddenly slips back and barely manages to catch on five yards below. By now the flames are about half way up. Then he gets panicky, gets another tremendous burst, and goes about ten yards. He hangs on there and watches the flames increasing their momentum. . . . He goes on taking about a foot at a time, the flames getting nearer. He can't rest—very hard to rest hanging on to a rope. He finally gets about ten yards from the top, that's the last thing he remembers."[41]

This story provides a fascinating contrast with Grope's earlier statement that he is waiting for an "inner fire" to propel him up the ladder of success. Here we have virtually the same image. We see the fire but it is outer rather than inner and dangerous rather than helpful. Though he leaves the conclusion up in the air, so to say, we assume that the hero goes, as did Phaethon, from strength and self-confidence ("starts out like fury"), through exhaustion and panic, to final death in a flaming fall.

Murray's suggestions about the etiology of the "Icarus complex" are fragmentary. But he does wonder whether "Grope's ardent desire to ascend is a counteractive disposition excited by one or more experiences of descent" (specifically by his childhood accidents and enuresis, followed by the several "falls" in status, which started with the birth of his two-year younger brother). Thus Murray is thinking of the Icarian pattern as an attempt to master a fall and deny the possibility of its repetition. It is a defensive attempt, which by its very concern with dramatic ascent opens the door for the sudden return of the awareness of catastrophic descent.

More recently, Jerome Weinberger and James Muller[42] have found Murray's formulation valuable in understanding what they see as an increasingly common clinical picture: a young man who complains of apathy and lack of satisfaction in spite of considerable personal success and whose life, in both love and work, shows a pattern of peaks of intense involvement interspersed with plateaus of restless boredom. Typically there are feelings of having already passed one's physical, intellectual, and sexual peak. The resultant sense of emptiness and helplessness lends a strange quality of later life depression to these men who are really only just beginning their adult lives (as we will see, Weinberger and Muller describe the inner dilemma in ways that would fit well with our earlier discussion of the male mid-life crises).

Weinberger and Muller appreciate Murray's portrayal of Icarus's rise, but feel more attention needs to be paid to his fall. Thus the case study they present is focused on exploring the dynamic relation between the apathy, listlessness, and dissatisfaction on the one hand and the intense need for ascendency and admiration on the other. L.F., as they call their exemplary case, is competitive, ambitious, and has an insatiable need for "ultimate peak experiences." He has devoted himself to rigorous body building and in his extensive sexual life he values stamina over pleasure. The goal is to be unique and unsurpassable in intercourse, the most satisfying proof of this being his ability to reduce a woman to exhaustion. But he is never successful enough: he quickly loses interest and each relationship, which he began with intense hopes, soon "runs a downhill course." His early family experience fits the pattern we've come to expect: he was in essence a first or only son (he had a brother fourteen years older), his father was heavily involved in his work and often absent, and L.F. remembers his father as an intimidating and angry figure.

L.F. had two serious childhood illnesses, each of which required hospitalization and each of which left him with a physical defect. It was after the second of these that his passion for physical fitness developed. The material produced in the course of the therapy suggested that this sequence was not accidental, and led to Weinberger and Muller's first dynamic hypothesis. They report a dream that, among other things, suggests that L.F.'s sexual athletics are an attempt to master a persistent inner experience of helplessness and physical vulnerability by turning it into strength and potency. They conclude that "his sexuality and body-building are his antidote against the anxiety of illness, castration and death."[43]

Their second hypothesis is similar but broader. It has to do with L.F.'s long struggle to free himself from a doting, entangling, and over-whelming mother. The intensity of his need to be masterful and independent is a statement of just how difficult that struggle is. The Icarian trappings of glory serve the dynamic function of trying to conceal their opposite: "Beneath the facade of phallic supremacy, uniqueness, being first, exceeding everyone, is the passivity, the softness, the need for tenderness and dependency, the wish to trust, and the fears of helplessness, and therefore distrust."[44]

There is a third explanatory notion that Weinberger and Muller put forward, one harder to evaluate because it is not fully integrated with the rest of the piece and no particular evidence is presented to support it. They suggest that the boredom, dissatisfaction, and repetitive falling short of expectations that these young men experience are connected with their pursuit of an unattainable unconscious goal. "The peak experiences sought by our patients are attempts to realize incestuous goals which in reality are impossible; an ecstasy of oedipal triumph which, although dangerously approximated, is fated to be, in William Wordsworth's phrase, 'a forever receding shore.' This sheer unapproachability of their goals, rather than inability to cope, is the key to their manifest distress—clinical boredom."[45]

It is true that the phallic-narcissistic character, except when in anxious and depressed phases, leans heavily on sexual overtones and metaphors. There may be overt sexual athleticism, or at least a doting on one's own body (or intellect) as a fine machine meriting sexual admiration. The compulsive urge toward sexual conquest, with its overtones of attack, may be, as in the instance of Grope, primarily evident in fantasy and not in behavior. But there is still likely to be a pattern of intense interest followed by disillusionment. It is this sequence in relationships that leaves people who have had a whirl with one of these fellows feeling that they've been used, been "had." Words like "prick" and "screwed" seem to fit the experience even if everyone kept their clothes on the whole time.

But while recognizing the importance of sexuality, we may still hesitate to see incestuous wishes as a separate and autonomous motive in the unfolding of this character type. One of the valuable aspects of Weinberger and Muller's presentation is the way in which it allows us to grasp the defensive function of a "phallic" style. Aggressive sexuality, physical strength, pride, and ambition—all these are used in part to cover and compensate for something quite different. The experience that is warded off is that of the frightened, overwhelmed, and probably envious little boy. It both simplifies and unifies our understanding if we see the boy's Oedipal strivings as, in part, another step in his struggle to effect his emancipation from his mother and to turn a feeling of being dominated into one of domination. Thus incestuous wishes become a special instance of the more general dynamic of the phallic character: the attempt to turn passive into active.

What sort of pathology is the Caring pattern subject to? We would expect the theme of emotional ties to others to be prominent. Whatever the external behavior, the inner drama is likely to involve the search for a particular loved one with whom all good feelings will be restored. The search requires patience, an ability to wait, and a willingness to take what comes. This in turn requires an inhibition of some of one's active impulses. The underlying fear is that there may be something destructive inside one that will destroy the hoped for relation and make the waiting in vain. When the theme of self-sacrifice becomes dominant we are likely to see the stance of the Victim or the Altruist. The Victim is a professional sufferer, forever fearing, and finding, desertion, and abuse. The Altruist takes a slightly more positive approach in the sense of being generous and giving. But at the pathological extreme there is the same deliberate neglect of one's own needs, and the constant undertone of "see how little I get back for all that I give."

Masochism is the character style closest to the core of pathological Caring. The word "masochism" is a slippery one, worn smooth by overuse. In this context it does *not* refer to the type of sexual perversion in which pain is a prerequisite for pleasure—that is a different matter, and if anything tends to be more frequent in men than in women. Instead we mean an approach to life in which the stance of the sufferer, the sacrificer, is dominant. Freud describes it succinctly: ". . . the true masochist always turns his cheek wherever he has a chance of receiving a blow."[46] Theodor Reik speaks of a person whose life motto is Victory Through Defeat.[47] But for a detailed example we turn to a case study presented by Margaret Brenman.[48]

"Allerton" was an adolescent girl whose main social resource was her ability to evoke laughter and teasing. At her best she could be a witty court jester, at worst a pathetic creature who bought acceptance by being an all-purpose slave and victim. This pattern went back as least as far as early childhood, when she attempted to win the affection of a cold and disinterested mother by elaborate acts of ingratiation and solicitude. But her mother found this distasteful, a form of "fawning," and reacted with sarcasm and ridicule. Allerton's role as "teasee" in the family became well-established. She later shifted her attentions to her older sister, becoming a virtual lady-in-waiting who put both her wit and her weekly allowance at the service of her sister's whims.

By the time Allerton came to psychotherapy her conviction that it was her lot to be constantly "used" and then "dropped" by others had ample daily confirmation in her life. But she had no awareness of the ways in which she helped to bring this about. Brenman says that "it was as if everyone felt in her unprovoked look of terror and pleading an unjustified accusation of evil intent and an undefined implicit demand."[49] This insightful description reveals an important piece of the complex transaction that resulted in Allerton's arousing anger and sadistic responses in others.

Allerton said that her fantasy life consisted of one story, which she had repetitively told herself, and dreamt, for years: she is ill with a fatal disease that is not her "fault" and as she is about to die the members of her family gather around her; her mother and sister suddenly discover that they love her, and tell her so, and her father discovers, after she dies, that he too loves her. Early in life she had resolved to make this fantasy come true before she reached eighteen. In the course of her psychotherapy urges to damage herself came to the fore. She went through a protracted period of self-injury, beginning with attempts to make herself ill by depriving herself of food and sleep and finally progressing to repeated episodes of cutting and burning herself (this obsession with the repeated inflicting of small but bloody injuries is a clinical nightmare that occurs much more frequently in women than in men).

This picture of Allerton gives us a better idea what is meant by "masochism" as a character style and we can see it on the various levels of interpersonal style, fantasy, and how one treats one's own body. The case of Allerton also provides an obvious point of contact with the Caring fantasy pattern: the remarkable story that seems to have dominated her imagination both while awake and asleep. Her fantasy of evoking love by way of a tragic death is so well-polished and so common a plot that we are likely to overlook its sadness and its destructive potential as a plan around which to organize a life. *"Then* they'll appreciate me!" Immediate associations which come to mind are Camille and the "succumbing" lady in the parody with which we opened chapter V. But on a less clichéd level, this is the journey of Persephone again. Persephone's disappearance into the underworld *does* call forth impressive evidence of her mother's love. The trick of course is being able to come back to life in order to enjoy the fruits of one's death.

From the point of view of Allerton the omniscient constructor of this fantasy, it is a pure example of an extreme of the Caring pattern; as a life plan it is a disaster. The fantasy has become genuinely masochistic by means of two small but vital shifts: implicitly the suffering has become the *only* means of evoking love, and the reward of the love itself has become so atrophied that it is now small compensation indeed. The emphasis is on the suffering and not on the resulting pleasure. The deathbed scene is also a way of punishing those who have not loved her. The masochistic character's "pardon-me-for-living" attitude tends inevitably toward the grotesque benevolence of suicide on the doorstep of those people who have not been properly loving. Here the similarities with Mrs. Lauder are apparent, especially her suicide attempt, which took place in her therapist's waiting room.

There is an odd detail included in Allerton's fantasy. The fatal illness is not her "fault." It is unlikely we would have thought it *was;* why does this have to be specified? Something about intent and responsibility is being deliberately disowned. Likewise in her daily life she was able to remain unaware of her own active participation in her victimization, though when she became more disturbed there was no doubt that the hand wielding the whip was hers.

There is an intriguing conjunction in the masochistic character: on the surface a studied renunciation of any self-interest or active seeking of pleasure, yet they routinely provoke considerable guilt and anger in those around them. These facts can be linked by understanding masochism as a disorder in which anger is consciously denied only to be smuggled back in the form of spiteful and guilt-provoking self destruction—"See how I suffer!"

The case of Allerton is valuable because Brenman traces these relationships in convincing detail. She shows the link between Allerton's inner strategies to banish her own anger and her corresponding ability to bring anger out in others. The Victim needed a Victimizer in order to maintain the fiction that all the anger, exploitativeness, and sadism resided in someone else. Forcing people to play the brute was a well-disguised channel through which to express some of her own urges for domination and revenge. The course of Allerton's therapy offered confirmation of this understanding. Her acute distress began when someone accused her of being that which her character style was most bent on concealing: destructive. The resultant period of turmoil, when her assaults on herself reached a frenzied peak, coincided with her first awareness that she was full of sadistic fantasies. The road out led through an acceptance of her own anger and "bossiness."

Brenman helps us to see the ways in which masochism is a complex transformation of anger. But she also takes up the question of the origins of Allerton's anger. As we might expect from the deathbed fantasy and from the picture we're given of Allerton's mother, Brenman traces the anger back to an intense, and intensely frustrated, demand for love. We imagine Allerton's rage at her unresponsive mother, and the impossible dilemma of hating the very person you want so much from. Her attempted solution was to transform the rage into self-sacrifice. This relieved the fear of destroying the valued relationship, allowed the search for affection to continue, and at the same time provided an entirely new way of exacting revenge. Brenman ends up describing the masochistic character style as "a highly organized, hierarchically stratified set of functions designed to express aggression, however circuitously, and to obtain gratification of infantile needs in fact or fantasy, however long delayed."[50]

We can now see three important aspects of the masochistic character. There is a willing acceptance of pain or humiliation, which, depending on the person and the circumstances, ranges from altruistic self-denial to actual mutilation. It is also a pattern that involves an intense and dependent attachment to another person (Freud described the masochist's wish for punishment as the desire to be treated like a naughty child). The masochist is a vivid example of the metaphor that describes an important relationship as "the tie that binds." Lastly there is a paralysis and denial of ordinary human aggressiveness; in its stead there is covert revenge and hidden tyranny.

These same three aspects are the main points of thematic similarity between the masochistic style and the Caring pattern (as we saw it in chapter IV) or, for that matter, the traditional female role. There has been considerable dispute about whether there is a special affinity between femininity and certain forms of masochism. Helene Deutsch is the most blunt exponent of the notion that a species of masochism is a natural and appropriate part of the "feminine core."[51] She links "feminine masochism" with a partial renunciation of activity. This in turn is due to the woman's lower constitutional level of activity and aggression, to the fact that her genital organ is not as appropriate for the expression of such impulses anyway, and to the way in which society exerts pressure on the girl to further forsake such activity. Deutsch sees this trend as adaptive in the sense that a certain amount of masochism aids a woman in accepting and affirming the inevitably painful parts of her sexual and reproductive function.

Others, Karen Horney being the best example, have argued that culture is more important than biology in these matters and have denied that any sort of "masochism" is part of the healthy woman. But even Horney acknowledges "a certain preparedness in woman for a masochistic conception of their role."[52] Women *are* less strong, intercourse *does* involve being penetrated, menstruation, defloration, and childbirth *do* involve blood and pain, and society *does* encourage women to inhibit their aggression and assertiveness. Thus, says Horney, when "masochistic motives" arise in a woman's life they are likely to invade her definition of her sexual role.

We would want to add to Horney's list the female emphasis on maintaining close attachments—this too can be conducive to a masochistic stance. With both Allerton and Mrs. Lauder we saw the link between a frustrated hunger to have more from a parent and the development of pathological self-sacrifice. But it is important to make clear that these are extreme instances. To repeat what was said in chapter IV, masochism can be an unfortunate development from the Caring pattern. It may well be a liability inherent in the pattern, but it is not identical with it. In that sense we are more in agreement with Horney than with Deutsch.

The first element that drew our attention to the possible affinity of Caring and masochism was in fact the structural resemblance of the fantasy patterns. Speaking of the fantasies that belong to feminine masochism, Deutsch says that "often the fantasy is divided into two acts: the first, the masochistic act, produces the sexual tension, and the second, the amorous act, supplies all the delights of being loved and desired."[53] Reik, apropos of the masochistic character says, "The fantasies are comparable to an anticipated memorial to the ego of the daydreamer . . . the enduring person becomes victorious, is appreciated and loved, is most honored where he had been rejected before. . . . The aggressive and ambitious, revengeful and violent instinctual aims, the parrying of which resulted in the genesis of masochism, rise again in the fantasied satisfaction."[54] Though Deutsch puts it in terms of sexuality and Reik in terms of aggression, they both describe a distilled version of the Caring fantasy pattern. The suffering, the privation, and the tension are all allocated to the first act of the story and the reward to the last act.

Looking at the male pathology of phallic narcissism helped us to see more clearly one of the dynamics that may underlie the structure of the Pride fantasy pattern, even in its less extreme version: the attempt to deny dependence and weakness. Our excursion into a case study of masochism now allows us to do the same for the Caring pattern. Here the hidden aspects of the self, revealed only in the last installment, have to do with triumph, vindication, and the seizing of the pleasures one has been hungering for. In a more narrow sense, if the extreme version of Pride attempts (unsuccessfully) to defend against an image of the self as small, damaged, and helpless, then the extreme version of Caring attempts to defend against an image of the self as a sadistic attacker who will take whatever she wants.

We spoke of the phallic narcissistic character as founded on the principle of turning passive into active. The masochistic character works in reverse, turning active into passive. To make this contrast more real, think of two reactions we've seen to the childhood experience of being immobilized and invaded while in the hospital. L.F., the case example of the phallic narcissist, responded to this physical and psychological insult by redoubling his efforts to be strong, independent, and masterful. He was determined to be always the doer and never the victim. Mrs. Lauder, on the other hand, reacted by stifling the fury that her telling of the tale suggests she must have felt. Instead she took on the role of the helpless victim and followed it out with a vengeance; the experience of being abused and neglected remained a major theme in her life and the possibilities of expressing her own active or angry wishes constantly receded.

From the way in which these two character types complement each other it is obvious that they are a match made in heaven—but made in a malevolent heaven, since they are attracted to each other for all the wrong reasons. Each embodies to the other parts of the self that have been disowned. A consequence of erecting firm barriers against the recognition of aspects of one's inner experience is that these same qualities will then be attributed to, and even sought out in, the external world. To put it another way, a person who defines himself or herself as *not* being soft, or nasty, or intelligent, or whatever, is likely to show a special interest in those who, to his or her eye, show that very trait. The emotional tone of this interest will be quite mixed and subject to sudden shifts. Ordinarily it will be compounded of an unacknowledged empathy, which we might think of as a wish to reclaim that which has been denied, an anxious curiosity, and an urge to master or dominate.

Imagine a relationship between these caricatures of Caring and Pride, the masochist and the phallic narcissist. She has all the responsiveness, tenderness, patience, and willingness to give. He has all the open self-assertion, competitive energy, initiative, and bravado. Each thus confirms the other's conscious self-definition. At the same time each has the opportunity to explore and learn to manage this polar Other. She can unconsciously partake of his aggression and he of her ability to become attached and dependent. But it is a precarious balance. If the partaking, the living through the other, goes too far it then touches on those feared inner images: the greedy rapist inside her and the tattered victim inside him. Then anxiety surges up and the partner must be demeaned and cast aside. In all but the most lucky circumstances such a pattern obscures any vision of a relationship where *both* people are active and responsive by turns and both are relatively at ease with the two sexes inside them.

# Chapter VII

⊱◈⊰

# The Dream
# of Androgyny

The words at the end of the last chapter may sound to some ears like another voice added to the recently growing chorus that is singing the praises of "androgyny." It is not; at least not in the way the term has begun to be used.

By the New Androgyny I mean a social and ideological position that has emerged most clearly in some writings in psychology and literary criticism, but bits and pieces of which are scattered through our popular culture. What began as a feminist critique of "sex roles" has become an attempt to construct an ideal that will radically diminish the importance of the distinction between male and female. This is, after all, a natural step. Once "sex role stereotypes" are seen as the source of considerable injustice and evil, then the stage is set for a program to abolish them. The difficulty and sheer frustration of finding a way to talk and think sensibly about men and women makes it tempting to cut the knot with one sharp thought: we will no longer speak of men and women but rather of human beings who can be either masculine or feminine, or both, depending on the moment and on his or her (developing androgynous pronouns is a growth industry in itself) inclination.

Here are some examples of this new ideal:

When we use the word androgyny in this book, we mean flexibility of sex role. We refer not to individuals with male and female sex organs but to individuals who are capable of behaving in integrative feminine *and* masculine ways, who are assertive and yielding, independent and dependent, expressive and instrumental.

It is the flexibility and union of positively valued traits that is critical. . . .

Androgynous people, from our view, are "hybrids" who have moved beyond the scientific and cultural stereotypes.[1]

All of this indeed does sound appealing. The androgynous ideal calls for freedom from arbitrary restrictions on our ability to be and feel as best suits us, and in that sense is of a piece with the broader American ideology of individual choice, freedom, and equality. This is not a tradition to be lightly dismissed. John Stuart Mill made the case for the equality of women over a hundred years ago. His elegant and convincing argument has yet to be improved on. There are in fact similarities between his position and that of the advocates of androgyny: they share an ideology that sees individual freedom and individual choice as the highest goods, they both make a split between "nature" and the influence of society, they both distrust any assumption of "natural" differences between the sexes, and are inclined to see the effects of society as oppressive and coercive. But the androgynists have shifted the argument in at least one crucial way: no longer is the goal the abolishing of unjust laws but rather now the goal is a change in our character. The goal is a new sort of person. The rights in question are no longer political or economic rights but instead we see a very modern notion, that of the right to have whatever personality traits we wish.

We cannot help but admire the image held out to us: a person both "feminine" and "masculine," uniting in one form dependence with independence, assertiveness with the ability to yield, expressiveness with executive efficiency. The modern androgyne is a fusion of "positively valued traits," a construction made only of the best of both genders. And above all flexible. The androgyne's behavior is grounded in "the sociocultural context of situations" rather than in any persistent self-definition by sex. I gather that this means an effective and graceful rising to the occasion, whatever the occasion may be. We are also told that by transcending sex roles we will be able to "integrate personal characteristics and adopt alternative life styles, new careers, and new relationships throughout our lives." A Person For All Seasons.

It may seem undemocratic—or at the least, churlish—to hold back one's enthusiasm for this ideal of androgyny. There is, after all, much of value in the critique of rigid sex roles, and much that is beneficial in the exhortation to be whatever we want to be. Yet much as we might want to believe in it, when it is taken to the extremes I have quoted, there is no mistaking the hollow ring: something is missing, it's all a bit too good to be true. It is this quality that signals the fact that some important fantasy, some persistent magical hope, is quietly at work underneath the rhetoric. And it is here that we can learn from looking at the Old Androgyny, as it were. Although the New Androgyny does not seem eager to acknowledge its ancestors, in fact this notion does have an ancestry that can help us understand its current shape and popularity.

Androgyny is a concept with a long, complicated, and honorable history. As a word it refers originally to an hermaphrodite, or more specifically to Hermaphrodite, the son of Hermes and Aphrodite in Greek mythology. Hermaphrodite was, so the myth goes, joined in one body with a nymph. Ovid tells it in florid detail: Hermaphrodite has spurned the romantic overtures of the nymph, but when she sees him bathing in a pool she is overcome with desire:

> [She] Dove, swam to him, and held him fast, resisting,
> Sought his reluctant kisses, touched his body,
> Stroked his unwilling breast, embraced and held him
> Whatever way she could. He fought and struggled,
> But she wrapped herself around him, as a serpent
> Caught by an eagle, borne aloft, entangles
> Coils around head and talons, or as ivy
> Winds round great oaks, or an octopus extends
> Its prey within its tentacle.[2]

Her successful prayer makes the union permanent. This vision of female power is one of the persistent threads in the idea of androgyny, at least as seen through male eyes. More importantly let us note two other aspects of the tale. In its original context the word andro-gyny has qualities both of fatefulness and of concrete physicality: it refers to the merging of male and female bodies in a fashion that is beyond the control and wishes of at least one member of the pair. These are two overtones of the word that have been sloughed off in its new incarnation. The New Androgyny aims at enshrining free will and leaving bodies behind.

The story of Hermaphrodite is just one moment, more fully formed and literary than most, in a long chain of cults, fables, and parables about androgyny. It is a tradition that can be traced from Oriental and Near Eastern creation myths through classical Greece, the Gnostics, and early Christian mystics, the alchemists, medieval heretics, and on up to the romantics.[3] Each period has of course added its own twist to the story but even across this tremendous expanse of time and cultures there are common elements, elements that are relevant to understanding the heritage and appeal of the New Androgyny.

Myths of androgyny are statements of the attempt to overcome separation, to achieve a re-union.[4] There is in the background of these tales the assumption of a time when all was whole, seamless. The wholeness was split by some misfortune and the vision of the androgyne is an intermediate stage, a way station on the reparative trip back to the primal unity. We can see these elements, for in-stance, in the Christian creation myth, which is ambiguous about whether God first created an androgyne ("male and female He created them") or shaped woman from man's body, and which pro-ceeds on to the shattering Fall as the advent of human sexuality and reproduction. Likewise Aristophanes' discourse on love in Plato's *Symposium:* here heterosexual love is seen as the desperate urge on the part of the separated halves of the androgyne to reunite.

It is likely that the myths of androgynous gods were invented to explain and give a context to various surviving fragments of prehis-toric ritual. Transvestism, a masquerade or disguise using the clothes of the other sex, played an important part in many rituals of transition —but particularly in rites of initiation and in the ritual of marriage. There are many surviving fragments that involve the curious custom of the bride and/or groom dressing up as the other sex on the wedding night. In some instances what seems to be intended is a disguise to protect against the envy or anger of a malevolent demon, in other instances the cross-dressing concretely embodies the sharing of the powers of the other sex that is felt to happen through sexual intercourse. In either case the moment of union is fraught with power for both good and ill. The androgynous gods (Hermaphrodite and Dionysius) are persistently associated with sexual union. Even Hermaphrodite's name is the straight forward coupling of mother and father; the word *androgynos* is a rare construction in Greek, a "copulative compound," which unites two polarities.

The coming together of male and female was seen to be freighted with potent magic. The androgyne came to symbolize fertility (Dionysius as an androgynous transformation of Priapus and other phallic figures), wisdom (Tiresias is only one of many androgynous shamans and soothsayers), and immortality (the Phoenix, reborn from its own ashes, is a derivative of an androgynous deity). In the image of the androgyne we can imagine eternal reduplication, giving birth unaided, being both parents in one. There is considerable awe associated with these notions, awe that shades over into more fearful thoughts such as the fantasy of overwhelming attack that Ovid pictures, or the band of murderous Maenads who were thought to follow Dionysius.

The fact that the image of the androgyne has been kept alive over the centuries speaks to a deep interest in the nature of the boundary between the sexes (as does our often excited, annoyed, or anxious curiosity about impersonation of one sex by the other, about homosexuality, and about that latest technological miracle of border crossing, surgical sex change).

Looking at a statue of an hermaphrodite is an odd experience.[5] It is a mixture of fascination and unease. The attempt to fuse male and female compels our attention, yet rarely seems to work—in most cases what we see does not appear genuinely androgynous but rather looks like a woman with a penis or a man with breasts. It is not, I am sure, just that the artists who took this subject happened to lack skill. Rather it is again a matter of an inherently unrealizable obsession, something we can't let go in fantasy but yet refuse to accept in any particular real form. In looking at these statues we can feel that double pull: on the one hand the intense and excited wish to see what it *would* be like to have both, and on the other hand the sense of relief when we decide, inevitably, that it's really *a man* with breasts or *a woman* with a penis. It is in this tension between union and differentiation that much of the power of the androgyne lies.

The existence of two separate and different sexes is an insult to our dearly held narcissistic image of ourselves and our own limitless possibilities. Human psychological life begins with no sense of a difference between "me" and what is "out there." It is in this original infantile state of oneness that we can see the individual analogue, perhaps even the source, of the mythic and religious conviction of a primal unity. It is no mean trick to develop a stable and tolerably accurate sense of oneself in relation to the world outside the boundary of one's skin. The course of human development, at least in the early years, is a series of grapplings with the fact of separateness and differentiation. And each step in that process is a painful shock to our diffusely proud sense that we *are* the world. We react to these shocks with disbelief and envy. Something different from us is quite likely to seem intriguing, mysterious, and desirable; we want it, or want to *be* it.

Perhaps the first such lesson the child learns is that the world consists of children (little people) and adults (big people). The latter are manifestly more powerful and we imagine that they control or possess all those things we want, so we resolve to become them. The second lesson is that the world contains male and female. In the mind of the child, given to a mixture of concrete thinking and fantasy, and vitally concerned with his or her origin, this is a very important difference indeed. It is important in part because it is absolute. We learn gradually that an adult is something we can be, will be, later. We may cháfe at the delay but we have hope. But in the child's eye, undimmed by modesty, the most admirable part of being grown-up is having children. This aspiration runs head on into the fact of sexual differentiation. It is impossible to be a parent on one's own, reality tells us. The lesson about the sexes is severe; we *are* one and cannot realistically expect to be both or to become the other. And over time we listen, giving up large fragments of our narcissistic aims and finding happy consolation in the possible. But some of the earlier hopes merely retreat into the psychic interior. And so envy of the opposite sex begins.

The annals of envy are long and complex. It is a uniquely demoralizing emotion. It carries with it no suggestion for satisfying action, as do anger or lust. Episodes of envy occur along a continuum from admiration to self-hatred. As it shades into admiration, envy becomes a more benign and positive feeling, a feeling that we might enjoy having and that can lead us to some action, some emulation, some set of ideals with positive and lasting results. But as we move along the continuum toward envy's roots in self-hatred and greed, it becomes an increasingly disturbing and corrosive experience. It emphasizes the distance between us and whatever we desire or value. At the same time envy includes a strong temptation to destroy or degrade the very object of desire. In this context trying to possess the envied person or quality by becoming it seems a very good solution, in fact the only one that might heal the breach without destroying the goal.

It is important to remember here that we are talking of mental processes that are neither very sophisticated in the sense we usually mean by "thought," nor often conscious. It is a magical sort of thinking, which itself strives to blur the boundary between that which is inside us and that which is outside. Thus envious thoughts inevitably exaggerate the happiness, power, or desirability of the envied. We invest a person or thing with all our fantasies of how splendid life could or should be and then we proceed to envy our own largely mythical creation. And then we reclaim our vision through the process of trying to become it. The process is also deeply magical in that parts stand for wholes (thinking, for instance, that if I were tall as she I would feel as good as I imagine she must), and our sense of inner consistency, and of the difference between inner and outer, is put in abeyance. Thus we develop a host of fragmentary inner images, each invested with powerful feeling and each an attempt to endow ourselves with an envied attribute.

Due to the concrete mode of childhood thought, envy is likely to begin with a focus on a visible, palpable part of someone else's body and to assume that various wonderful qualities or abilities are vested in that part. Though the history of our growing up is in part one of tremendous strides in the ability to think in a more rational and organized way, this original mode persists quietly and gives envy both its vivid impact and its bedeviling complexity in our mental life. The aspect of envy between the sexes that has received the most public attention recently is the psychoanalytic concept of "penis envy." It is a notion that has been harshly criticized both within and outside the profession. This criticism is justified, but not because girls don't at times experience a wish to have a penis and those powers that they imagine go with it. Rather the problem is that this partial theory has been emphasized to the extent of avoiding or denying the equally powerful envy that boys feel about women and their functions. In the usual dialectical fashion of these things, men can use a partially true notion of female enviousness to disguise and assuage their own envy. There is reason to think that, because of the importance of the early relationship with the mothering person, envy of the other sex is if anything more endemic and troublesome in men than in women. Since it needs more attention, we will use the male instance to illustrate further.

A little boy's first career aspiration is to be a mommy. It is a considerable blow when he finally accepts the fact that his body won't permit it. Even before he begins to assemble hazy bits of theory about the process of birth, the fact that his most constant and intense relationship is likely to be with a woman leads the boy to admire, wish to emulate, and possess her. In time large parts of this relationship can be based on the particulars of his being a boy with her, but the earlier amorphous wish remains, the wish to *be* this wonderful other creature. And then in the midst of this already complicated process, his infantile researches into the origins of life begin to turn up some facts. The facts are none too pleasing: not only are there two radically different types of bodies in the world but also the type he's endowed with appears to have a rather brief and minor role in what he modestly sees as that most basic of events, the creation of new people like himself. To settle for being a daddy seems thin stuff indeed when compared with the concrete realities of gestation, birth, and nursing.

There are three routes out of this impasse. All of them remain alive in our fantasy, although we ordinarily settle on one as a major theme. The first route involves a denial of the troublesome difference between the sexes; we continue to imagine that we *are* all it takes, both male and female, androgynous. The second route is the continuing wish to have the equipment and abilities of the other sex. But of course this requires us to think about losing or giving up what we have. We can try to evade the starkness of this choice, as in a young man who dreams that he possesses a set of female genitals that he can attach to himself and remove at will. But the dream has to be deliberately fuzzy about the anatomical details of where this portable vagina would fit and how it would share space with his own equipment. So this route sooner or later brings us to anxious thoughts about the integrity of our bodies—to which, envy or no, we are attached. This is the area of thinking that Freudian theory has referred to as "castration anxiety," although it is traditionally seen as linked to a fear of punishment rather than to envy of the opposite sex. The final, and perhaps most typical, route is to set about exaggerating and puffing up the value and importance of one's own sex. Thus the whole panoply of assertions of male primacy in the process of reproduction and birth. These range from elaborate rituals in more so-called primitive cultures, through the Biblical picture of a male God giving birth to woman through the body of a man, to elaborate legal structures that have until recently made the father lord and owner of both women and child, thus compensating for the fact that in nature paternity is hard indeed to prove.[6]

But let us take a more humble example. A forty-year-old man dreamt the following:

> There were two of me; one was a diver, with a black suit on—you know, one of those rubber things—and the other me was sort of a foreman. And we were in the Nile, which was probably three or four inches deep and clear. And the me that was a diver had to dive into a thing that was slanted down, a long tunnel, and then there was a cavern down at the bottom of that. And in the cavern was some little guy on a little bulldozer who was turning out . . . the bulldozer would lift up and hand me mummies, in the wooden part, not just wrapped in sheets. And I was supposed to take them up.

This dream occurred at a time in this man's life when he had been exploring, in psychotherapy, some of his wishes to be a woman. The dream was linked with finding out that his ex-wife had gotten pregnant and had had an abortion. A pregnancy was something they had tried for fruitlessly during many years of marriage. When he found out that it had now happened without him he felt cheated, "ripped off," and envious; mostly envious. Whatever competitive feelings, and sense of inadequacy, he did have in regards to the other man involved seemed less powerful and full of sadness than was his frustrated competition with his ex-wife, his bitter sense that she had gone and done this without him, and that he was helpless and without any role in the important matter of babies.

He felt angry at men whom he saw as strong, the "jocks, all of them breeding children all over the place, every time you turn around, and spitting kids out over the bed." The enviously angry exaggeration, and idealization, is clear. But even more interesting is the way in which this fantasy manages to do away with women: it sounds as if these "jocks" are having babies on their own. The notion that this fantasy is a defensive maneuver is supported by the fact that, in the session, anger at these imagined men was less painful than the grief and frustration of feeling closed out of the birth process.

Which brings us back to the dream. The dream also attempts to displace women and to put men at the center of it all. We easily accept the dreamer's statement that he thought he was dreaming about a female body and the dream has something to do with birth. Indeed it seems to be a stylized attempt to recast the story of where babies come from. The remarkable aspect of this particular creation myth is its utter maleness. There are two men, both the dreamer, and on the inside "some little guy on a little bulldozer." These three men are responsible for the delivery of the "mummies" (the pun was obvious in the telling). The exclusively male quality of this birth is emphasized by the machines, equipment, and hierarchical authority: bulldozers, wet suits, and a foreman. But all this male efficiency and daring is going on, we gather, in and around a cavernous female body. It is here that the wishful universe of the dream begins to break down. The dream tries to maintain that instead of mummies bearing babies, in fact the bulldozer-riding homunculus is the motive force behind it all. But see how small he is. As we step back to take in the whole scene this little guy on a little bulldozer seems more and more a comic figure. And the "babies" that emerge have been long dead. The dream ended unpleasantly for the dreamer: after one shuttle trip to the surface he noticed that the Nile was crawling with snakes and in panic he refused to go down again, and then awoke. So much for male mastery over the process of birth.

Notions of androgyny are rooted in ambivalent wishes, in irreconcilable hopes. The context is one of inner conflict. This turns out to

be an element strikingly absent in the world view of the New Androgynists. One of the distinguishing characteristics of the picture they
paint for us is that it relies on bright colors. Except for an occasional
shadow added as a concession to reality, it is a purely positive image
of human potential: "Consider, first, the androgynous male. He performs spectacularly. . . . He stands firm in his opinions, he cuddles
kittens and bounces babies, and he has a sympathetic ear for someone
in distress"; again the Person For All Seasons, the individual who
combines the best of each of us and has no apparent blemishes or
even limitations.

The new ideology of androgyny achieves this shining vision of
human nature in three ways: by minimizing the importance of our
bodies, by overlooking the tenacity of our individual histories, and by
externalizing evil.

Let us consider the latter strategy first. It is a familiar human
technique, used both by individuals and by whole nations. We purify
ourselves by assembling all the bad and troubling impulses and locating them somewhere outside ourselves. We become all good and *they*
become all bad. The way this works in the ideology of androgyny is
bound up with another curious fact, something else we would have
wanted to understand about this literature: the controlling metaphor
is often that of a prison. Thus: "the restricting prison of sex role
stereotyping," "when gender no longer functions as a prison,"
"locked into," "restraints," and so forth. The image evoked is of a
good, struggling person imprisoned by a bad, oppressive society. Society or culture becomes the villain in the piece, the repository of all
that is bad. Once the ambivalence is split and apportioned in this
fashion then we can indeed be carried along by the exhilaration of
our own potential goodness and the hope of "liberation."

But the fact that this feels good doesn't make it right. Who is the
"society" that has done all these terrible things to us? Perhaps people
very like ourselves? Perhaps, in the first instance, those people we
grew up with? Were we so passive and helpless in all that, so at the
mercy of our jailors? Are we still? What this stance of blaming the
Other gains in making us feel good it loses in distorting reality. In
particular it obscures the way in which our personal characteristics
are, and have been, created in a complex interaction with the people
we care about. In terms of character structure or personality it is as

true to say that we create our society as to maintain that it creates, let alone oppresses, us.

Which brings us to the second implicit theory that supports the vision of androgyny: a strong commitment to an environmentalist stance and vigorous opposition to any implication that heredity might play a role in psychological differences between the sexes. This position follows from a dedication to the possibility of change and a belief that genetic effects are immutable while anything shaped by the environment can rather more easily be reshaped. The linking of "genetic" with fixed and "social conditioning" with malleable has a certain intuitive appeal and is heir to a much older tradition that distinguished the effects of God's will from the more arbitrary and ephemeral doings of man. However, as we have seen in chapter V, it is not a useful dichotomy. All human traits worth thinking about almost certainly develop through a complex interaction of genetic potential and life experience. And even if some aspect of our character may be due primarily to our experience with the social world, that does not therefore make it any the more easily changed.

The concept of "role" plays its subtle part here by invoking connotations of the theater, as if aspects of the way we are could be altered with about as much effort as an actor puts into learning a new part. Enough is known about human development to give us a deep respect for the formative effects of early experience. Our history is not simply grafted onto some cloistered inner "us" but rather is the very stuff, the building blocks, of our character. We shape ourselves through repeated acts of attempting to become like someone who matters to us, or to distinguish ourselves from someone we loathe. These childhood acts of loving choice are not undone without considerable grief and pain, even when we may dearly wish to change. Our character is the living residue of our loves and hatreds and we pay our past little honor by pretending we can shed it easily.

Along with minimizing the roots that our current life has in our past, the new argument for androgyny strives to put firm limits on the importance of our bodies. We have already touched on one way in which this is done, by denying that our genes set any limits on our possibilities. There is also a push to separate an idea of "self" from our bodies and then to downgrade or delimit the sphere of the body. For instance: "We envision that the future effect of sex on behavior will become as innocuous as current reactions to hair color." This simile reduces our physical maleness and femaleness to something cosmetic which can be, and often is, changed with only a trip to the drugstore.

Another recent statement begins: "By sex-role transcendence [held up here as the ideal] we mean the achievement of a dynamic and flexible orientation to life in which assigned gender is irrelevant"; the word "assigned," with its connotations of arbitrariness and reversibility, plays the same minimizing function here. Or again: "But beyond being comfortable with one's body, one's gender need have no other influence on one's behavior or on one's life style." Gender exists, this argument holds, in a different realm from behavior or "life style." And the demands of gender should be rather easily satisfied: "One's gender does dictate the nature of one's body, after all, and hence one ought to be able to take one's body very much for granted, to feel comfortable with it, and perhaps even to like it." The "perhaps" is a delightful touch. I would hope it was meant with a certain irony, but nothing in the text supports that hope. It seems that the most our bodies can hope for under the New Androgyny is a benign tolerance. As long as they don't interfere with our behavior or life style, that is.

There is a fantasy here of liberation from our physical being. As I have said, the metaphor of a prison is the characteristic description in this literature of things as they are now. Although the vision of what is to come is less clear, it involves phrases such as "a freedom of choice unhindered by sex stereotypes," "self-renewal," "self-determination," and "an unlimited range of personal destiny." Once the prison doors are thrown open we will enter a world of individual freedom and choice, the unhampered exercise of our will. Perhaps the most apocalyptic statement of this vision comes from Shulamith Firestone:

> What we shall have in the next cultural revolution is the reintegration of the Male (Technological Mode) with the Female (Aesthetic Mode), to create an androgynous culture surpassing the highs of either cultural stream, or even of the sum of their integrations. More than a marriage, rather an abolition of the cultural categories themselves, a mutual cancelation—a matter-antimatter explosion, ending with a poof! culture itself. We shall not miss it. We shall no longer need it: by then

humanity will have mastered nature totally, will have realized in *actuality* its dreams.[7]

Curiously enough, we can see here the classical notion taken to its furthest limit: not even the ancient Greeks saw *so much* power in the union of male and female that the ensuing explosion would obliterate culture and vanquish nature at one stroke. Firestone openly states the faith underlying the New Androgyny: dreams *do* come true.

The paradise pictured by the New Androgynists thus has much in common with the mythic context in which the word grew up: the hunger is for ecstatic union and an overcoming of all those boundaries that so painfully limit us.[8] But an important difference is that this more modern heaven has been brought down to earth and is held out to us as something that ordinary mortals, with the right social and mechanical technology, could really achieve. It is a promised land only to be reached through the overthrow of our bodies, since our physical existence is the most concrete and persistent reminder we have of our own limitations. While being the source of our most intense pride and pleasure, the body also speaks to us of what we most probably cannot have. The tasks we cannot accomplish, the people we cannot entice to love us, and our certain aging and death—all these are thus embodied.

Where does all this leave us? Is there anything wrong with an ideology that seeks to "liberate" people and give them a sense of an ideal future state, especially when the other alternative may sound like a counsel of despair and resignation? While admiring much of the impulse behind the New Androgyny, it seems to me that there are two things wrong. The first is that it is not true enough. We do not know so much about human life and development that we can afford to bury large chunks of hard-won knowledge. It does often appear that every advance in consciousness, especially when it aspires to a revolutionary thrust, is bought at the price of forgetting things we once knew. But to accept the disembodied, inspirational, and purely conscious psychology that the New Androgyny offers would be a considerable loss indeed. The second problem is a more practical matter, following on the first. Certainly we can all use hope, encouragement, and ideals for which to strive. But when those ideals are too close to a narcissistic fantasy rather than a real possibility, then we play a cruel trick on ourselves—cruel because the hopes we raise are unlikely to be fulfilled, but also because we will have to blame ourselves if we do not attain the goal. In this sense the call for androgyny has the same risk as the broader American ideology of freedom and opportunity: if you do not succeed the fault must lie somewhere within you, you must be either weak or bad.

Contending with our notions of the other sex, and our own inner bisexuality, can be a rich and fertile area of our life. But it is rich in part because it is not easy. It requires an effort of imagination and a tolerance of anxiety. It is clear that an overly harsh split within us between male and female is impoverishing. And rigidly exclusive definitions of male and female only increase the envy that troubles us in the first place. All this we can agree on. The part we are tempted to forget is that we work always within the limitations of our life histories and our bodies. But perhaps that isn't such a curse, since it may be that the pleasure is intimately, even perversely, connected with the struggle and that in evading the one we lose the other. In any case there seems fully enough to be done without losing ourselves in dreams of androgynous perfection.

# Appendix A

## Deprivation/Enhancement Scoring System

This scoring system was developed in order to distinguish certain patterns of emotional and physical movement described within a brief story or fantasy production. For instance, consider the following four stories: the first two were told about a picture of trapeze artists, a man and a woman, in mid-air, and the second two were told about a picture of a young bullfighter standing in the middle of the ring:

1–A: The man and woman are performing a trapeze act in a circus tent. The two people are members of a family of trapeze artists. One member of the family has recently plunged to his death during an aerial performance, and these two people are proving that the show must go on (even though a relative of theirs has died doing the same thing, e.g., the Flying Wallendas). No one has forced the two people to perform their aerial act in the face of such tragic circumstances. Thus they are doing it just for their own self-respect. They will be successful.

1–B: This is a man on a trapeze catching a woman, and they are up at the top of the tent. The man and woman are close friends. He is gripping her very tightly because there is no net below them, very dangerous. He would rather give up his own life than have her fall or miss her hands as she flew toward him. But I think that sometime from when this picture happened, sometime afterwards, that they will miss, there will be an accident. He'll drop her. She'll be crippled, or killed. The man will never forgive himself for this.

2–A: It's just before the bullfight. The matador is so frightened but he mustn't show it. He is saying a prayer that God will make him brave and that he will defeat the bull in an honorable manner. If he isn't brave in facing up to the bull he will lose the love of Theresa, a rich Spanish girl. He fears this because he's always been so poor and this is his chance to get ahead in life by becoming a famous matador and by marrying a rich woman. He has such perseverance that he will do well in life. He will defeat the bull and get Theresa.

2–B: A cocky Latin-American aristocrat has decided to be a bullfighter and achieve further eminence for his playboy name. He just lost a love battle in competition with the champion bullfighter. He wants to show his opponent in love, and the world as well, that he is the better of the two men, in fact the best man in the world. He hopes that his actions will retrieve his lover. The battle will leave the arena and be settled by a duel. The aristocrat will be killed.

If one thinks in terms of two very broad categories of experience, with Deprivation representing such negative things as suffering, failure, obscurity, or disappointment, and Enhancement representing such things as success, joy, eminence, and pleasure, then these stories can be distinguished from each other in terms of the sequence of these categories, in terms of the movement from one to the other. In each pair the first story (A) moves from Deprivation in the beginning to Enhancement at the end, and the second story (B) shows the opposite pattern. The scoring system outlined below is aimed at identifying and ranking these patterns. Since it is not possible to do word-by-word scoring with this kind of material without losing too much of the context and meaning, it is important to keep in mind the general idea of these patterns and sometimes to be willing to bend a rule slightly in order to do justice to the whole story. While satisfactory reliability between scorers has been established several times, and while I shall give examples here to try to make the various categories clear there are still bound to be large areas where it is a matter of judgment and interpretation. The scoring system has been applied successfully to stories told by children as well as adults, and both to stories that were written and ones that were given orally and either written down by the examiner or transcribed from a tape. Most of the work so far has been done with three special pictures: two trapeze artists, a bullfighter, and a middle-aged couple sitting on a bench. The scoring was developed on the trapeze picture, so many of the examples of scoring categories below have to do with acrobatics and performance. Theoretically, the scoring system could be applied to any story, but it is obvious that stories with a clear sequence of dramatic action and a definite outcome are considerably easier to score. Some preliminary work has been done in trying to apply this scoring system to the standard Murray TAT cards, with the most encouraging results being on card 1, card 3 BM, and card 15.

The first step in the pattern scoring is to establish an anchor point that determines what is before and what is after. This is called the pivotal incident (PI). It is the dramatic turning point in the story, the central act or feeling that mediates between what went before and the ultimate outcome, the fulcrum or hinge around which the story turns. The pivotal incident can be a literal fall, a mistake, a high point of desire or wishing for something, a state of tension just before what is going to happen happens, a point of decision, an intense feeling or some critical action that determines what is to come, or an interlude between past and future. If there is a change of tense in the story from present to future, the pivotal incident is usually located somewhere in that neighborhood. Phrases or sentences involving the words "climax," "peak," or "is going to" are often likely choices. It is a rare story that does not offer two or three possible pivotal incidents, and the decision must be made in terms of one's feeling for the trajectory of the story. If the outcome of the story involves a strong wish either being fulfilled or disappointed, then the statement of that wish in the story would be a logical pivotal incident. If there are two closely linked, parallel elements, both of which would be acceptable pivotal incidents in the above terms, and one is an action incident while the other is a feeling or thought, the action incident should be preferred. An emotion or thought needs to be strong and clearly related to the following action or outcome in order to be acceptable as a pivotal incident (the only exception to this rule is if taking the action incident as PI then makes the story unscorable). The pivotal incident, which is itself not scored, can be a phrase or a sentence, or even two sentences. The extent is determined by the consistency of meaning. If there is a discontinuity or shift of meaning, phrases can be split at such natural connecting points as "and," "and will," "but," and "until." Phrases that involve more than one dramatic happening and a rather definite outcome, such as "falls to the ground and dies," are usually split, with the outcome being scored as a unit. Clauses beginning with "if" (e.g., "if they are adept") are not acceptable as pivotal incidents except in the most dire straits.

There are three overall categories that stories fall into: unscorable stories, doubtful stories, and stories that are simply scored. The unscorable category should be avoided whenever possible. The emphasis is on making stories scorable, but there is always a certain percentage (five to fifteen percent in past trials) that defies scoring. These are stories that lack any action or outcome, incomplete stories where the author has just given up, or stories not having scorable units on both sides of the pivotal incident. Stories do not have to have a neat chronology or a "serious" tone in order to be scored, and one should always give the story the benefit of the doubt in this regard. Even if an outcome is given conditionally ("maybe they will succeed"), it is scored unless it is one of a number of contradictory and evenly weighted alternatives.

The "doubtful" category is simply a convenience in scoring and reliability. It identifies those stories for which the scorer has some real doubt about the proper scoring and feels that there are serious and dubious issues involved. Ordinarily, these stories are later conferred on by more than one scorer in order to arrive at the best score. But each individual scorer must first arrive at his own best possible score, since how many of these doubtful stories can be conferred upon depends on their proportion in the total group. If there are a large number of them, it is often useful to distinguish between several degrees of doubt over the proper score.

As an example of the kind of thing that might lead to marking a story doubtful, it is sometimes necessary to rearrange the time sequence of a story and treat some part of it as if it came before the pivotal incident, when on paper it comes afterwards. This rarely happens with a written story (particularly when there are short guideline questions going from past through present to future), and when the stories are told by fairly well-put-together subjects. It is most likely to happen in children's stories or in the transcript of a clinical TAT with an inquiry by the examiner. A person may tell a story with a definite outcome but then be asked by the examiner about something he said previously, or be asked how the people in the picture feel (a question referring to present state rather than future). If this inquiry brings a major elaboration or addition, it should be scored as if it were in its logical time position before the pivotal incident.

Once the pivotal incident has been located, the story is then scored for all the units (words, phrases) that fit the categories below. The important scoring distinction is between Deprivation and Enhancement. Deprivation and Enhancement units (referred to below as D and E scores) are scored throughout the story, with no limit on the number of times a given category can be scored for one story. (As was mentioned above, units within the pivotal incident are not scored.)

DEPRIVATION

1. Physical tension.
   Hunger, intense sexual desire, or other such physiological or biological needs.
2. General physical discomfort, poverty, professional or vocational obscurity.
   Illness, exhaustion, or fatigue, "just starting out," "young bullfighter," "newcomer," "losing their property" in the context of poverty.
3. Physical harm or injury.
   People being killed, shot, injured, disfigured; someone dying; concern with, or mention of, any of the former.
4. Physical exertion or striving.
   "Running endlessly for hours," "working hard," "training," "long hours of practice," "worked since they were children," "practicing a difficult act," "rehearsing to perfect the act," "trying to lead a good and hard-working life," "trying to show his courage and skill," "difficult battle"; but not "doing their act" or just "practicing" unless the context clearly connotes difficulty or long duration.
5. Falling.
   Falling, slipping, losing control in the course of a trapeze act, "going down" (except when deliberately and under control). Concern with or awareness of these things can also be scored, although something like "afraid of falling" is better scored under category 8. "Without a net" would be scored as awareness of the danger of falling (but "falls in a net" would get one D and one E score). "Thinking about dropping her" would not be scored since it is from the point of view of the dropper rather than the

dropped. The phrase "fell and killed himself" would be given two D scores. A phrase such as "she has to trust him or she'll fall" would also be scored for awareness of the danger of falling. Something like "they are thinking they won't fall" is marginal and I would be inclined not to score it—see the discussion of denial and negation below. "Jumping," "jumped off," and "leaping" are scored when a stated or clearly connoted risk, a launching of oneself into space, is involved (but "she jumped at the right time" or "she jumped into his arms" would receive E scores). "Falling in love" is not in the falling category.

6. Physical decline or defect.
   Growing weak, being "unable to," running out of ambition or skill; growing old (unless it implies something good, such as increased knowledge or comfort); being "a cripple," "ugly."

7. Failure.
   Falling short of a goal, losing one's job; "can't get along with people," "crazy," "alcoholic," "prostitute," "they just got drunk all the time," "they were poor"; dull and routine conditions or outcomes such as "it's over and they go home."

8. Negative feelings.
   Doubt, nervousness, dislike, hate, anger unless it is righteous or enjoyed, discord, fear, "bluffing," feelings of rejection, loneliness, alienation, unhappiness, despair, jealousy, envy, feeling bad about one's self, apathy, or boredom; expressions of bad feelings, such as screaming, crying, complaining, and moaning are also scored.

9. Unpleasant pressures.
   Being under orders, external compulsion, an obsession that sounds or feels alien to the person, to "have to" when there are overtones of its being against the person's wishes; command performances, "practicing for an audition," "first public performance," "fierce competition" (just having "an audience" is too weak for a score unless it's an expectant audience); being blamed, reprimanded, scolded, criticized, ridiculed, punished; being "caught" in the sense of trapped or found out, imprisoned; rejection, having one's desire directly denied; being threatened or chased; repeating the same activity over and over again when the context is one of external necessity and some negative feeling on the part of the person involved.

10. Tension, dissatisfaction, generalized desire.

   To desire, yearn, wish, "need" when it means desire; "hope" when it means wishing and a tension rather than category 7 under Enhancement; to have an urge, to seek, "he would like to be able to do it very, very well," to want to become great, to have a driving aspiration; extreme mental effort such as "concentration" in the context of danger or of striving to do well; being in a situation that demands or requires that one trust someone else (see category 5 under Enhancement); people in the process of learning something that requires courage and skill; needing to be reassured. The word "want" is sometimes not enough in itself to be scored, depending on the strength of its context; "he wants to be a trapeze artist" could be scored, especially if it is elaborated on or if the person finds his progress blocked.

11. Ignorance of something important.

   "He fails to realize," "never to consider the morality of his actions." This should be scored in the context of the specific morality given in the story.

12. Self-sacrifice.

   To give something important of one's self with no internal or external reward stated.

### ENHANCEMENT

1. Physical satisfaction.

   "Have physical contact," "sleep together" when a desire for this has been stated earlier; to sleep when one is tired, or eat when hungry; to be "well-rested."

2. Ability, physical excellence, or accomplishment.

   "Skill and daring," "powerful precision," "perfect form," "bulging sinews," "beautiful bodies," "handsome," "perfect harmony," "magnificent performance"; someone is described as an experienced or accomplished performer, "well-practiced," "finds learning easy," "mastered the trade"; the description of tricks or feats ("a double back flip").

3. Height, rising, flying, stopping a fall.

   Flying, soaring, floating, "flying trapeze," "highwire act"; being caught or saved from a fall; "luckily he fell in the net" would be scored as long as there had been a previous separate score for the element of having fallen; images such as "came up to the big time," "worked his way up," "greater heights," but not "from such heights they can only go down" or references to routine ladder climbing ("go up to the next platform" is a marginal instance that I would lean toward scoring, depending on the context). Allusions to heights such as "the crowd below watches the artists above" are scored, so long as the height reference is not a fearful one. "Swinging" is not scored but "freely swinging through the air" would be scored. "High trapeze" would be scored, but not "mid-air" or just "aerial act." "Hold" or "holding" would be scored as stopping a fall unless it is described as a continuing condition and routine part of the act. Names that include flying ("The Flying Flanigans") are not scored.

4. Growth.

To grow up, grow strong, grow fat (unless in the context of ugly or weak); "having grown up with the circus," "bigger and better."

5. Positive feeling.

Happiness, love, satisfaction, contentment; "cheerfully," "intimate relation," "close friends" but not simply "friends," "union," "join each other," "mutual concern," establishment of significant communication, "remained together quite a while"; a positive attitude toward one's self, feeling "free" or expansive, excitement, "fascination" when the context is positive, pleasant memories; expressions of positive feeling, such as laughing, are also scored. References to "trust" bring up complicated issues with the trapeze picture. The basic question is whether trust is something that *exists,* in which case it would be scored under this category, or whether it is *required* in the sense of Deprivation category number 10; phrases such as "they must trust each other" are ambiguous and cannot be scored unless the context indicates whether the author means that these people are *forced* to trust each other, which would be Deprivation category 10, or whether he means that they obviously *do* trust each other because they're doing what they're doing, which would be scored here. Instances such as "they derive immense pleasure from the trust that is demanded" would be scored only for the positive pleasure element.

6. Positive shift in tension level.

"Relieved," "her tension will become less and less," "adjust," "get used to," "he's lived with fear so long it doesn't bother him"; to forget about a negative experience, to relax, or recuperate.

7. Positive anticipation.

To be looking forward to something expectantly, "readiness," to be confident, to have faith in someone; "hope to" is scorable if there is a positive context, an indication that the hopeful outcome is expected or taken for granted rather than just desired or wished for; dreams of grandeur, the imagining of glory or fame, are scored here rather than in category 10 under Deprivation, since it is a matter of imagining the goal, of mentally leaping over obstacles in an unreal way; the description of someone as "pompous" implies some of these qualities and would be scored here; also something like "the crowd is watching for extraordinary feats" if the context is one of confident expectation.

8. Receiving help, affection, or concern.

To have someone concerned for you, to have someone "grateful," to receive a wanted gift or help, to be loved or mourned, to have someone wish you well or be concerned with your well-being; someone trying to save someone else; "finally get their chance," "asked to join the circus"; to stick together in the face of trouble, to work together as a team in a positive context that is more than just "in the past they have worked together"; being trained by someone to do something well ("she trained him to do the whole act").

9. Success.

"Successful," to achieve one's goal or desire, to win, to be "very good," "was accepted," "wealthy"; only facts are scored here and not desires or wishes. This can include the "completion of the act" if the sense is of success or if the outcome was in doubt. Names such as "The Great Zambini" also are scored.

10. Publicity, attention, fame.

"Big publicity," "received many awards," to receive applause or attention, "a huge crowd has come to see him," "he has a large following," to be respected, to be famous, "parading about," "star billings," "the biggest act in the circus," "playing in Madison Square Garden" (but not just "performing in front of a crowd").

11. Revenge, retaliation, successful resistance.

Avenging one's self, overcoming obstacles, escaping, courage in the face of danger, carrying on some desired activity in the face of adversity or previous trouble, successfully holding out for what you want.

12. Insight, realization.

Achieving an awareness, recognizing a previously unknown fact or situation even if it is a negative one, understanding, "one day they realized they hadn't been doing what they really wanted to do with their lives." The "awareness of danger" only is not enough for a score in this category.

The examples given under each category above are by no means exhaustive. Every group of stories will provide many specific phrases that are not listed above but that fit the meanings of the categories. The examples above are guidelines rather than absolute definitions.

Since the scoring system does not go mechanically word by word, questions come up about how many scorable units there are within a given phrase or sentence. In order to have more than one unit scored there must be independent elements with clearly separate meanings. For instance: "They are poor, tired, sad" would receive three scores since these three words refer to clearly different things; "she has been shunned or humiliated by her lover" would receive only one score because "shunned" and "humiliated" are rather close in meaning and because it is not clearly stated that they both happened but rather that one or the other did. "He is very sure of himself that he will, as always, be able to maintain their balance" would receive two scores, but "he feels sure that he can keep their balance" would receive only one. "Fantasies of warmth, love, tenderness" is a more difficult instance where I would incline toward one score since I think it is only a global, fuzzy feeling of comfort being referred to, but it would also be possible to argue for two scores—three separate scores would be too many.

A similar issue comes up with repetition in a story. Restatement of a given unit or phrase is not scored when it appears to be simply narrative or dramatic repetition (involving exactly the same words and usually occurring in the same paragraph or section of the story). This rule holds even if the repeated phrase is applied to another character. For instance, "she's tired too" would not be scored in a story where "he's tired" has already been scored. Exceptions to this rule against scoring repetitions are direct statements about flying and about falling (in stories about the trapeze card) and direct references to death (excluding, however, the death of the bull in stories about the bullfighter picture).

There are some references for which one must be careful not to read in positive feelings. For instance, such things as "physical contact," "married," and "affair" are only scored if there was previously a stated desire for this outcome or if happiness or pleasure is implied (thus the phrase "love affair" would be scored because of the connotations of love). If, however, the happiness or pleasure is openly stated in the same phrase, then the happiness or pleasure is scored as a unit and the rest ignored. In general, such a construction as "they take great pleasure from . . ." would be scored only for the pleasure unless what they're taking pleasure from is strong or striking in its own right (for example, "they take great pleasure from being the best trapeze artists in the world," or "they were very happy about the news of their lifetime contract," both of which would receive two scores, whereas "he's glad that his grip is firm" would receive one score).

Sometimes the author of a story will go out of his way to deny the possibility of something bad happening. One wants to be able to score strong instances of this because the fact of having to bring it up and deny it shows that such a thought has at least occurred to the storyteller. But this scoring of denial or negation as a deprivation must be reserved for very strong instances. Negating references to falling, blood, and death would be scored ("they will not die," "there will be no blood on the floor of the circus ring"). One does not split units here the way one would in positive instances, and thus the phrase "they don't fall and die" would receive only one score. "There will be no tragedies" and "I don't see a sad ending" are both weaker examples but ones that I would lean toward scoring. "They are thinking that they won't fall" is too weak to be scored.

When there is an introjection of the author's first-person comments into a third-person story, such as "they lived happily ever after. I can't believe it all turned out so well," the first-person phrase should be scored for the emotion connoted (in this case for the negation) and the change in point of view ignored.

The numerical scoring of units is done on the basis of their position before and after the pivotal incident, and is arranged such that a story moving from Deprivation to Enhancement receives a positive score and a story moving from Enhancement to Deprivation receives a negative score. A Deprivation unit before the PI is scored $+1$, an Enhancement unit before the PI is scored $-1$. A Deprivation unit after the PI is scored $-1$, and an Enhancement unit after the PI is scored $+1$. The unit scores are summed to get a score for the whole story. The mean of any group of stories is not necessarily zero, this being dependent on the particular group of people and the picture used. No distinction is made between relative and absolute shifts: that is, a story with twice as much Deprivation before the PI as it has after it could receive a score equivalent to a story having a small amount of Deprivation before the PI and a small amount of Enhancement after it.

Occasionally a story will have two independent themes, involving several heroes and a different outcome for each, or two very different possible outcomes. Such a case may have two separate pivotal incidents or only one, depending on the degree of divergence of the themes. These kinds of productions can be treated as two separate stories, with a score for each and the final score for the subject being the average of these two separate scores. Double-theme stories should be rare and a story should not be scored this way unless there are two very clearly divergent story lines. A story that is scored as a double theme should always be put in the doubtful category. Only one of the themes need have scorable units after the pivotal incident in order for the whole story to be scored in this fashion.

# Appendix B

EMPIRICAL STUDIES OF DEPRIVATION/ENHANCEMENT
FANTASY PATTERNS

Bramante, Michael. "Sex Differences in Fantasy Patterns: A Replication and Elaboration." Ph.D. dissertation, City University of New York, 1970.

Bramante was curious whether D/E patterns would be affected by a deliberate attempt to enhance people's sense of their own gender. The scheme he evolved was to recruit about sixty male and sixty female undergraduates, divide them randomly into two groups, and then treat each of these groups to a private showing of a film in a rented commercial theater. The so-called experimental group watched a romantic film including sexual love (it was not, we are assured, pornographic), while the "control" group got Laurel and Hardy. Immediately after the film each group was given a written form of the TAT with the trapeze, bullfighter, and dejected couple pictures. The notion underlying this experimental design was that the experimental group would be stimulated by the film into a heightened awareness of their own gender and sexuality, and we might then see whether D/E patterns are sensitive to such feelings.

Bramante's control group showed a highly significant sex difference when males and females were compared on the average score for all three pictures (for comparative purposes we may note that the mean scores on the trapeze picture alone were $+.77$ for the women and $-.59$ for the men). And Bramante found that the arousing film increased even further this D/E difference between the sexes. For instance, if we categorize people as having positive or negative D/E scores, in the control group fifteen out of twenty-five men and nineteen out of twenty-five women were in the category predicted for their sex; in the experimental group these proportions rise to twenty-six of thirty-one women and twenty-three of twenty-nine men. In the experimental group the mean scores on the trapeze picture are $+1.90$ for the women and $-1.89$ for the men. An analysis of variance showed statistically significant effects both for the experimental treatment and for the particular picture. As was true in the first validating study, the overall baseline shifts from picture to picture, with the shift being in the negative direction for the bullfighter picture and in the positive direction with the couple. Regardless of this absolute shift, each picture shows a significant difference between the sexes, and in Bramante's study each picture responded the same way to the experimental condition.

Bramante went on to look more carefully at what the experimental change consisted of. Still comparing the romantic film situation with the comedy, the major effect is that the romantic film prompts women to invent stories with an even greater preponderance of deprivation before the pivotal incident, and it prompts men to tell stories with greater deprivation after the pivotal incident. This is useful information since we might have thought, for instance, that the experimental effect could as well have been due to the distribution of references to joy and satisfaction. But no, the arousing film works on the balance and position of suffering in the story. And it works especially on men. Statistically the greater part of the difference between the two groups is that after watching the romantic film the men are much more uniformly "male" in their scores. Bramante had previously asked his participants to fill out a questionnaire comparing themselves to their own idea of the "usual" man or woman. This enabled him to show that in the experimental group, but not in the control group, it is those men who see themselves as least typically masculine who write the most extreme "masculine" stories. Bramante goes on to argue that what has happened here is that a group of defensively nonassertive men, the type who produced non-male scores in the control group, have been goaded by the romantic film into facing previously avoided sexual facts and they respond with stories full of disastrous outcomes.

Cramer, Phebe, and Bryson, Jane. "The Development of Sex-Related Fantasy Patterns. *Developmental Psychology* 8, no. 1 (1973):131–34.

They compared a group of children with an average age of five and a half years to a group of children with an average age of nine and a half years (the groups were equally divided between boys and girls, and their backgrounds and intelligence were comparable to Saunders's children—see below.) Testing was done individually and the pictures used were the trapeze, a child running, and two pictures from the standard Murray TAT (a man clinging to a rope and a young child looking at a violin). The overall results of this carefully done study are quite confirming. The young children do not show a significant sex difference in D/E patterns, while the older children do. And, as with Saunders's work, it is the girls who change more, with their scores becoming significantly more positive over the age range covered here (the difference in scores between the five and nine-year-old boys is not significant).

The general sex and age trends found by Cramer and Bryson held true when they looked separately at the different pictures, but the pattern of statistical significance was a bit more complicated. Although the spread between the sexes on the trapeze card increased from 1.5 points in the younger group to over two points in the older group, yet because of a large increase in the variance of the older boys' scores the sex difference was not significant for them while it was significant for the younger group. The other three pictures all reveal a significant age effect with girls but not with boys. Cramer and Bryson conclude: "The results of this study provide strong support for the hypothesis that boys and girls, at the time they are entering school, do not show the sex-related patterns of fantasy that have been found to differentiate adult men and women. However, by the age of about 9 years, sexual differentiation in fantasy patterns is clearly evident [and] . . . it is the female child who changes." [p. 133]

Cramer, Phebe, and Hogan, Katherine. "Sex Differences in Verbal and Play Fantasy. *Developmental Psychology* 11 no. 2 (1975): 145–54. See also Phebe Cramer, "The Development of Play and Fantasy in Boys and Girls," *Psychoanalysis and Contemporary Science* 4 (1975):529–67.

Forty children of average age five and a half and forty children of average age eleven and a half were tested individually, using the trapeze picture and the picture of a man climbing a rope. With both pictures the sex difference was negligible in the younger group but highly significant in the older group (the trapeze means for the older group were −1.72 and +5.14 respectively). The older girls were more "female" in D/E than the younger girls to a highly significant extent, while the older boys showed only a tendency toward more "male" scores than the younger boys. The bulk of Cramer and Hogan's paper is given over to an interesting investigation of sex differences in play construction. The only part of that which should be mentioned here is that they found

no relation between this more concrete mode of expression and the
D/E patterns.

## Cramer, Phebe, and Carter, Trudy. "The Relationship between Sexual Identification and the Use of Defense Mechanisms. *Journal of Personality Assessment* 42 (1978):63–73.

By using an inventory of preferences and attitudes as a measure of
conscious "sex-role adoption" and D/E as a measure of less conscious
"gender identity," Cramer and Carter wished to prove that these are
indeed two independent levels, and more importantly to investigate the
relationship of each to a series of psychological "defense mechanisms"
or modes of coping with stress. Since the latter are presumed to be
rooted in one's character and strongly influenced by nonconscious factors, they expected defenses to be related to D/E but not to the more
superficial measure of sexual identity.

Fifty female and fifty male college students responded to the trapeze
picture, an interest and attitude scale, and a measure of typical defense
mechanisms. As we have come to expect by now, there was a highly
significant difference between men and women in D/E scores ($-0.04$
versus $+3.92$; we have no explanation at hand for the unusually high
score of these college women). While the interest and attitude questionnaire also discriminated men and women, scores on it had no
significant relation to D/E scores. Cramer and Carter conclude that
one can indeed think of sex-role adoption and gender identity as two
independent levels of sexual identity.

While the interest and attitude scores were not related to the use of
particular defense mechanisms, there were interesting linkages between
defenses and D/E (the brief summary I am about to give is by no means
an adequate substitute for a close reading of the original paper). Of the
five defenses measured, two turned out to be typically male: Turning
Against the Object (dealing with conflict by blaming or attacking
someone) and Projection (seeing a specific malevolent other person as
the root of the difficulty). Two were definitely more female: Turning
Against the Self (self-blame, feeling responsible and at fault) and Principalization (diluting one's feelings through rationalization or an appeal
to abstract principle). Reversal (various modes of denying that one ever
felt bad in the first place) was marginally female.

Women high on Reversal are also significantly higher (more in the
female direction) in D/E scores. Men high on the typically male
defense of Projection are significantly more in the male direction on
D/E. With the other three defenses the pattern is a cross-sex one.

Males who were high on the typically female defense of Turning Against the Self scored more in the female direction on D/E; women who scored high on the typically male defense of Turning Against the Object also were significantly more in the male direction on D/E. Likewise men who frequently indulged in the statistically more female defense of Principalization were more female on D/E than men low on Principalization.

These results fully deserve the careful attention and space that the authors give them, and we cannot repeat that here. For now let us quote Cramer and Carter: ". . . it is clear that the use of defenses is related to gender identity as measured by D/E. The two female groups with the most feminine gender identity scores were those who were high scorers on the feminine defense of Reversal and those who were low scorers on the male defense of Turning Against the Object. Similarly, the two male groups with the most masculine gender identity scores were those who were high scorers on the masculine defense of Projection and those who were low scorers on the female defense of Principalization, followed closely by those who were low scorers on the female defense of Turning Against the Self."

Fakouri, M. Ebrahim. "Relationship Among Differences In Fantasy Pattern, IQ, And Sex-Role Adoption." *Psychological Reports* 44 (1979):775–781

In testing thirty boys and thirty girls in early grade school, Fakouri found that the predicted sex difference in fantasy patterns appears from age eight or nine years on. He found that D/E patterns were not related to intelligence, and not related to teachers' ratings of masculinity, but they were related to teachers' ratings of femininity.

Johnson, Jeffrey. "The Measurement of the Development of Sex Differences." Honor's thesis, Williams College, 1974.

Johnson's work adds another successful replication with young adults, and some evidence for the independence of the D/E measure from questionnaire-type measures of sex-role adherence. Johnson tested fifty male and fifty female college students. He employed the rope climber and trapeze pictures. The former yielded a significant sex difference and the latter an highly significant one (means of +1.94 and −1.54). A curious sidelight is that he also inquired about siblings and found that having an older brother is associated, in men, with more "masculine" scores. But the main question he was asking was whether D/E scores would be related to scores on two standardized tests which assess the degree to which one's interests, activities and vocational goals fit the usual sex-role stereotypes. One of these was the same test used in my 1969 study, below. Johnson expected to find that D/E patterns would not be related to these other measures, arguing that D/E is concerned with a more private, "inner" aspect of sexual identity. His expectation was confirmed.

Malmaud, Roslyn. "Sex Differences in Fantasy Patterns: A Replication And Refinement." Master's thesis, Department of Psychology, University of Massachusetts, 1975.

Malmaud set out to test her notion that the previous results had been due to the nature of the trapeze picture, and that a redrawing of the picture that put the male acrobat in the more dependent and physically unsupported position would reverse the usual D/E sex difference. Her hypothesis was not confirmed in that there was no significant difference between the stories evoked by the redrawn picture and those evoked by the standard one. However, her group of fifty college students also failed to show a significant difference between men and women (the means on the standard trapeze were +1.39 for men and +1.75 for women). These subjects also showed atypical patterns on a standardized test of personality traits, with the women being higher than the men on the need to achieve and the wish to dominate. So there is some reason to think of Malmaud's group as unusual.

In spite of the lack of overall sex difference Malmaud was able to look at some of the correlates of D/E. Still using a standard inventory, the Gough Adjective Check List, she found that the best predictor of a woman's D/E score was her score on the scale "Nurturance" (defined as the wish to engage in behaviors that provide material or emotional benefits to others). Other positive factors in female D/E scores were Succorance (the wish to solicit sympathy, affection, or emotional support from others) and Endurance (the tendency to persist). A woman's D/E score was negatively related to her scores on the need for Achievement (to strive to be outstanding in some publicly valued way), Autonomy (to act independently of others and of social values or expectations), Exhibitionism (to elicit the immediate attention of others), and Deference (to seek and maintain a subordinate role in relation to others). In the male instance, the only useful predictor of D/E was the need for Achievement: the higher that need the more "male" the D/E score.

May, Robert. "Sex Differences in Fantasy Patterns." *Journal of Projective Techniques and Personality Assessment* 30 no. 6 (1966): 576–86.

This first attempt to validate the Deprivation/Enhancement method of looking at thematic material used one hundred and four college students, sixty of them female. Along with the main aim of seeing whether the scoring system would reveal the predicted sex difference, it seemed a good idea to broaden the range of pictures involved. So to the trapeze picture were added a picture of a young bullfighter walking in the ring with an expression that could be either arrogance or fear, a picture of a dejected, shabby couple slumped on a stone bench, and a picture of a child running or leaping in a field. The students came from a large urban university, a large college of engineering, and a small, private women's college. They were tested in a classroom context and were asked to write a brief story about each of the four pictures. Taking the average score for these four stories, there was a highly significant difference, in the predicted direction, between men and women (the female mean score was +.80 and the male mean −.24). If we ask only about the proportion of positive and negative scores, the difference between men and women is still highly significant (dropping those with scores of zero, forty-three of fifty-nine women have positive scores and twenty-six of forty-one men have negative scores). Looking at the four pictures separately, we find that all but the last showed a significant sex difference (the means for the trapeze picture alone were −.71 and +.79)—the picture of the child does not, perhaps because that picture tended to evoke rather stereotyped rhapsodic tales from these college-aged people.

A number of other questions were asked in this first study, to try to ensure that the scoring system was measuring what we wanted it to. Were we simply picking up optimism versus pessimism? When we looked at the total number of Deprivation units and the total number of Enhancement units for each of the three significant pictures, only one of these six comparisons yielded even a marginally significant sex difference. The overall emotional tone of the story was not determining the result. What about the possibility that women are taught to believe more in the traditional happy ending—could our scoring system be measuring only this? Most likely not, since a comparison of the scores for the part of the story before the pivotal incident yielded a significant sex difference for the first two pictures and a tendency toward significance for the third. Only a pattern hypothesis seems adequate to the data.

May, Robert. "Deprivation-Enhancement Fantasy Patterns in Men and Women." *Journal of Projective Techniques and Personality Assessment* 33 no. 5 (1969):464–69.

This study aimed at both a replication of the original result and a first step in connecting these fantasy patterns with other aspects of the person. The group studied was smaller (sixteen men and eighteen women) and somewhat older than with the first study (fewer than half of them were students). Only the trapeze picture was used and rather than being written the stories were told, and tape-recorded, in the context of individual sessions, which included a lengthy personal interview. With this smaller group it was possible to match the men and women carefully for age, intelligence, and social class (none of these factors was significantly related to D/E scores).

Again there was a significant sex difference in fantasy score (trapeze picture means of $+.89$ for the women and $-2.25$ for the men). The interview paid particular attention to impressions of one's parents, what it was like to grow up as a boy or girl, and current feelings about one's gender. This is the picture that emerged of the man who shows a strongly "male" D/E pattern (as compared to less extreme men): he sees his father as a very "masculine" figure and views him with admiration and awe; the father is described as tough and/or competent and the son strives to be like him or to prove his own worth next to the father. The son reports passing through a period of uneasiness about his manliness, an anxious period when he was stung by mockery or abuse from other boys or by rejection on the part of a girl. He needs to feel in control and assertive and thinks that men are properly "the boss" as far as women are concerned. He refers to the extraordinary pressure that men feel to prove their competence and sees this as one of the liabilities of the male role. He speaks of envy for women's supposed greater warmth and ability to depend on others. And on a rating of sex-role discontent (derived from the interview) the more "male" D/E score is significantly related to greater discontent. In line with this, there was a positive relationship between a male D/E score and "masculinity" as rated by a test that focuses on conscious sex-typed aspirations and on the tendency to deny any fears or timidity—in general a test on which a highly "masculine" score indicates self-conscious toughness and bravado.

For a woman a more "female" D/E score is associated with a perception of her mother as demanding conformity to a definition of girls as "nice," loving and well-behaved. Also, the woman herself talks of disliking the notion that women should be quiet and responsive and stifle their own initiative, especially where men are concerned. She either openly envies men or reports a happy period of being a "tomboy" before being forced to become more "feminine."

Thus for both sexes it seems that more extreme D/E patterns are associated with a feeling of strain and dissatisfaction about one's gender. One of the ways in which this comes about *may* be seen in an unexpected and puzzling finding: in both sexes the people with the more extreme and traditional fantasy patterns report that they felt isolated, lonely, and cut off from peers in early adolescence. Being mindful of Harry Stack Sullivan's comments about the crucial role of a "chum" relationship (see chapter VI), we can entertain the hunch that these people were thrown into the sexually demanding turmoil of adolescence without having had an intimate relationship in which they could find out that their particular frailties are shared and that one need not always live up to an ideal image of maleness or femaleness.

May, Robert. "A Method for Studying the Development of Gender Identity." *Developmental Psychology* 5 (1971):484–87. See the reference to Jean Saunders, below.

May, Robert. "Further Studies on Deprivation/Enhancement Patterns. *Journal of Personality Assessment* 39 (1975):116–22.

There are three projects here, all attempts to explore the limits and correlates of D/E in various clinical groups. The first asked whether the patterns would hold up in people diagnosed schizophrenic. Seventeen men and fifteen women were selected. They had been hospitalized for a relatively short time (seventeen to twenty weeks) with a diagnosis of acute schizophrenia. All were, at the time of testing, sufficiently recovered to be in the process of returning to school or work. These people were matched for age, intelligence, and social class with the group cited in my 1969 study above. The men who had been schizophrenic scored −1.53 on the trapeze and the women −0.20. These scores are significantly different from each other, even though in absolute terms the women score slightly on the negative side. Comparing these scores with the matched group of nonpatients we see that they are less extreme than, but not significantly different from, the "normal" group. Thus the D/E phenomenon is lessened, but still present, in a recently schizophrenic group.

If D/E patterns are an expression of some aspect of sexual identity, we would expect them to vary along with major shifts in sexual orienta-

tion. Putting aside for the moment a number of complex questions
about levels of sexual identity and their relation to sexual behavior, one
working hypothesis is that male homosexuality would be associated with
a more "female" D/E pattern. To test this, the trapeze picture was
used as part of a more extensive TAT series in a study of treatment
methods for homosexuality. (For a description of the project and the
subjects, see Lee Birk, Bertram Cohler, William Huddleston, and Elizabeth Miller, "Avoidance Conditioning for Homosexuality," *Archives of
General Psychiatry* 25 (1971):314–23. My thanks to Bert Cohler for
including the trapeze picture.) The subjects were fourteen young men
(average age, twenty-three) who had requested psychotherapy. All but
one were in college or graduate school at the time and the mean IQ
of the group was estimated to be between 115 and 120. "Homosexual"
was defined for the purposes of this project as someone who reported
deriving most of his sexual pleasure from contacts with other men and
was "active/promiscuous" (and, of course, unhappy enough with this
state of affairs to seek treatment). The mean D/E score for this group
was +.71, the most "female" score of any male group tested to date.
In deciding on the best comparison group we could make a case either
for using the men in the 1969 study or, if we wanted to emphasize the
"patient" status of this homosexual group and their probable anxiety
and unhappiness, the recently schizophrenic men we just finished discussing. The homosexual group is significantly more "female" in score
than either of these possible comparison groups.

  In the work so far, D/E scoring had been done without any attempt
to define who the hero of a story might be. We assumed that all the
characters are in some degree expressions of the author's feelings and
expectations. But a reading of the stories told by these homosexual
young men suggested that the D/E pattern might vary according to the
sex of the central figure. Some simple rules were established to determine whether the hero or central figure in the trapeze story was the
male acrobat, the female acrobat, or an anonymous and neuter "they."
Although the numbers in each group are of necessity very small, the
results were suggestive: for the homosexual group the two "he" stories
have a mean score of −2, the seven "they" stories +.71, and the five
"she" stories +1.80. This is in contrast to the 1969 comparison group
that has seven male-identified stories (−3.14), six neuter stories
(−3.33), and three female-identified stories (+1.67). It becomes clear
that the overall difference between the homosexual and nonhomosexual
groups is due both to the distribution of identification (the homosexuals
telling more "she" stories and the others more "he" stories) and to the

fact that the neutral or undifferentiated story is more female in pattern for the homosexual group and more male in pattern for the non-homosexual group. We might say that the homosexual young men equate the general case with the female while the nonhomosexuals see the general as another example of the male pattern.

The last part of this series of studies was undertaken to further explore the personality context and correlates of D/E patterns. We shall give it more space because it is rather more complex than the other 1975 projects. The subjects were thirty-two women and twenty-nine men who were patients at a private residential center for intensive psychotherapy.

The men were somewhat older than the women, with an average age of twenty-seven as opposed to twenty-three, but otherwise the sexes were similar: their average IQ level was between 110 and 120, and their socioeconomic background was upper-middle to upper class. There was considerable variation in the length of "patienthood" when tested, with a range from two weeks to over four years. There was also a wide spread in diagnosis, from neurosis or character disorder to acute schizophrenia. The routine of the institution involved psychological testing within six weeks after admission and at yearly intervals thereafter. For the period of a year, every willing patient who came up for routine testing was also given a D/E TAT.

The major predictions were:

1. The "hysterical" end of the diagnostic continuum will be associated with more positive (Deprivation leading to Enhancement) D/E scores and the "obsessive-compulsive" end with more negative scores. In brief, this expectation is based on the correspondance between hysterical character traits and an exaggeration of the stereotyped female role: emotionality, seductiveness, dependence, a disinclination for "rational" thinking, and a combination of seeming helplessness with impressive interpersonal skills and impact. Likewise the obsessional end of the diagnostic range, with its emphasis on rationality, competence, impersonal objectivity, self-control, and power, is an extreme example of the stereotyped male role. No relationship was predicted between D/E scores and psychosis, a functional dimension relatively independent of character type.
2. "Field dependence" will be associated with more positive (deprivation leading to enhancement) D/E scores. Field dependence/independence is a perceptual and cognitive dimension that has been

extensively studied by Witkin and his co-workers. In its simplest form it refers to the ability, or inclination, to make judgments irrespective of the perceptual context—for instance, to identify the "true" vertical while sitting in an artificially tilted room or, the measure used in this case, to pick out a simple figure hidden in a confusing and competing perceptual field. Witkin's work has shown that men do this more readily than women.

3. D/E scores will be related to other likely indicators of sexual identity. Specifically, D/E scores more in the direction typical of one's own sex will be associated with: drawing a same sex figure when asked to draw "a person," the degree of sexual differentiation shown in figure drawings, and a sex-appropriate Semantic Differential (Osgood, et al.) rating of the concept "me" on a scale of "masculine-feminine."

Turning to the results, the D/E sex difference in this group turns out to be a tenuous one. The means were +.82 for women and −.35 for men, which is only marginally significant (in large part due to an unusual amount of variation within the female group). One might argue that it shouldn't be surprising to find sexual identities blurred in a group that, whatever else may be true, consists of people with psychological difficulties. But this seems too simple in view of our previous findings with a schizophrenic sample. There must certainly be differences between people who, as in the previous study, have reorganized themselves after an acute schizophrenic episode and are beginning to reenter their ordinary lives, and the subjects in this study who typically were entering, or in the middle of, lengthy intensive treatment (and whose difficulties were most often long-standing character problems). But such post hoc speculation seems of little use. It is worth noting that the present group also failed to show the usual sex difference in field dependence scores.

There were no significant relationships between D/E score and age, intelligence or social class.

The specific predictions were tested separately for men and women, with the expectation that there might be different patterns of relationship for the two sexes. The results will be summarized by prediction:

1. The diagnosis used was the psychological test diagnosis as entered in the patient's clinical record, arrived at independent of any knowledge of D/E scores. Two groups of categories were set up. The first classified subjects as nonpsychotic (neuroses, character disorders, etc.), psychotic (primarily "schizophrenia" but also including "borderline" states and "schizophrenic character"), or paranoid (which

in all cases but one involved also being diagnosed psychotic). The second classification referred to the character type, or basic personality, in the diagnosis, with the categories of primary interest being "hysterical" and "obsessive-compulsive." As might be expected, the most popular character diagnosis for women was hysterical (fourteen out of the twenty-seven women who received a character diagnosis) and for males it was obsessive-compulsive (fourteen out of twenty-two), thus lending weight to the link between sex roles and diagnosis suggested above. Men and women did not differ in the proportion of psychotic-nonpsychotic diagnoses, although it did appear that "paranoid" is primarily a male attribute (ten out of the twenty-nine men, and no women).

There was no significant difference in D/E scores within either sex along the nonpsychotic/psychotic/paranoid dimension, although there was a suggestion that, as previously, psychosis is associated with a lessened sex difference in D/E patterns. Only two men were diagnosed as hysterical and although the means are in the predicted direction, the difference in D/E scores between hysterical men and obsessive-compulsive men ($-.50$ versus $-.71$) naturally does not begin to approach significance. But with the women, the hysterical group had scores significantly further in the female direction ($2.45$ versus $-1.07$ for the obsessive-compulsive women). The highly "female" score of the hysterical group is, so far, matched only by the preadolescent girls studied by Saunders and by Cramer.

2. Field dependence was measured by the Embedded Figures Test. There was no significant correlation between field dependence and D/E for either men or women. But an inspection of the data suggested that a few extreme cases might be obscuring a more general pattern. Splitting the female group into those who have positive D/E scores (twelve women) and those who have negative D/E scores (ten women), one finds that the field dependence scores are significantly different. Women with positive D/E scores are more field dependent than women with negative D/E scores, in line with the prediction. The results for the men are in the opposite direction but not statistically significant due to the small number of subjects and large variance within the groups.

3. All but three subjects had drawn human figures as part of their routine clinical testing. Although the sex of the first drawing has had a rather checkered career as far as empirical research is concerned, yet it has an appealing validity on the face of it: it *ought* to be significant whether someone draws a figure of the same or the other sex when asked simply to "draw a person." And it has been a

consistent finding that at all ages a majority of men draw a man first
and a majority of women draw a woman first. In this study the mean
D/E score for women who drew a woman first was $+2.54$ while for
those who drew a man or a totally ambiguous figure first it was
$-.71$. This difference is statistically significant. The male group
produced far fewer opposite-sex or ambiguous first drawings (only
nine out of twenty-seven) and the difference between the D/E
means was not significant. The figure drawings were also rated on
a simple five-point scale according to the degree of sexual differentiation present, and then given a score for the number of specific
gender attributes (genitals, sex-typed clothes, etc.); neither of these
measures correlated with D/E in either women or men.

May, Robert. "Mood Shifts and the Menstrual Cycle." *Journal of
Psychosomatic Research* 20 (1976):125–30.

Among other things this study looked at whether D/E patterns in
women varied according to the phase of the menstrual cycle. In this
group of thirty young women, they did not.

McClelland, David, and Watt, Norman. "Sex-Role Alienation in
Schizophrenia." *Journal of Abnormal Psychology* 73 (1968):226–39.

McClelland and Watt report that a group of working-class housewives
show a preponderance of "feminine" (positive) D/E patterns, but that
women who are employed do not. They also found a reversal of the
usual patterns in men and women diagnosed schizophrenic. These
interesting results are hard to interpret because McClelland and Watt
do not use the standard scoring system for D/E. It is thus not clear
whether their results are comparable with the rest of the literature.

Rabinovitz, Sharon. "The Relationship of Expectancy of Success and
Performance to Fear of Failure, Fear of Success, and Deprivation-
Enhancement in Men and Women." Master's thesis, Department of
Psychology, University of Miami, 1976.

One hundred thirty-one male and 115 female introductory psychology
students in a large southern university had virtually identical mean D/E
scores (both means were positive). While this part of the study remains
puzzling, there is much else of interest. Rabinovitz started with the
well-established finding in psychological research that men typically
overestimate their probability of success in a task while women typically
underestimate it. This is true even when the task is virtually meaning-

less and when both groups have been given the same "feedback" about their actual success during a trial run. Rabinovitz wondered whether there might be a relation between D/E and these patterns of expectancy. She predicted, and found, a significant negative correlation in both men and women. Translated this means that the male D/E pattern goes with tending to overestimate one's chances, while the female D/E pattern goes with underestimating. This makes considerable sense if we look at it thusly: someone who habitually overestimates his chances of success is arranging a continuous series of incidents of high hopes followed by disappointment, a constant repetition of the male fantasy pattern; someone who habitually underestimates her chances of succeeding is arranging a repeated confirmation of the notion that worry, doubt, or demeaning oneself can be followed by a pleasant surprise. Without trying to decide which might come first, Rabinovitz's results point to a striking parallel between fantasy patterns and habitual levels of expectation.

Saarni, Carolyn. "Social-Cohort Effect on Three Masculinity-Feminity Instruments and Self-Report." *Psychological Reports* 38 (1976):1111–18.

She studied four groups of women: nursing trainees, undergraduate psychology students, skilled workers, and "feminists." These groups differed considerably in average age (ranging from twenty for the psychology students to forty-three for the skilled workers) and education (twelve and a half years for the workers, eighteen and a half for the feminists). While this represents a complication in Saarni's experimental design, since it confounds different variables, for our purposes it affords another glimpse at whether the assumed D/E patterns exist outside the rather young and highly educated groups of adults with whom most of the work has so far been done. Scores on the bullfighter picture did not differentiate the four groups in this study, but scores on the trapeze picture did. The feminists came out slightly negative $(-.48)$, the nurses and psychology students slightly positive $(+.20$ and $+.58)$, and the skilled workers highly positive $(+3.18)$. Saarni's main purpose was to study "masculinity" and "femininity" on a number of different levels so she had her subjects fill out the Gough Femininity scale (the same measure used in May, 1969, and Johnson, 1974), a structured self-rating on various sex-stereotypic traits, and an unstructured self-report of the degree of one's femininity.

Her basic argument is marred by the assumption that differences between groups must be due to the effect of belonging to that group (what she refers to as a "social-cohort effect") rather than the just as

plausible notion that people with different interests and character structure choose different occupations and associates. But this flaw need not
interfere with using her data to learn more about the correlates of D/E.
We see that the trapeze stories order the groups in the same series as
do Saarni's other measures of femininity: the feminists are least "feminine," the nurses and psychology students next, and the skilled workers
most feminine. At the same time there is a difference in level of
measurement. The three self-report measures, all relatively transparent
in terms of what they are asking, are significantly related to each other.
But the D/E measure is uncorrelated with any of them. This is consistent with the findings of Johnson and of Cramer and Carter. In Saarni's
results all measures of femininity, including D/E, are correlated with
education. The more years one has spent in school the lower the
"femininity" score. We must keep in mind, however, the fact that one
cannot partial out in this study the influence of education as opposed
to group membership, occupation, or basic personality structure.

## Saunders, Jean. Reported in May (1971) and May (1975).

The first investigation of D/E scores in children was carried out by Jean
Saunders. She studied a group of seventy-five third through fifth graders
(forty-six girls and twenty-nine boys) in a predominantly white and
middle-class school. As part of a "creative writing" class they were asked
to make up stories about the trapeze and bullfighter pictures. The
predicted sex difference was significant for both pictures (the means for
the trapeze picture were +.19 for boys and +1.54 for girls).

After this preliminary test, Saunders went on to a more extensive
project. This time there were 190 students from the third, fifth, and
eighth grades. It was a group of above average intelligence and middle-class background. The same two pictures were used. The D/E
score that Saunders worked with was the average for the two stories
or, since some children wrote unscorable stories, the score for the one
usable story. When the results are looked at both in terms of age and
sex, we find a highly significant overall sex difference but no overall
difference by age. But a closer inspection of the data shows that while
the scores for boys do not change much (−.09 in third grade versus
−.26 in eighth grade), the scores for girls change considerably (+.46
in the third grade to +2.23 in the eighth). This suggests that these
fantasy patterns begin to become differentiated in the early school
years and that the important change is a sharp rise (obvious by age
ten and increased by age thirteen) in the strength of the female pattern.

Wilsnack, Sharon. "Psychological Factors in Female Drinking." Ph.D. thesis, Harvard University, 1972. (Since Wilsnack's complex project involved numerous TAT pictures and some alterations in the D/E scoring system, the results reported here came from a rescoring, by an expert in the standard D/E system, of the trapeze picture only.)

> Two dozen women diagnosed as alcoholic had a mean D/E score of +1.21, while a matched comparison group of nonalcoholics scored +.64. This difference does not reach statistical significance. But if we simply classify the stories as positive or negative in score then we see that the alcoholic women tell significantly more positive stories, that they more unanimously show the female pattern. Interesting, but one doesn't know what to make of it beyond wondering about a link between the alcoholic life of repetitive descents into chaos and the fantasy schema that hopes that exaltation will follow degradation. And in fact these alcoholics were all in a treatment program at the time they were tested and might be expected to be showing the reformist zeal and optimism that comes so regularly, and briefly, to heavy drinkers. But the data here are too weak to support much speculation. Wilsnack's work is certainly significant in a narrower sense: it was the first evidence that the female D/E pattern held in a group of older (average age of forty-four), high-school-educated and largely working-class women.

Winter, Sara. "Characteristics of Fantasy while Nursing." *Journal of Personality* 37, no. 1 (1969):58–72.

> Sara Winter was interested in the mother's experience while nursing and contrived to have two dozen young mothers tell TAT stories into a tape recorder while actually breast-feeding their first child. A matched group of mothers responded to the same pictures while in the presence of a child they had recently weaned. Winter used the trapeze picture and a somewhat simplified version of the scoring scheme whereby a score of plus one is given to any story which shows a progression from deprivation to enhancement. She found that the nursing mothers showed a significantly greater incidence of the deprivation followed by enhancement sequence. While Winter was primarily interested in explaining other parts of her findings, she suggests that this heightening of fantasy pattern may have to do with the feeling, and reality, of gaining pleasure by giving of oneself in the baby's behalf.

# Notes

## INTRODUCTION

[1]Diana Trilling, "Daughters of the Middle Class," *Harper's*, April 1977, p. 34.

## CHAPTER I. THE MYTHS OF MALE AND FEMALE

[1]Rolfe Humphries has given us a beautiful and moving translation of Ovid's version of the tale. I have resisted the temptation to quote the whole piece, but if you find the excerpts and summary intriguing, it's well worth reading: Ovid, *Metamorphoses* (Bloomington: Indiana University Press, 1955), pp. 28–38.

[2]Ovid, *Metamorphoses*, trans. F.J. Miller (London: William Heinemann, 1916), pp. 55, 57.

[3]Unattributed quotes are from *Hesiod, the Homeric Hymns and Homerica*, translated by H. G. Evelyn-White, Loeb Classical Library (London: William Heinemann, 1936). Another good translation is that of Apostolos Athanassakis, *The Homeric Hymns* (Baltimore: Johns Hopkins Press, 1976).

[4]See G. Mylonas, *Eleusis and the Eleusinian Mysteries* (Princeton, N.J.: Princeton University Press, 1961).

[5]Jane Harrison, *Prolegomena to the Study of Greek Religion (1908)* (New York: Meridian Books, 1966).

## CHAPTER III. TWO LIVES

[1]Sigmund Freud, "Some Character-Types Met with in Psycho-analytic Work" (1916), *The Complete Psychological Works of Sigmund Freud*, trans. James Strachey (New York: W.W. Norton, 1976), vol. XIV, pp. 311–33.

[2]Erik Erikson, *Childhood and Society* (New York: W.W. Norton, 1950), p. 83.

[3]Ibid., p. 224.

CHAPTER V. THE CASE FOR SEX DIFFERENCES

[1]Roger Brown, *Social Psychology* (New York: The Free Press, 1965), p. 161.

[2]Judith Bardwick and Elizabeth Douvan, "Ambivalence: The Socialization of Women," in Bardwick, ed., *Readings on the Psychology of Women* (New York: Harper & Row, 1972), p. 53.

[3]Julian Silverman, "Attentional Styles and the Study of Sex Differences," in David Motofsky, ed., *Attention: Contemporary Theory and Analysis* (New York: Appleton-Century-Crofts, 1970), p. 89.

[4]See Eleanor Maccoby, "Sex Differences in Intellectual Functioning," in Maccoby, *The Development of Sex Differences* (Stanford: Stanford University Press, 1966). Also Judith Bardwick, *The Psychology of Women* (New York: Harper & Row, 1971), p. 133.

[5]See Jerome Kagan, "Acquisition and Significance of Sex Typing and Sex Role Identity," in Martin Hofmann and Lois Hofmann, eds., *Review of Development Research* (New York: Russell Sage Foundation, 1964). Also: Maccoby, "Sex Differences in Intellectual Functioning," and Bardwick, *Psychology of Women.*

[6]Henry Biller, "Paternal and Sex-Role Factors in Cognitive and Academic Functioning," in *The Nebraska Symposium on Motivation* (Lincoln, Ne.: University of Nebraska Press, 1973), p. 106.

[7]Jerome Kagan and Howard Moss, *Birth to Maturity* (New York: John Wiley & Sons, 1962).

[8]Marjorie Honzik's review of *Birth to Maturity* points out both that other longitudinal studies have found dependence to be a stable trait in women and aggression a stable trait in men, and more importantly, that such stability says nothing about the social versus biological origin of these traits. Kagan and Moss's data is interesting and valuable, but their conclusions go beyond it. "Prediction of Behavior from Birth to Maturity," *Merrill-Palmer Quarterly,* 11 (1965): 77–88.

[9]Elizabeth Douvan, "Sex Differences in Adolescent Character Processes," in Bardwick, *Readings on the Psychology of Women,* pp. 44–48.

[10]Rae Carlson, "Sex Differences in Ego Functioning: Exploratory Studies of Agency and Communion," *Journal Consulting and Clinical Psychology,* 37 (1971): 267–277. For an interesting study of sex differences in time perception, see Thomas Cottle, *Perceiving Time* (New York: John Wiley & Sons, 1976). Another important contribution is Carol Gilligan's "In a Different Voice: Women's Conceptions of Self and Morality," *Harvard Educational Review* 47 (1977): 481–517.

[11]Alfred Heilbrun, "Parent Identification and Filial Sex-Role Behavior:

The Importance of Biological Context," in *The Nebraska Symposium on Motivation*, p. 141.

[12]Robert Bales and Talcott Parsons, *Family, Socialization and Interaction Process* (Glencoe, Ill: Free Press, 1955), p. 23.

[13]David Bakan, *The Duality of Human Existence* (Boston: Beacon Press, 1966), p. 15. The complex duality Bakan outlines is rich in potential connections. To cite one example: Andreas Angyal's *Neurosis and Treatment* (New York: John Wiley & Sons, 1965) describes what seems to be an identical polarity, but here called "autonomy" vs. "homonomy" and explored from the viewpoint of individual psychological development and psychopathology.

[14]Bardwick, *Psychology of Women;* Corinne Hutt, *Males and Females* (Hammondsworth, England: Penguin Books, 1972); Maccoby, *Development of Sex Differences.*

[15]Kate Millett, *Sexual Politics* (New York: Doubleday, 1969), p. 93.

[16]Laurence Kohlberg, "A Cognitive-Developmental Analysis of Children's Sex-Role Concepts and Attitudes," in Maccoby, *Development of Sex Differences*, pp. 82–173.

[17]Naomi Weisstein, "Psychology Constructs the Female, or the Fantasy Life of the Male Psychologist," in V. Gornick, and B. Moran, eds., *Woman in Sexist Society* (New York: Basic Books, 1971), pp. 133–146.

[18]Miriam Rosenberg, "The Biologic Basis for Sex Role Stereotypes," *Contemporary Psychoanalysis* 9 (1973): 374–91.

[19]Gary Mitchell, "Paternalistic Behavior in Primates," *Psychological Bulletin* 71 (1969): 399–417.

[20]Irven DeVore, *Primate Behavior* (New York: Holt, Rinehart & Winston, 1965).

[21]Since much of this work is associated with the name of Harry Harlow, and he comes in for considerable personal attack at the hands of Miriam Rosenberg, it is worth stating that others have reported the same observations. See the references in Bardwick, *Psychology of Women*, p. 91.

[22]Gary Mitchell, "Attachment Differences in Male and Female Infant Monkeys," in Bardwick, *Reading on the Psychology of Women*, pp. 18–22.

[23]Corinne Hutt, *Males and Females*, p. 54.

[24]Donald Broverman et al., "Roles of Activation and Inhibition in Sex Differences in Cognitive Abilities," *Psychological Review* 75 (1968): 23–50. A good recent summary of the evidence for the effects of sex hormones in shaping aspects of the central nervous system is in Robert Briscoe, David Quadagno, and Jill Quadagno, "Effect of Perinatal Gonadal Hormones on Selected Nonsexual Behavior Patterns," *Psychological Bulletin* 84 (1977): 62–80.

[25]Robert Rose et al., "Androgens and Aggression: A Review and Recent

Findings in Primates," in R. Holloway, *Primate Aggression, Territoriality, and Xenophobia: A Comparative Perspective* (New York: Academic Press, 1974), p. 300.

[26]H. Persky et al., "Relation of Psychologic Measures of Aggression and Hostility to Testosterone Production In Men," *Psychosomatic Medicine* 33 (1971): 265–277.

[27]This phrase is used by Anke Ehrhardt and John Money, *Man and Woman, Boy and Girl* (Baltimore: Johns Hopkins University Press, 1972), p. 24. The animal data are covered by Rose, "Androgens and Aggression."

[28]Ibid., p. 269.

[29]Margaret Mead, *Sex and Temperament* (New York: William Morrow, 1935), p. 191.

[30]Steven Goldberg, *The Inevitability of Patriarchy*, (New York: William Morrow, 1973). This book is worth reading in tandem with *Sexual Politics.* Goldberg is just as fervent—rabid might be more accurate—in defending traditional sex roles as Millett is in attacking them.

[31]See Mead's piece in Jean Strouse, ed., *Women and Analysis* (New York: Dell, 1974), especially pp. 126–27.

[32]Deborah Gewertz, "An Historical Reconsideration of Female Dominance Among the Chambri of Papua New Guinea," in Sherry Ortner and Harriet Whitehead, eds., *Sexual Meanings,* in press.

[33]Clyde Kluckhohn, "Variations in the Human Family," in Norman Bell and Ezra Vogel, eds., *A Modern Introduction to the Family* (Glencoe: The Free Press, 1960), pp. 45–51.

[34]Roy D'Andrade, "Sex Differences and Cultural Institutions," in Maccoby, *Development of Sex Differences,* p. 179.

[35]For references on authority, see D'Andrade, ibid., and Goldberg, *Inevitability of Patriarchy.*

[36]Morris Zelditch, "Role Differentiation in the Nuclear Family: A Comparative Study," in Norman W. Bell and Ezra F. Vogel, *A Modern Introduction to the Family* (Glencoe, Ill.: The Free Press, 1960), pp. 329–38. It is important to note that this argument does not depend on the power of the actual biological father. Thus it is not contradicted by Evelyn Reed's recent assertion of the importance of matriarchy, *Woman's Evolution* (New York: Pathfinder Press, 1975), since she classes as "matriarchal" societies where the mother's brother is the main source of instrumental authority within the extended family.

[37]Beatrice Whiting, ed., *Six Cultures: Studies of Child Rearing* (New York: John Wiley & Sons, 1963).

[38]John Whiting, cited in Hutt, *Males and Females,* p. 130f.

[39]Carolyn Pope Edwards and Beatrice Whiting, "A Cross-Cultural Analy-

sis of Sex Differences in the Behavior of Children Aged Three through Eleven," *The Journal of Social Psychology* 91 (1973): 171–88.

[40]D'Andrade, "Sex Differences and Cultural Institutions," p. 191.

[41]H. Barry, et al., "A Cross-Cultural Survey of Some Sex Differences in Socialization," *Journal of Abnormal and Social Psychology* 55 (1957): 328–29.

[42]See Irving Howe, "The Middle-Class Mind of Kate Millett," *Harper's,* December 1970, pp. 110–29.

[43]Melford Spiro, *Children of the Kibbutz* (Cambridge: Harvard University Press, 1958).

[44]Anneliese Korner, "Sex Differences in Newborns with Special Reference to Differences in the Organization of Oral Behavior," *Journal of Child Psychology and Psychiatry* 14 (1973): 27.

[45]Jerome Kagan and Michael Lewis, "Studies of Attention in the Human Infant," *Merrill-Palmer Quarterly* 11 (1965): 126.

[46]Susan Goldberg and Michael Lewis, "Play Behavior in the Year-Old Infant: Early Sex Differences," in Bardwick, *Readings on the Psychology of Women,* pp. 30–34.

[47]Howard Moss, "Sex, Age, and State as Determinants of Mother-Infant Interaction," in Bardwick, *Readings on the Psychology of Women,* pp. 22–29.

[48]See Richard Bell's "Stimulus Control of Parent or Caretaker Behavior by Offspring," *Developmental Psychology* 4 (1971): 63–72. The following article, by Harper, in the same volume is also useful.

[49]Erik Erikson, "Sex Differences in the Play Constructions of Preadolescents," *American Journal of Orthopsychiatry* 21 (1951): 667–92.

[50]Ibid., p. 690.

[51]See Millett, *Sexual Politics,* and Elizabeth Janeway, *Man's World, Woman's Place* (New York: William Morrow, 1971). See also Erikson's recent response and elaboration in Strouse, ed., *Women and Analysis.*

[52]Marjorie Honzik, "Sex Differences in the Occurrence of Materials in the Play Constructions of Preadolescents," *Child Development* 22 (1951):-15–35.

[53]Phebe Cramer and Katherine Hogan, "Sex Differences in Verbal and Play Fantasy," *Developmental Psychology* 11 (1975), no. 2: 145–54; and Phebe Cramer, "The Development of Play and Fantasy in Boys and Girls: Empirical Studies," in D.P. Spence, ed., *Psychoanalysis and Contemporary Science,* vol. 4 (New York: International Press, 1975).

[54]Patricia Minuchin reports a similar sex difference in play themes: "Sex-Role Concepts and Sex Typing in Childhood as a Function of School and Home Environments," *Child Development* 36 (1965):1033–48.

55Cramer and Hogan, "Sex Differences in Verbal and Play Fantasy," p. 154.


CHAPTER VI. MALE AND FEMALE DEVELOPMENT

1Irving Howe, "The Middle-Class Mind of Kate Millett," *Harper's*, December 1970, p. 126.

2Erik Erikson, "Once More the Inner Space: Letter to a Former Student," in Jean Strouse, ed., *Women and Analysis* (New York: Dell, 1974), p. 376.

3Erik Erikson, "Sex Differences—The Play Configurations of Pre-Adolescents," *American Journal of Orthopsychiatry* 21 (1951): 691.

4Erik Erikson's first book, *Childhood and Society* (New York: W.W. Norton, 1950), is still the best place to begin.

5For criticism, see the contributions of Elizabeth Janeway and Margaret Mead in Strouse's *Women and Analysis*. For recent modifications, see Roy Schafer, "Problems in Freud's Psychology of Women," *Journal of the American Psychoanalytic Association* 22 (1974):459–85; and Janine Chassequet-Smirgel, "Freud and Female Sexuality," *International Journal of Psychoanalysis* 57 (1976):275–86. For an example of a careful willingness to consider Freud from a feminist point of view: Juliet Mitchell, *Psychoanalysis and Feminism* (New York: Pantheon, 1974).

6Sigmund Freud, "On the Universal Tendency to Debasement in the Sphere of Love" (1912), *The Complete Psychological Works of Sigmund Freud*, trans. James Strachey (New York: W.W. Norton, 1976), vol. XI, pp. 179–90.

7Ibid., p. 189–90.

8Sigmund Freud, The *Origins of Psychoanalysis: Letters to Wilhelm Fliess, Drafts and Notes*, 1887–1902 (New York: Basic Books, 1954), p. 288.

9Sigmund Freud, *Three Essays on Sexuality: The Complete Psychological Works of Sigmund Freud* (1905), trans. James Strachey (New York: W.W. Norton 1976); vol. VII, p. 220 note.

10Sigmund Freud, "Analysis Terminable and Interminable," (1937), *The Complete Psychological Works of Sigmund Freud*, trans. James Strachey (New York: W.W. Norton, 1976), vol. XXIII, pp. 216–53.

11Sigmund Freud, *Beyond the Pleasure Principle* (1920), trans. James Strachey (New York: W.W. Norton, 1961), pp. 14–15.

12Briffault's work of the 1920s has a recent champion in Evelyn Reed. See note 36, chapter V.

13Erik Erikson, "Identity and the Life Cycle," *Psychological Issues* 1, no. 1 (1959):89.

14Harry Stack Sullivan, *Conceptions of Modern Psychiatry* (New York:

W.W. Norton, 1940), p. 56. See also his extensive description of preadolescence and adolescence in *The Interpersonal Theory of Psychiatry,* (New York: W.W. Norton, 1953).

[15]For instance, see Peter Blos, *The Young Adolescent* (New York: Macmillan, 1970). Or for a briefer summary, see the introduction to "The Initial Stage of Male Adolescence," *Psychoanalytic Study of the Child* 20 (1965):-145–64.

[16]Joseph Adelson and Elizabeth Douvan, *The Adolescent Experience* (New York: John Wiley & Sons, 1966).

[17]Ibid., pp. 347–48.

[18]Both of Erikson's articles, "Womenhood and the Inner Space" and "Once More the Inner Space" are in Strouse, *Women and Analysis,* pp. 333–64, and pp. 365–87.

[19]Peter Blos, "The Initial Stage of Male Adolescence."

[20]Saint Augustine, *The City of God,* trans. Marcus Dods (Edinburgh: T & T Clark, 1871), p. 32 (xiv,17). Augustine talks at length about the penis as the only part of our body that is out of our control. This state of affairs is a just punishment—because of Adam's disobedience to God, man must now suffer a disobedient penis.

[21]Simone de Beauvoir, "Joie De Vivre," *Harper's,* January 1972, p.34.

[22]Karen Horney, "The Denial of the Vagina," in *Feminine Psychology* (New York: W.W. Norton, 1967).

[23]Judith Kestenberg, *Children and Parents: Psychoanalytic Studies in Development* (New York: Jason Aronson, 1975), chapter 5.

[24]Ibid., p. 105.

[25]Leslie Farber, "He Said, She Said," in *Lying, Despair, Jealousy, Envy, Sex, Suicide, Drugs, and the Good Life* (New York: Basic Books, 1976), p. 170.

[26]Ingrid Bengis's *Combat in The Erogenous Zone* (New York: Alfred A. Knopf, 1972) is a moving and sophisticated autobiographical exploration of this persistent source of conflict and misunderstanding between men and women.

[27]John Updike, "London Life," *Picked-Up Pieces* (New York: Alfred A. Knopf, 1975).

[28]Aristotle, "On the Generation of Animals," *The Basic Works of Aristotle,* ed. Richard McKean (New York: Random House, 1941), book I, chapter 18, p. 675.

[29]Robin Lane Fox, *Alexander the Great* (London: Allen Lane, 1973) p. 57.

[30]John Osborne, *Look Back in Anger* (London: Faber and Faber, 1957), pp. 37–38.

³¹Elliot Jacques, "Death and the Mid-Life Crisis," *International Journal of Psychoanalysis* 46 (1965):502–14.

³²Ibid., p. 506

³³Another bit of evidence here is Colby's finding that, in a sample of seventy-five "tribal" societies, men dream of death considerably more than do women. See Eleanor Maccoby, *The Development of Sex Differences* (Stanford: Stanford University Press, 1966), p. 198.

³⁴David Gutmann, "An Exploration of Ego Configurations in Middle and Later Life," in Bernice Neugarten, ed., *Personality in Middle and Late Life* (New York: Atherton Press, 1964); "Mayan Aging—A Comparative TAT Study," *Psychiatry* 29 (1966):246–59; and with A. Krohn, "Changes in Mastery Style with Age: A Study of Navajo Dreams," *Psychiatry* 34 (1971), :289–300.

³⁵David Gutmann, "Women and the Conception of Ego Strength," *Merrill-Palmer Quarterly* 11 (1965):240.

³⁶A similar theme is emerging in the writing of Daniel Levinson. See *The Seasons of a Man's Life* (New York: Alfred A. Knopf, 1978), especially pp. 228–36. He also comments that men in middle adulthood are "less tyrannized by the ambitions, instinctual drives, and illusions of youth." "The Mid-Life Transition: A Period in Adult Psychosocial Development," *Psychiatry* 40 (1977):99–112.

³⁷Daedalus lends himself so well to technology that Haldane entitled a paean to progress: "Daedalus, or Science and the Future." Bertrand Russell wrote a blunt rejoinder that suggested that science mainly serves to put more powerful weapons at the disposal of human aggression and avarice, and that it will likely kill us all. The title? What else but: *Icarus, or the Future of Science* (New York: E. P. Dutton, 1924).

³⁸Henry Murray, "American Icarus," in *Clinical Studies of Personality,* Arthur Burton and Robert Harris, eds. (New York: Harper & Brothers, 1955), pp. 615–41.

³⁹Ibid., p. 636.

⁴⁰For a more detailed and technical discussion of these matters, see Anny Katan, "Distortions of the Phallic Phase," *The Psychoanalytic Study of the Child* 15 (1960):208–14; and Annie Reich, "Pathologic Forms of Self-Esteem Regulation," *The Psychoanalytic Study of the Child* 15 (1960): 215–32.

⁴¹Murray, "American Icarus," p. 634.

⁴²James Muller and Jerome Weinberger, "The American Icarus Revisited: Phallic Narcissism and Boredom," *International Journal of Psychoanalysis* 55 (1974):581–86.

⁴³Ibid., p. 584.

[44]Ibid., p. 584.

[45]Ibid., p. 585.

[46]Sigmund Freud, "The Economic Problem in Masochism" (1924), *The Complete Psychological Works of Sigmund Freud*, trans. James Strachey (New York: W.W. Norton, 1976), vol. xix, p. 165.

[47]Theodor Reik, *Masochism in Modern Man* (New York: Farrar & Strauss, 1941).

[48]Margaret Brenman, "On Teasing and Being Teased: The Problem of 'Moral Masochism,'" in *Psychoanalytic Psychiatry and Psychology,* Cyrus Friedman and Robert Knight, eds. (New York: International Universities Press, 1954), pp. 29–51.

[49]Ibid., p. 32.

[50]Ibid., p. 48.

[51]Helene Deutsch, *The Psychology of Women* (New York: Grune and Stratton, 1944), vol. 1.

[52]Karen Horney, "The Problem of Feminine Masochism," in *Feminine Psychology* (New York: W.W. Norton, 1967), p. 232.

[53]Deutsch, "Psychology of Women," p. 255.

[54]Quoted in Brenman, "Teasing and Being Teased," p. 36.

## CHAPTER VII. THE DREAM OF ANDROGENY

[1]Unless otherwise noted, the quotes I use in outlining the New Androgyny are from:

Sandra Lipsitz Bem, "Beyond Androgyny: Some Presumptuous Prescriptions for a Liberated Sexual Identity," paper given at the APA–NIMH Conference on The Research Needs of Women, May 1975, to be published in F. Denmark and J. Sherman, eds., *Psychology of Women: Future Directions of Research* (Psychological Dimensions, in press); Carolyn Heilbrun, *Toward a Recognition of Androgyny* (New York: Alfred N. Knopf, 1973); Joan Bean and Alexandra Kaplan, eds., *Beyond Sex-Role Stereotypes: Readings Toward a Psychology of Androgyny* (Boston: Little, Brown & Co., 1976). For additional examples see *Women's Studies* 2, no. 2 (1974).

[2]Ovid, *Metamorphoses,* trans. Rolfe Humphries (Bloomington: Indiana University Press, 1955), p. 93.

[3]See A. J. L. Busst's article "The Image of the Androgyne in the Nineteenth Century," in Ian Fletcher, ed., *Romantic Mythologies* (New York: Barnes & Noble, 1967).

[4]The most comprehensive discussion of this theme is in Mircea Eliade's *The Two and the One* (London: Harvill, 1962), chap. 2.

[5]For more background and photographs of such statues, see Marie Del-

court, *Hermaphrodite: Myths and Rites of the Bisexual Figure in Classical Antiquity*, trans. Jennifer Nicholson (London: Studio Books, 1961).

[6]For a fascinating literary example of these themes see Edward Kaplan's recent book, *Michelet's Poetic Vision* (Amherst: University of Massachusetts Press, 1977). A French historian of the romantic period, Michelet elaborated a theory of male and female aspects of the mind: it is the intercourse between these aspects which leads to creativity. He speaks of his intellectual creations in a vivid flood of images ("conceived," "fecundity," "incubated," etc.), which suggest that his dearest wish was to have a baby. At the same time his picture of women oscillates between tender idealization and fearful derogation (e.g., they have a monthly "wound" and "sickness").

[7]Shulamith Firestone, *The Dialectic of Sex*, quoted in Juliet Mitchell, *Woman's Estate* (Harmondsworth, England: Penguin Books, 1971), p. 90.

[8]Alan Friedman's *Hermaphrodeity* (New York: Alfred A. Knopf, 1972) is a novelistic romp through the same fantasy terrain. Bawdy, bizarre, and deeply tongue-in-cheek, the book nonetheless portrays, in vivid and even pornographic fashion, the same themes: the original envy of the other sex, the Utopian fantasies of power and divinity associated with being both sexes, and the ultimate utter narcissism of the androgynous state.

# Index